x Sarah Evans

Nomads of the Present

TEMPLE UNIVERSITY PRESS

NOMADS OF THE PRESENT

SOCIAL MOVEMENTS
AND INDIVIDUAL NEEDS IN
CONTEMPORARY SOCIETY

Alberto Melucci

Edited by John Keane and Paul Mier

TEMPLE UNIVERSITY PRESS
Philadelphia

Temple University Press, Philadelphia 19122
Published 1989

First published in Great Britain by Hutchinson Radius 1989

© Alberto Melucci

Printed in Great Britain

Library of Congress Cataloguing in Publication Data
on file
ISBN 0–87722–599–0

Contents

Editors' Preface

During the past few decades, there has been a remarkable growth of new forms of collective action, such as the black and civil rights campaigns, student and youth movements, feminism and the peace and ecology movements. In western Europe and North America, these social movements draw their support in novel ways from across class and regional boundaries. They also place a high value upon grass-roots, informal and 'hidden' forms of organization, and they consequently tend to be suspicious of business organizations, trade union hierarchies, political parties and state bureaucracies. Since they develop largely outside and 'underneath' these dominant institutions of civil society and the state, social movements raise important questions about the distribution and legitimacy of macro-power relations. But they do more than this. Social movements also publicize grievances and uncertainties about everyday life, as well as challenge the less visible power relationships crystallized in its shared conventions and sense of normalcy.

Considerable intellectual interest in the origins, patterns of development and socio-political effects of social movements has quickly followed their growth. Alberto Melucci is today recognized in Europe and North America as among the foremost researchers in this field – despite the fact that, until this volume, surprisingly few of his writings on social movements have been available in English.

Nomads of the Present is a highly original attempt to provide a new framework for analysing social movements in contemporary or 'complex' western societies. Melucci's arguments are broad-ranging in scope, and they blend together empirical and

1

theoretical perspectives. The theoretical approach he defends is illustrated with empirical examples, many of which are drawn from field research conducted in Milano by Melucci and his co-researchers. Different types of contemporary movements – of urban youth, ecologists, women and others – are described and analysed; the relationship between these movements and the institutions and individual needs of complex societies is examined; and the key methodological problems peculiar to the field of social movements research are explored in fresh ways.

The central theme of this book concerns the need to rethink fundamentally the conventional social science interpretations of social movements. Melucci not only rejects the early nineteenth-century metaphysical image of social movements as heroes or villians acting out a script on the stage of human history. He also questions the assumptions of those twentieth-century approaches, influenced by Marxism, the Freudian tradition and theories of deprivation, which emphasize either the objective causes of collective action – the structural contradictions and crises of the social system – or its subjective dimensions, that is, the psychological motivations and preferences of individuals which lead them to band together as a social movement. Melucci argues that each of these nineteenth- and twentieth-century perspectives was founded upon the questionable assumptions that movements are a *personnage*, and that collective action is a unified empirical entity, whose deeper significance can be unravelled by its observers.

Traditional assumptions of this kind continue to grip present-day discussions about social movements. Many observers are still inclined to speak about movements as if they had a personality of their own, while considerations of their origins continue to emphasize either the institutional processes and 'interests' generated by 'the system' or the psychological preferences of their participants. Melucci argues that these traditional assumptions are no longer plausible, in part because the conflicts, actors and forms of action in complex societies have become highly mobile and differentiated. He also points out that more recent analyses of collective action have attempted to transcend the received sociological and psychological traditions of analysing social movements.

Melucci devotes particular attention to three types of

interpretation which have dominated the field of social mo
ments research since the early 1970s. Structural approaches –
Habermas's theory of the colonization of the life-world is an
example – draw upon a form of systems analysis, and attribute
the new forms of collective action to institutional changes in
post-industrial or late capitalism. But in so doing, Melucci
argues, these structural approaches only explain why and not
how movements are formed and maintained. Resource mobilization approaches – evident in the work of McCarthy, Zald and
other American sociologists – attempt to fill this gap. These
theories explain the growth and development of social movements
by emphasizing the fundamental importance of pre-existing
organizations and the availability of resources such as money,
professional expertise and recruitment networks in civil society.
Melucci accepts this insight, but he claims nevertheless that
resource mobilization approaches suffer from an opposite
problem. They tend to explain how, but not *why* social
movements emerge and develop. That is, resource mobilization
approaches view collective action as 'data' which is merely given,
thereby inadequately examining the meanings and wider social
repercussions of a movement's action. Finally, political exchange
theories, developed by Pizzorno and others, interpret contemporary social movements mainly in political terms. Political
exchange theorists emphasize their efficacy (or lack of efficacy)
of movements within the political system. Melucci does not deny
this point. Indeed, he recognizes that movements affect the
political system in various ways, for instance by instigating
institutional and policy reforms, and by providing a pool of new
political elites. But he argues that political exchange approaches
understate the *non-political* aspects of social movements. Movements not only operate mainly in the pre-political terrain of
everyday life; they also remind us that institutional politics has
its limits, that there are certain social problems and dilemmas
which are irreducible to negotiation, decision-making and
administrative control.

Melucci's critique of these recent approaches is informative
and refreshing. It also forms the basis of his own creative
account of how and why complex and diverse issues, organizations
and actors crystallize as collective action. Among Melucci's
principal arguments is that social movements must be considered

3

as fragile and heterogeneous *social constructions*. Collective action is always 'built' by social actors, and thus what needs to be explained in concrete terms is how movements form, that is, how they manage to mobilize individuals and groups within the framework of possibilities and constraints presented them by the institutions of our complex societies. Collective action must be understood in terms of the processes through which individuals communicate, negotiate, produce meanings and make decisions within a particular social field or environment. Collective actors never act in a void. They establish relations with other actors within an already structured context, and through these interactions they produce meanings, express their needs and constantly transform their relationships. By means of these multiple and diverse processes – which are well illustrated by Melucci's own empirical research on movement networks in the Milano area – actors construct what Melucci calls a collective identity: a movable definition of themselves and their social world, a more or less shared and dynamic understanding of the goals of their action as well as the social field of possibilities and limits within which their action takes place.

Melucci's emphasis upon the self-production of social movements is perceptive and important, and it provides a framework for understanding why, during the past few decades, new forms of action have emerged in areas previously untouched by social conflicts. According to Melucci, conflicts develop in those areas of complex systems where there is greatest pressure on citizens to conform to institutions which produce and circulate information and symbolic codes. Complex societies, in contrast to their late nineteenth-century industrial capitalist predecessors, are systems in which the production of material goods depends increasingly upon the production of signs and social relations. The factory and the state executive are no longer the exclusive *loci* of power. Relations of power become more heterogeneous and less 'naked'. They become 'saturated' with deliberately produced symbolic codes. And society's capacity to organize life and to produce meanings for its members expands from the factory and government office to those areas which formerly escaped controls from above. Emotional relationships, sexuality, health and even birth and death are subjected to new forms of administrative regulation.

4

These trends, Melucci argues, stimulate the growth of social movements, and they help explain why complex societies are not 'iron cages of unfreedom' (Weber), and also why contemporary conflicts concentrate more and more on questions concerning individual identity, democracy and the relationship between society and its natural environment.

These themes evidently bear upon recent theoretical debates concerning what is 'new' about present-day social movements. Do present-day movements signal the permanent decline of the workers' movement? Are they indicators of major transformations of power in countries such as the United States, Britain and the Federal Republic of Germany? Are today's movements actually new and, if so, in what sense? This book has much to say about these questions. While Melucci is uncomfortable with the term 'new social movements', he parts company with most other contemporary commentators by specifying at least four unique features of today's movements.

First, unlike their nineteenth-century counterparts, contemporary social movements are not preoccupied with struggles over the production and distribution of material goods and resources. They challenge the administrative logic of complex systems primarily on symbolic grounds. Today's movements are more concerned with the ways in which complex societies generate information and communicate meanings to their members. This emphasis on the central role of information extends from demands for the right of citizens' access to 'factual information' (such as missile testing plans and the extent of ecological damage caused by industrial spills) to debates over symbolic resources, such as the challenge of the women's movement to sexist advertising.

Second, the constituent organizations of today's movements consider themselves more than instrumental for attaining political and social goals. Actors' participation within movements is no longer a means to an end. Drawing upon Marshall McLuhan, Melucci argues that the very forms of the movements – their patterns of interpersonal relationships and decision-making mechanisms – operate as a 'sign' or 'message' for the rest of society. The organizations of the women's movement, for instance, not only raise important questions about equality and rights. They also, at the same time, deliberately signal to the rest of society the importance of recognizing differences within complex societies. Participation within movements is considered a goal in itself because, paradoxically, actors self-consciously practise in the present the future social changes they seek. Collective actors are 'nomads of the present'. They are no longer driven by an all-embracing vision of some future order. They focus on the present, and consequently their goals are temporary and replaceable, and their organizational means are valued as ends in themselves.

Third, present-day social movements also rely on a new relationship between the latent and visible dimensions of their collective action. Social movements normally consist – here Melucci's work is at its most original – of 'invisible' networks of small groups submerged in everyday life. These 'submerged' networks, noted for their stress on individual needs, collective identity and part-time membership, constitute the laboratories in which new experiences are invented. Within these invisible laboratories, movements question and challenge the dominant codes of everyday life. These laboratories are places in which the elements of everyday life are mixed, developed and tested, a site in which reality is given new names and citizens can develop alternative experiences of time, space and interpersonal relations. For Melucci there is a complementarity between these 'private', submerged networks and their publicly visible dimension. Movements appear relatively infrequently as publicly visible phenomena – for instance, during public demonstrations in favour of abortion or against nuclear power – and yet their involvement in observable political action is only temporary. Movements are only part-time participants in the public domain, precisely because they practise new forms of everyday life.

Finally, contemporary movements are acutely aware of the planetary dimension of life in complex societies. Their emphasis upon the interdependence of the world system helps stimulate a new consciousness of ourselves as members of a human species which is situated in a natural environment. Melucci places considerable emphasis on the peace and ecological movements, precisely because they are testaments to the fragile and potentially self-destructive connections between humanity and the wider universe. These movements publicize the fact that local events have global ramifications – that nuclear war would bring with it the end of civilization, and that every Chernobyl and chemical spill ultimately affects all individuals and their environment.

Throughout this book, Melucci's reconsideration of social movements is twinned with a deep concern about individual needs and experiences. His interest in the 'subterranean' dimensions of contemporary social life provides a succinct account of changing patterns of individual experience in such matters as time and space, birth and death, health and illness, sexuality and our relations with the natural environment. Melucci examines these experiences within the context of a deep-seated contradiction of complex societies. He argues that these systems comprise a multiplicity of large-scale organizations which strive to regulate and control every aspect of the lives of individuals. And yet these organizations also place various resources – of knowledge, money and communicative skills – at the disposal of these same individuals. These resources facilitate individual autonomy by widening the range of possibilities available to them. Choices made by individuals in various realms of life potentially become *individual*, which is why Melucci rejects the old image of 'one-dimensional societies' populated by atomized and unthinking individuals. Melucci instead emphasizes the contemporary opportunities for individuation: the availability of resources in complex society makes possible individuals' attempt to realize their full potential as individuals. Melucci argues that individuals can take responsibility for developing a new culture of individual needs which gives prominence to individual self-expression and to the need for a new definition of dynamic freedom and for new democratic rights of everyday life.

Melucci's stress on individual needs and experiences explains why he argues for a 'post-industrial' democracy. In his view, contemporary social movements are deeply reticent about politics. They tend to act at a distance from the world of official politics and are equally suspicious of Leninist political organizations and strategies: contemporary movements are not interested in capturing state power and they have an aversion to violent confrontations with government and state authorities. The new movements raise issues that cannot be mediated fully by institutional party politics, and they consequently publicize the limitations of the political decision-making process. According to Melucci, there is a developing crisis of political representation in complex societies. Social movements are 'homeless', in the sense that their concerns cannot be represented easily by political parties, parliaments and other political mechanisms. Melucci proposes that this impasse can be attenuated and the autonomy of individuals and social movements be preserved by creating and expanding legally guaranteed, independent public spaces within the realm of civil society. These officially recognized public arenas would not be dominated by political parties and governments. They would instead function as open spaces in which a plurality of individuals and groups could meet to negotiate democratically their social demands and to formulate social policies independent of the prerogatives of political parties. Temporary public spaces, such as research institutes, task forces, local committees and other 'bio-degradable' forms of representation, could thereby provide a forum for social movements to publicize the basic dilemmas and problems of complex societies and to express the concerns and demands of civil society. Based on the principles of democratic rights, citizenship and equality, these public spaces could help reinforce the democratization of everyday life, as well as help to force the established policy-making bodies to be more accessible and responsive to the needs of citizens. Within these public spaces, in short, movements could help ensure that the anonymous and impersonal power relations of complex society are rendered visible and negotiable, and that those who exercise power are subject to greater control.

Melucci's arguments – summarized here only briefly – constitute a highly original attempt to synthesize and evaluate the best current European and North American research on social movements. His conclusions are deliberately open ended and therefore leave many questions unanswered. For example, Melucci recognizes the need to specify concretely the institutional processes of 'complex' societies, and yet he fails to provide a convincing model of the kind of society we are living in. Moreover, his argument for new public spaces poses many difficult strategic questions: can the new cultural codes of movements – supported by organizations such as women's presses, alternative theatres and small manufacturers of environmentally safe products – survive in a market dominated by large-scale economic and cultural enterprises? Doesn't the need for movements to seek political recognition and legal guarantees compel them to participate in political parties and state institutions, which at the same time threaten their very autonomy and survival? These types of questions are explored in the concluding interview. Readers who are unfamiliar with either his work or the recent debates about contemporary social movements will find this interview a helpful starting point. The interview, which was prepared especially for this volume, highlights this book's main themes and untreated questions in a style that is personal, lively and accessible.

We should like to express our thanks to Alberto Melucci, whose patience, thoughtful comments and friendly support made this project all the more worthwhile. Thanks are also due to Neil Belton for his editorial assistance, and to Penny Gardiner for her work on the text. And we gratefully acknowledge the time and facilities made available to us by Capilano College, Vancouver, and the Centre for Communication and Information Studies at The Polytechnic of Central London.

John Keane, London
Paul Mier, Vancouver

June 1988

Introduction

This book proposes a new theoretical and methodological framework for analysing contemporary social movements and individual needs. It replaces the conventional, originally nineteenth-century idea of movements as characters acting on the stage of history with a view of collective action as composite action systems which are socially constructed. This book also examines the ways in which present-day collective action emerges in areas of society traditionally immune from conflict, and it shows how this conflict assumes the form of symbolic challenges which publicize novel dilemmas and problems, the clarification of which requires new definitions of freedom and the recognition of new rights and responsibilities.

All these issues simultaneously touch upon the meaning of individual existence and the destiny of the human species. My arguments therefore deliberately cut a circuitous path between collective social and political processes and the subjective personal experiences of everyday life. Areas of collective experience and conflict which cannot be reduced to politics are considered, and an attempt is made to grasp the collective effects of phenomena that are 'hidden' or appear to have significance only for individuals. It is argued that social movements play a vital role in contemporary or 'complex' systems. Without the challenges posed by these movements, complex societies would be incapable of asking questions about meaning; they would entrap themselves in the apparently neutral logic of institutional procedures.

In complex societies, the power of organizations to construct social codes is considerable but not overwhelming. The

11

definition of the self and the biological and motivational structures of human action become targets for intervention. The generation of meaning is subject to systemic regulation and control. At the same time, individuals (potentially) enhance their control over the conditions and orientations of their action. As organized systems increasingly intervene in the perception of representation of action, there is a corresponding growth in the individual and social capacity for self-reflection, the production of information and the development of communication. Complex systems are marked by a deep ambiguity. They develop networks of high density information, the participants of which require a measure of autonomy: without developed capacities for formal learning and action, the individuals and groups could not function as dependable, self-regulating components of the system. At the same time, however, the high degree of differentiation which results stimulates a need for greater systemic integration and intensified control, which shifts its focus from content to codes, from patterns of conduct to the pre-conditions of action.

This book argues that new conflicts develop in those areas of the system where both symbolic investments and pressures to conform are heaviest. These conflicts act increasingly at a distance from political organizations. They are interwoven with the fabric of everyday life and individual experience. The new conflicts are often temporary and they are not expressed through 'instrumental' action. Contemporary movements operate as signs, in the sense that they translate their actions into symbolic challenges to the dominant codes. This is understandable, since in complex societies signs become interchangeable: increasingly, power resides in the codes that order the circulation of information. In this respect, collective action is a *form* whose models of organization and solidarity deliver a message to the rest of society. Collective action affects the dominant institutions by modernizing their cultural outlook and procedures, as well as by selecting new elites; but it also raises questions that transcend the logic of instrumental effectiveness and decision-making by anonymous and impersonal organizations of power. Contemporary social movements stimulate radical questions about the ends of personal and social life and, in so doing, they warn of the crucial problems facing complex societies.

12

INTRODUCTION

The reader should note that this book does not develop its arguments in a straightforward narrative style, and that it deliberately presents a variety of overlapping themes and levels of analysis. This mode of presentation may appear strange, especially since the mass communications media have accustomed us to discourses which claim to mirror social reality – and encourage each individual to recognize and reconfirm him- or herself in the obviousness of common sense. This book attempts to develop different viewpoint, through which the less obvious can be rendered visible. It requires us to see that in complex societies fundamental aspects of human experience are presently undergoing profound changes, and that new needs, together with new powers and new risks, are being born; all of which affect the experience of time and space, birth and death, health and sickness, and the meaning of individual and collective existence.

One way of looking at these changes is merely to register what is already known and familiar. But this fails to reveal the novelties of our situation. For this purpose, another way of seeing – the kind of 'eye' developed in this book – is required. This unusual point of view is preoccupied with the unfamiliar. It resembles a journey into the unfamiliar territory between individual experience and collective action – an uneasy and uncertain adventure, since it lacks the sense of security produced by undivided belonging. Although often accompanied by a feeling of 'homelessness', it provides unique views of the social landscape, at times uncovering landmarks which are impossible to see from deep within the heartland.

The exploration of unfamiliar territory necessitates the special methods of presentation evident in this book. The confident and purposeful stride of one who walks the open road is ill-suited to unmapped terrain. Exploration requires *bricolage*, the gathering and piecing together of clues, the following of tracks that lead back to the starting point, the recognition of signs that are instantly recognizable, and the discovery of other signs that were missed the first time round. This results neither in confusion nor in the simple accumulation of knowledge. The journey into unfamiliar territory leads to the discovery that identical things can be given different names, and that each name conveys a different meaning. It teaches us to recognize ambivalence, encourages us to acknowledge different points of view, and thereby stimulates awareness of potential freedoms, the realization of which depend upon the choices and responsible actions of each and every individual.

Milano
May 1988

I

TOWARDS A THEORY OF COLLECTIVE ACTION

1

Collective action:
a constructivist view

Traditional approaches

At the screening of the current box-office attraction, an audience is simultaneously moved to tears, laughter and applause.

A larger number of people at a soccer match cheer a goal and boo the referee, while groups of supporters wave flags and banners.

Workers on an assembly line down tools and strike without the official backing of their trade union.

Upon first rumours of an imminent rise in the price of petrol, filling stations are besieged with long queues of drivers.

A terrorist group carries out a series of bombings as part of a wider campaign to claim political rights for ethnic minorities.

Groups of demonstrators converge on the capital city to take part in a large rally against the deployment of nuclear missiles.

Following the example of a successful punk group, urban teenagers dye their hair vivid colours; the trend spreads quickly to other parts of the country.

Such phenomena, typical of modern complex societies, have been analysed by social scientists under a variety of headings: as collective behaviour, mass psychology, crowd behaviour and as social movements. These categories assume in each case that these phenomena share certain common features, yet from a strictly phenomenological perspective, they have in common only their 'collective' character: they comprise a number of individuals exhibiting, at the same time and in the same place, behaviour with relatively similar morphological characteristics. Beyond these traits, it is difficult to show that they have a qualitative unity without introducing *conceptual* assumptions. The very classification of these phenomena as 'collective behaviour' or as 'collective action' always involves theoretical and methodological assumptions, which are rarely made explicit.

This problem is evident in traditional analyses of collective phenomena, of which there are two recurrent variants. Emphasis is sometimes placed on the simple facts of collective action, which thus appears as *action without actors*, as an accidental sum of individual events. For example, both the classic analysis of crowd behaviour (Le Bon, Tarde) and the Freudian tradition, emphasize imitation, irrationality, contagion or suggestion. In the sociology of collective behaviour, similarly, collective action is represented as a reaction to the crisis or disorders of the social system. Another traditional view, found especially in Marxism, focuses on the 'objective' social foundations of collective action. It also derives the meaning of action from its analysis of the social conditions which the actors appear to have in common. Here collective action appears as *actors without action* – while the gap between 'objective conditions' and the empirically observed collective behaviour proves impossible to explain. Marx's old problem – how to explain how a class-in-itself becomes a class-for-itself – remains in the background, unsolved.

These traditional approaches, which continue to be influential, share certain epistemological assumptions. The collective phenomenon – whether a panic, a social movement, or a revolutionary process – is treated as a *unified empirical datum* which, supposedly, can be perceived and interpreted by observers. It is supposed that, first, individuals' behaviour forms a *unitary character* or *gestalt*. Second, this assumption is then transferred from the phenomenological to the conceptual level and acquires ontological consistency: the collective reality is seen to exist as a thing. This process of reification of 'collective action' transforms social action into an incontrovertible fact, a *given* that does not merit further investigation.

In recent years social scientists have begun to question these assumptions. Changing historical conditions and the evolution of theoretical debate have contributed to this scepticism. The social conflicts of the nineteenth century – reactions to the crises of the old order produced by industrialization, new industrial conflicts, as well as struggles for citizenship – stimulated the classical theory of collective action. The action of the working class in the phase of industrial capitalism served as a model for the study of collective phenomena. Its resistance to the disruption of traditional ways of life in decline, its demands for political rights and for the extension of citizenship, and its opposition to capitalist domination in the workplace and the market combined the problem of nation-building with class relationships in the development of the factory system. In this historical context the idea developed of social movements as historical agents marching toward a destiny of liberation, or as crowds in the grip of suggestion and under the control of a few agitators.[1]*

This era of industrial conflict is over, not because struggles for full citizenship are complete or because there are no remaining democratic spaces to conquer, but because the different dimensions of collective conflicts have become increasingly separated. In present-day complex societies, conflicts affecting the dominant social relationships and struggles for the extension of citizenship tend to become distinct and to involve diverse constituents. Moreover, new forms of collective resistance to the global expansion of modern industrial ways of life have emerged. This differentiation of fields, actors, and forms of action no longer conforms to the stereotypical image of collective actors moving on the historical stage like characters in an epic drama, and the image of an amorphous crowd guided by its gregarious instincts has become equally suspect.

These changes in historical circumstances have been accompanied by a renewed theoretical debate within the social sciences. The assumption that collective phenomena are unified empirical data has been questioned. Current research in sociology and social psychology suggests the need to examine collective phenomena as the outcome of multiple processes, which are seen either to enhance or to impede the formation of cognitive frameworks and systems of relationships necessary for action. Collective phenomena are viewed as the result of various types of action and elements of structure and motivation. The

---

* Superior figures refer to the Notes and references sections following each chapter.

analytical problem, then, is to explain how these elements are held together, and how a 'collective actor' is formed and maintained.[2]

An important corollary of this theoretical development is our increased understanding of collective phenomena in terms of *action*. Cognitive and constructivist theories of human action (see note 2) help us consider collective phenomena as processes through which actors produce meanings, communicate, negotiate, and make decisions. In other words, the actors are seen to be capable of transcending the linear logic of stimulus and response. Consequently, collective action cannot be explained either by structural determinants (e.g., in terms of crisis, relative deprivation or class condition) or by a theory of the instincts (e.g., in terms of suggestion, imitation or manipulation).

The traditional approaches, by assuming collective action as a unified datum, also impeded the formulation of several fundamental questions:

– Through which processes do actors construct collective action?
– How is the unity of the various elements of collective action produced?
– Through which processes and relationships do individuals become involved in – or defect from – collective action?

If we seek answers to these questions in the traditional approaches we find two recurring forms of explanation. Emphasis is given either to structural contradictions and dysfunctions of the social system, or to the values, the psychological differences and the motivations of individuals. Neither approach is capable of satisfactorily addressing these questions. Each is weakened by an unbridgeable gap between the explanations they offer and the concrete processes that enable individuals to act together. An explanation founded upon the common structural condition of collective actors assumes their capacity to perceive, evaluate, and decide what they have in common. It ignores, in other words, the very processes that enable or inhibit actors to define the circumstances of common action. Individual differences and motivations, however cannot explain how certain individuals come to recognize themselves in a more or less shared sense of 'we'.

20

Beyond dualism

Philosophies of history, based on the belief that the course of history is guided to fulfilment by spiritual or material forces, to which human action is necessarily submitted, are a basic ingredient of modern thought. Dualistic thinking is the remaining legacy of this philosophy of history. In theories of collective action, it has been pointed out that dualism has been commonly formulted in terms of *breakdown/solidarity* models (Tilly, 1975; Useem, 1980). Breakdown theories – theories of collective behaviour and mass society – hold collective action to be the result of economic crisis and social disintegration, disregard its conflictual dimensions and thus reduce it to pathological reaction and to marginality. Solidarity models see collective action as an expression of shared interests within a common structural location, but are unable to explain the transition from social conditions to collective action. The Marxist dilemma mentioned above still persists and cannot be solved without taking into account how collective action is formed and maintained. It has been pointed out that approaches based on the *structure/motivation* dualism (Webb, 1983) are also problematic, in that they view collective action either as a product of the logic of the system or as a result of personal beliefs. The former stresses the social–economic context, while the latter emphasizes the role of ideology and values.

In Europe, during the 1970s, Touraine (1973, 1978) and Habermas (1976) tried to move beyond these dichotomies. Their analyses emphasized the need for a 'structural' or systemic approach which linked new forms of social conflict to changes in post-industrial capitalism. Across the Atlantic, some American theorists focused on processes of *resource mobilization* (McCarthy and Zald, 1973, 1977, 1979; Gamson, 1975; Oberschall, 1973; Tilly, 1978). This approach tried to explain how a movement is formed, how it persists through time, and how it relates to its environment.

Both theories leave certain problems unresolved. Structural theories, based on systems analysis, explain *why* but not *how* a movement is established and survives; they hypothesize potential conflict without accounting for concrete collective action. By contrast, resource mobilization models regard such action as mere data and fail to examine its meaning and orientation. In this instance, the *how* but not the *why* of collective action is emphasized. The two perspectives are not irreconcilable, however. While each frequently passes, sometimes implicitly, for a global explanation, each is legitimate within its own parameters.

Despite these unresolved problems, the theoretical work on social movements during the 1970s created what I call a 'sceptical paradigm': collective action is not perceived as a 'thing', and what movements say of themselves is not entirely taken at face value. Instead, attempts are made to discover the system of internal and external relationships which constitutes collective action. Analysis thus concentrates on the systemic relationships in place of the simple logic of actors' values or motivations. And action is not analysed only by referring to structural contradictions. Emphasis is given to their goals and to the field of systemic opportunities and constraints within which action takes place. Here, I think, the legacy of the research of the 1970s can be creatively consolidated through an analysis of the how, without neglecting the why of collective action.

Positive indicators of this possibility are evident in many recent contributions which take a systemic, relationship-oriented approach to collective action. Again the stress is on social opportunities and constraints, rather than on subjective orientations or merely objective factors. This stress is evident in recent developments in the resource mobilization approach (Garner and Zald, 1981; Zald and McCarthy, 1985; Oberschall, 1978, 1980; Ferrel and Miller, 1985) and in some analyses of protest (March, 1977; Tarrow, 1982, 1983, 1988; Webb, 1983a; Gamson, Fireman and Rytina, 1982). Protest, for example, is seen to be an aspect of a system of relations, which includes reactions of the political system and interaction between protest groups and elites. Tarrow's concept of a *political opportunity structure* – the set of opportunities offered to protestors by the political system, and, thus, by such factors as its degree of openness and flexibility, and the nature of political elites – is also relevant here because collective action is not reduced to a set of 'objective' interests. Finally, Kriesberg (1981, 1982) speaks of a 'multiple interaction paradigm' emerging from contemporary studies on social movements: movements are not considered as 'objects' but as actors operating within a field of interaction which includes political authorities, opponents and allies. These works are innovative, particularly when contrasted with traditional American studies, in which social movements were frequently reduced to beliefs or to aggregate mass behaviour. More significantly, these works broaden the field for further research. For instance, Tarrow's hypothesis of a link between cycles of protest and cycles of reform claims that protest is a stable 'physiological' function in complex societies, rather than a symptom of social pathology. Tarrow's approach also provides empirical support for the originally Marxian claim that social conflict is linked with change.

Many problems remain unresolved, however. The current interest in the resource mobilization approach is paralleled in Europe by the development of political exchange theories (Pizzorno, 1978a, 1978b; Crouch and Pizzorno, 1978). These theories analyse movements as collective actors seeking inclusion into a political market. Even though these approaches signal a shift from the paradigms based on either class interests or on shared values, they nevertheless concentrate their analysis on the political system rather than on civil society. Consequently, social conflicts are reduced to political protest and regarded as part of a political system. This emphasis exaggerates the function of politics. Participants in collective action are not simply motivated by 'economic' goals – calculating costs and benefits of their action – or by exchanging goods in a political market. They also seek goods which are not measurable and cannot be calculated.[3] Contemporary social movements, more than others in the past, have shifted towards a non-political terrain: the need for self-realization in everyday life. In this respect social movements have a conflictual and antagonistic, but not a political orientation, because they challenge the logic of complex systems on cultural grounds.

These diverse perspectives on collective action and social movements cannot be compared unless their key terms are defined more precisely. Tarrow (1983) observes that the field of social movements is elusive because movements are themselves conceptually hard to define. As a consequence, or so I would argue, most analyses make empirical generalizations rather than provide useful analytical concepts. Tarrow's helpful distinction

23

definitions

between *movements* (as forms of mass opinion), *protest organizations* (as forms of social organization) and *protest events* (as forms of action) is an attempt to isolate the various factors of collective action. However, he adopts Tilly's (1978) definition of movements which, unfortunately, remains based upon an empirical generalization: a social movement comprises an aggrieved, mobilized mass opinion in contact with the authorities. Defined in this way, Tarrow admits, a movement rarely acts in a concerted way and its existence must be inferred from the activities of its representative organizations (Tarrow, 1983, p. 5).

But how does one know that a movement exists behind protest activity? If one adopts this perspective, a movement resembles a metaphysical entity which triggers protest organizations and protest events. Contemporary American authors seem to call every form of non-institutional political action a social movement, to the extent that the word 'movement' is in danger of becoming synonymous with everything in motion in society. Furthermore, the concept of protest is defined weakly. Should protest be defined as every form of complaint by an aggrieved group? As a reaction which breaks established rules? As a confrontation with authorities? Or does it include all these variables? The resource mobilization approach begs such questions and fails to distinguish between empirical generalizations and analytic definitions. How, for example, does one differentiate between a drunken individual shouting anti-government slogans in the street, a trade union strike and a broad mobilization against nuclear policy? All of them can be viewed empirically as protest, but each of them has a quite different meaning. The definition of protest as *disruptive* behaviour demonstrates the inadequacies of empirical generalizations. Such a definition implies a system of reference – a set of limits or boundaries which are disrupted – and collective action is again reduced to political action because the only possible index of disruption becomes the confrontation with authorities. To avoid such misconceptions, a conceptual shift away from empirical towards analytic definitions is necessary.

To facilitate this shift, sociological analysis must abandon the traditional view of movements as characters moving on an historical stage. In the tradition of both progressive and conservative social thought, conflict is often represented through

24

the image of theatre. Social movements are cast as figures in an epic tragedy, as heroes or villains who are moving toward some grand ideal or dramatic destiny. There is a stage on which the characters act; the players follow a script that foreshadows a happy or tragic ending, usually defined from the point of view of the author. In addition, there is a public which has to side with one or other of the play's main characters – the hero or the villain – since this choice determines the destiny of the society, its progress into civilization or its descent into barbarism.

The currently dominant view of social conflicts still conforms to this traditional representation of collective action. We continue to speak of the workers' movement, the women's movement, the youth movement, the ecology movement or the peace movement as if they are living subjects who act as homogeneous entities, expressing the deepest contradictions of society or its values. The action of these movements is perceived as an event which takes place on a theatrical stage, acted out by characters defined by their role (and with intellectuals acting as playwrights, prompters or even directors). This kind of imagery has become highly questionable. Social movements cannot be represented as characters, as subjects endowed with being and purpose, as acting within a scenario whose finale is predetermined. Such misconceptions can be rectified only by rejecting the assumption of collective action as a unified datum. Only then can we discover the plurality of perspectives, meanings and relationships which crystallize in any given collective action. The problem, in politics as well as in theory, is to understand how and why these complex and diverse elements actually converge in relatively unified empirical entities.

Action Systems

This problem cannot be resolved by considering collective action either as an effect of structural conditions or as an expression of values and beliefs. Collective action is rather the product of purposeful orientations developed within a field of opportunities and constraints. Individuals acting collectively *construct* their action by defining in cognitive terms these possibilities and limits, while at the same time interacting with others in order to 'organize' (i.e., to make sense of) their common behaviour. Collective action is not a unitary empirical phenomenon. Whatever unity exists should be considered the result and not the starting point, a fact to be explained rather than assumed. When actors produce their collective action they define both themselves and their environment (other actors, available resources, opportunities and obstacles). Such definitions are not linear but are produced by interaction, negotiation and conflict. This process is often concealed by both collective actors and their opponents. Collective actors tend to emphasize the 'highest' meaning of their action and to claim a unity which they in fact rarely achieve. Those in power, conversely, tend to stress the 'lowest' meaning of collective action, for instance by dismissing it as pathological behaviour. Such reactions fail to acknowledge that whenever individuals act collectively they are situated within a *multipolar action system* (Figure 1). Individuals contribute to the formation of a more or less stable 'we' by rendering common and laboriously negotiating and adjusting at least three orientations: the *goals* of their action; the *means* to be utilized; and the *environment* within which their action takes place.

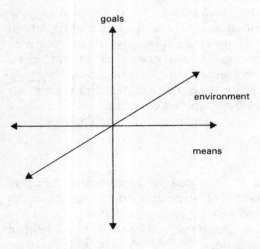

Figure 1

26

These three axes of a multipolar action system resemble a set of interdependent vectors in a state of mutual tension. Collective action has to satisfy multiple and contrasting requirements. It is never the simple expression of actors' intentions, but is constructed by actors who utilize the resources available to them within a particular environment of possibilities and obstacles. Ends, means and the environment continually tend to generate tensions within the action itself: the objectives may not correspond to the means, the environment may be rich or poor in resources, and the means may be more or less congruent with the field of action. In addition, there may be continual tensions even within the single axes: for example, between short- and long-term objectives, in the choice of means, between the use of resources to maximize the efficacy of action or to consolidate solidarity, and in actors' various relationships with their environment, which provides opportunities to a greater or lesser extent.

Collective actors continually negotiate and renegotiate each of these dimensions. Leadership patterns and organizational forms represent attempts to give a more durable and predictable order to these negotiations. This point is usually ignored in analyses of collective action. Attention is normally focused upon its more visible aspects (personalities and events, public mobilizations, acts of violence). These visible phenomena are, however, only manifestations of deeper processes which in turn depend upon the capacity of actors to negotiate the ends, means and environment of their action. Collective action constantly requires this 'social construction' – the failure or breakdown of which renders collective action impossible.

Having clarified the sense in which collective action is *produced*, some important distinctions should be introduced to highlight the *plurality* of dimensions which can be observed and analysed in the same empirical phenomenon. While all 'collective' events consist of several individuals who exhibit common patterns of behaviour within the same framework of space and time, it is easy to see that this behaviour comprises at least three analysable dimensions:

1 Some collective phenomena entail *solidarity*, actors' mutual recognition as members of the same social unit. Other collective

phenomena are based on *aggregation* (Alberoni, 1977), on purely individualistic behaviour which is directed exclusively to its external environment, rather than to the group itself. Thus, in a workers' strike solidarity normally prevails, whereas a shoppers' panic and other forms of crowd behaviour more closely resemble aggregative behaviour.

2 Collective phenomena sometimes involve *conflict*, an opposition between two or more actors competing for control over resources which they consider valuable. Collective phenomena can also emerge through actors' *consensus* about the procedures for controlling the distribution and use of valued resources. A demonstration against nuclear power normally entails conflict, whereas a peaceful march of enthusiastic football supporters after a match is usually based on consensus.

3 Some collective phenomena involve a *transgression of the limits of compatibility of the system* of social relationships in which action is embedded. These limits of a system are defined by the range of variations which it can tolerate without modifying its own structure. Collective phenomena may also comprise forms of *adaptation* which are situated within these limits of a system. Grievances centred on the distribution of rewards within a firm are good examples of adaptive behaviour; but when a struggle aims to alter the decision-making structures of the firm, collective action transgresses the given boundaries of the organization itself.[4]

These analytical distinctions permit the separation of different aspects of collective action. For example, any given collective action can contain competing interests which respect the limits of a given social order; actions that challenge the system's limits of compatibility; aggregative behaviour; deviant behaviour which transgresses a system's shared rules, but which does not imply conflict; and so on.[5]

A fundamental implication of this point about the plurality of possible meanings within collective action is that a social movement is not a unified 'subject' but always a composite action system, in which widely differing means, ends and forms of solidarity and organization converge in a more or less stable manner. The conventional term 'social movement' seems

28

unable to grasp this complexity. In recent years there have been attempts (including my own) to transform the term social movement into a clearly defined analytic *concept* which is not identical with empirical forms of collective action which contain many different dimensions: elements of deviance, controlled competition, aggregative behaviour, and so on. This research development creates a difficulty, in that the term social movement continues to be used by many researchers in a naïvely descriptive manner to refer to a supposedly unified 'subject', such as the 'youth movement', the 'women's movement' or the 'ecological movement', and even when the term is not used naïvely, its descriptive usage seems unavoidable in contemporary speech. There seems to be no easy way of resolving this problem without venturing into unexplored semantic territory (which would lead, as always, to the redefinition of the entire conceptual universe in this field). This adventure may have begun already in the sociology of collective action and, as often happens in the evolution of scientific concepts, the semantic change will be noticeable only after it has occurred. Until that time one conclusion seems inescapable: the present-day study of social movements necessitates a shift from naïve empirical generalizations to analytic concepts.

The need to define more precisely a 'social movement' is a case in point. In my view, this concept designates a specific class of collective phenomena which contains three dimensions. First, a social movement is a form of collective action which involves *solidarity*, that is, actors' mutual recognition that they are part of a single social unit. A second characteristic of a social movement is its engagement in *conflict*, and thus in opposition to an adversary who lays claim to the same goods or values. Conflict is analytically distinct from the idea of contradiction as used, for instance, within the Marxist tradition. Conflict presupposes adversaries who struggle for something which they recognize as lying between them. Third, a social movement *breaks the limits of compatibility of a system*. Its actions violate the boundaries or tolerance limits of a system, thereby pushing the system beyond the range of variations that it can tolerate without altering its structure (see note 4). In this analytical sense a social movement differs from other forms of action (such as conflicts taking place within a system of shared rules; deviance; or aggregative behaviour). Empirical forms of collective action comprise a combination of these analytical dimensions: actors play many different games at the same time, and the task of the analysis is therefore to reveal the existence of this pluralism.

Collective identity

Having clarified the need for a change from empirical generalizations to analytical definitions in the study of collective action, we can now return to the questions raised in the opening section. In particular, the question of how collective action is formed, and therefore how individuals become involved in it, assumes a decisive theoretical importance. What was formerly considered a datum (the existence of a movement) is precisely what needs to be explained. Analysis must acknowledge the heterogeneity of collective action and explain how its various aspects are combined and sustained through time. For this purpose, neither the macro-structural models of collective action nor those based on individuals' motivation are satisfactory, for they lack an understanding of an intermediate level of collective action. This level comprises the processes through which individuals recognize that they share certain orientations in common and on that basis decide to act together. Recent work in Europe and North America has concentrated on this intermediate level.[6] Klandermans (1986; Klandermans and Oegema, 1987) has usefully analysed this level by delineating three dimensions of collective action: mobilization potential, recruitment networks, and the motivation to participate.

The concept of *mobilization potential* refers to that sector of the population which identifies with a movement, or to some of the issues it raises. Mobilization potential, however, can be considered a subjective attitude based on objective circumstances. But such a dualistic foundation supposes a *deus ex machina* (the intellectuals, the party, the organization) capable of synchronizing the objective conditions and subjective attitudes and transforming the latter into action. If unity is not assumed from the beginning of the process it cannot be found at the end. Hence the mobilization potential must be conceived – in my view – as a negotiated view, among a number of individuals, of the opportunities for and the constraints upon action.

Recruitment networks play a fundamental role in the process of involving individuals. No process of mobilization begins in a vacuum and, contrary to the theory of mass society (Kornhauser, 1959), isolated and uprooted individuals never mobilize. The existing networks of social relationships facilitate the processes of involvement and decrease the cost of individuals' investment in collective action.[7]

In this context, Olson's classic argument of the 'free rider' (Olson, 1965) provides a useful comparison. He holds that the interest in obtaining a collective good is not sufficient to induce individuals to pay the cost of obtaining it (since the individual will equally enjoy the benefits of an action carried out by others). This argument, compared with the naïve assumption that collective action derives from the 'objective' common interests of individuals, plays a vital critical role. But it does not go beyond this critical function, and has prompted numerous objections.

Fireman and Gamson (1979), for example, note that individuals act to secure a collective benefit because they recognize that it could not be attained if each waited for the other to act. Still others draw attention to the importance of individuals' perception of the action's potential success, of the number of participants, and the importance of their contribution (Oberschall, 1980; Oliver, 1984). Pizzorno (1983a) has also emphasized that the presence of a collective identity is the condition for the calculation of the costs and benefits of action. For all these reasons, therefore, recruitment networks constitute a crucial intermediate level for understanding the processes by which individuals become involved in collective action. Within these networks, individuals interact, influence each other, negotiate and hence establish conceptual and motivational frameworks for action.

This is also why the *motivation to participate* which develops at the level of the individual, cannot be considered as an exclusively individual phenomenon. While motivation is rooted in individual psychological traits, it is constructed and developed through interaction. The incentives to act exert a dominant influence on individuals' motivation. But the criteria used by individuals to recognize and evaluate these incentives are always interactive, in that they develop within the networks to which individuals belong.

These considerations demonstrate that the models developed by the western political tradition to explain the involvement of individuals in collective action are inadequate. Two models – the 'Leninist' and 'Luxemburghian' – exemplify these weaknesses. The former includes Leninism and theories of crowd behaviour and mass society, which paradoxically share a common assumption: that involvement is the work of a minority that inspires an undifferentiated mass of individuals and leads them to recognize their real interests (Lenin) or to accept, through suggestion and manipulation, the aims of the agitators (crowd psychology theory). By contrast, the Luxemburghian model attributes to individuals a spontaneous capacity to mobilize on the basis of discontent, injustice, and deprivation. Both models disregard the fact that individuals define themselves as collective actors by means of a variety of negotiated interactions.

It is important to identify how this negotiation process develops. Individuals construct their goals and make choices and decisions within a perceived environment. Here the concept of expectations is fundamental in analysing the link between actors and their environment.[8] Expectations, which are socially constructed, enable actors to relate to their external world. I propose that only if individual actors can recognize their coherence and continuity as actors will they be able to write their own script of social reality and compare expectations and outcomes. Thus, any theory of collective action which incorporates the concept of expectations presupposes a theory of identity. This dimension, unfortunately, is rarely made explicit in those conventional models of collective action which involve a theory of expectations.

The most common models of collective action can be described briefly as follows:

1 rise and fall (Davies, 1962): these occur when a period of prosperity is followed by a sharp decline in the capacity of a social system to satisfy the needs of its population;

2 rising expectations: after a period of sustained growth, which

multiplies expectations, a gap appears between expectations and the satisfaction of needs, thereby causing social unrest;

3 relative deprivation: actors compare their position and rewards with those of a comparable group on the stratification scale; this comparison creates discontent and mobilization;

4 downward mobility: collective action is due to a particular form of relative deprivation, which results when actors lose their social position and compare themselves with their previous condition and the position of other social groups;

5 status inconsistency: social actors observe an inconsistency between the various elements of their status (income, prestige, power) and mobilize in order to eliminate this discrepancy.

These models imply a theory of expectations (based on previous experience or on comparisons with other groups). They also suppose that the gap between expectations and outcomes is the basis of collective action. As such, they are an extension of the well-known frustration/aggression paradigm: the gap between expected gratifications and actual outcomes (i.e. frustration) produces an aggressive response, such as collective protest and violence.

The over-simplification of this model has been criticized by resource mobilization theory (RMT) (McCarthy and Zald, 1976; for a review, see Jenkins, 1983; Gurney and Tierney, 1982). Its criticism focuses upon the relative deprivation theory but it is also applicable to the other models listed above. RMT points out that discontent is present in any society and hence is insufficient to explain processes of collective mobilization. It also emphasizes the importance of 'discretional resources' (i.e. resources available to and recognized by particular actors) and the 'structure of opportunities' (i.e. the set of opportunities made available by the existing system) in making action possible. This criticism correctly reveals the inadequacy of the frustration/ aggression models of mobilization as well as underlines the significance of the social preconditions of collective action. Unfortunately, the RMT criticism neither confronts the essential weakness of the frustration/aggression paradigm nor formulates a plausible alternative.

The frustration/aggression paradigm, indeed all other theories based on expectations, assumes that actors are capable of first, comparing expectations and rewards at different times; second, identifying the social sources of their deprivation; and third, recognizing the expected benefits of their action as not only desirable but just. In the absence of these conditions, it cannot be supposed that the simple deprivation of an expected gratification will produce a response of the 'voice' type, that is, a conflictual response. Many other 'exit' types of responses are in fact possible, including sublimation, symbolic escape, and the search for a scapegoat.[9]

The proponents of RMT correctly emphasize that expectations are constructed by evaluating the possibilities and constraints provided by the environment of action. In this way RMT reveals the importance of an intermediate level of action which is completely ignored by the models that assume a direct relationship between discontent and mobilization. But RMT is marked by the same limitations as the theories it criticizes. In fact, its key concepts, such as 'discretional resources' and a 'structure of opportunities', do not refer to 'objective' realities but imply the capacity of actors to perceive, evaluate, and determine the possibilities and limits afforded by their environment. RMT thus postulates a process of actors' construction of their identity, without, however, examining this process. RMT and the models based on expectations all presuppose a theory of identity. Expectations are constructed and compared with reality only by actors who are capable of defining themselves and the field of their action. The result of this process of constructing an action system I call *collective identity*.

Collective identity is an interactive and shared definition produced by several interacting individuals who are concerned with the orientations of their action as well as the field of opportunities and constraints in which their action takes place. The process of constructing, maintaining and altering a collective identity provides the basis for actors to shape their expectations and calculate the costs and benefits of their action. Collective identity formation is a delicate process and requires continual investments. As it comes to resemble more institutionalized forms of social action, collective identity may crystallize into organizational forms, a system of formal rules, and patterns of leadership. In less institutionalized forms of action its character more closely resembles a process which must be continually activated in order for action to be possible.

Considered as a process, collective identity involves at least three fundamental dimensions which are in reality closely interwoven: first, formulating cognitive frameworks concerning the goals, means and environment of action; second, activating relationships among the actors, who communicate, negotiate, and make decisions; and third, making emotional investments, which enable individuals to recognize themselves in each other.

Collective identity is thus a process in which actors produce the common cognitive frameworks that enable them to assess their environment and to calculate the costs and benefits of their action. The definitions which they formulate are in part the result of negotiated interactions and of relationships of influence and in part the fruit of emotional recognition. In this sense collective action is never based solely on cost–benefit calculations and a collective identity is never entirely negotiable.[10]

Collective identity thus defined indicates a key analytical dimension to be explored in the sociological analysis of collective phenomena. Its degree of stability or variability, concentration or diffusion, integration or fragmentation, varies considerably according to the degree of structuring of a collective phenomenon (which can range from purely aggregated behaviour to formal organization). It is nevertheless a chronic feature of collective action. The propensity of individuals and sub-groups to involve themselves in collective action always depends upon their differential access to resources, such as information, access to networks, and professional or communicative skills, which enable them to participate in the process of identity building. These differences also influence the starting point and the duration of their involvement, the intensity of their participation and the quality of their expectations. For example, studies show that militants and activists in social movements are typically recruited from those who are highly integrated into the social structure, play a central role in the networks to which they belong, and have at their disposal substantial cognitive and social resources. These studies also clarify the differences between the militants and individuals belonging to marginal, deprived, or declining social groups (such as peasants, marginalized workers and unemployed people). The latter become involved more slowly, for shorter periods of time, and at levels of participation which have lower costs.[11]

Even in less structured forms of collective action actors 'organize' their behaviour, produce meanings and actively establish relationships. Certainly these processes of construction of collective identity vary greatly, both in intensity and in complexity, according to the type of collective phenomenon in question. But researchers can no longer ignore these processes. Individuals' involvement in collective action calls for new explanations. These must give due weight to the ways in which actors make cognitive and emotional investments in the intricate process of building collective identity – and, hence, to the capacity of actors to construct their collective action in various ways.

Notes and references

1 See the definitive studies of Tilly (1975, 1986) and Moscovici (1981). The classic contributions of Bendix (1964, 1978) remain of fundamental importance.

2 Various studies contributed to this view: cognitive social psychology (for example, Eiser, 1980); the sociology of action (Touraine, 1973); constructivist approaches in the sociology of organization (Crozier and Friedberg, 1977) and decision-making processes (Simon, 1973, 1977; for a synthesis, see Gherardi, 1985). In the field of research on collective action an important role was played by the resource mobilization theory (a synthesis is provided by Kerbo, 1982; Jenkins, 1983). In the field of social movements research a constructivist approach has been adopted by Melucci (1984a, 1984b, 1985a, 1985b, 1986, 1987); Hosking (1983); Brown and Hosking (1984); and Donati (1984).

3 As Pizzorno himself has pointed out, identity is also a non-negotiable good for social actors, the pre-condition of their calculations; see Pizzorno (1983a), and Melucci (1982). This is also the basis for Pizzorno's critique of rational choice theories (Pizzorno, 1983b, 1986a, 1986b).

4 A corollary of this distinction is the importance of defining the limits of a given system, precisely because the same action's meaning (e.g., its disruptive potential) may differ dramatically from one system to another. It might be useful, for example, to distinguish between the system that ensures the production of the constitutive resources of a society, the

system within which decisions concerning the distribution of those resources are made, and the system of roles that permits the exchange and enjoyment of the resources. The meaning of a given action will vary according to which system is affected or 'disrupted' by collective mobilization (Melucci, 1974a, 1980).

5 For a detailed presentation of the types of collective action which can be derived from a combination of these analytical dimensions see Melucci (1982, 1984a).

6 I first proposed a comparison between these approaches in Melucci (1976, 1977, 1984b). For a critical survey, see Klandermans (1986). On the intermediate level of collective action see Tarrow (1986); McAdam (1986); Snow and Benford (1986); and Kriesi (1985, 1986). A psycho-social extension of resource mobilization theory, focusing on the intermediate level, is proposed by Klandermans (1984). A synthesis of the debate between American and European perspectives is provided by Klandermans, Kriesi and Tarrow (1988).

7 Among the many empirical contributions, see Oberschall (1973); Wilson and Orum (1976); Snow, Zurcher and Ekland-Olsen (1980); McAdam (1982); Rochford (1982); Walsh and Warland (1983) Melucci (1984a); Donati (1984); Diani and Lodi (1986); Snow, Rochford, Worden and Benford (1986); and Ennis and Schreuer (1987).

8 A critical discussion of expectation models is developed in Melucci (1982), chapter 2.

9 On the exit–voice alternative, see Hirschman (1970).

10 The concept of collective identity was introduced to recent sociological debate by authors such as Touraine (1973, 1978, 1984, 1985) and Pizzorno (1978, 1983a, 1983b, 1986a, 1986b); see also Cohen (1985). These authors fail to clarify the process of construction of collective identity by means of interactions, negotiations and relationships with the environment. In the case of Touraine, collective identity appears as a datum, as something essential to a movement; in the case of Pizzorno, collective identity seems to be based on mutual recognition and shared values, which are the condition for calculating the costs and benefits of collective action.

11 For an extensive survey of the empirical literature, see Grazioli and Lodi (1984) and McAdam (1986).

2

Movements as messages

Systemic conflicts

limits of a system

Among my criteria for defining a social movement is the extent to which its actions challenge or break the limits of a system of social relations. Defined in this way, the study of social movements raises a significant question for sociological theory: are there forms of conflict which are being directed against the intrinsic logic of complex systems?

Marx's mode of production

This logic may be analysed in terms of Marx's 'mode of production'. However, this term is problematic, especially because of its connotations of economic reductionism. Production not only impinges on the economic/material sphere but also affects the totality of social relations, including the cultural processes through which a system creates its basic resources. The important question is therefore whether we can identify a dominant 'mode of production' and pinpoint types of conflict that impinge upon the social relations which produce the key resources of complex society. In other words, do contemporary collective phenomena contain antagonistic conflicts which break or challenge the limits of the system? Or are we faced only with processes of marginalization, patterns of collective behaviour in the classic functionalist sense, or adjustments among actors competing in the political market?

The answers to these questions are difficult to verify. In political sociology, for example, the whole issue of antagonistic conflicts has been excluded from the realm of relevant inquiry. Political market or strategic behaviour theories, such as the recent rational choice approaches, reduce conflict to the

38

framework of exchange. Ironically, these theories represent the reverse side of orthodox Marxism, which clings to an increasingly outdated concept of class struggle to explain the forms and strategies of new conflicts. Political exchange theories deny the existence of antagonistic conflicts on a systemic level, while Marxism defends a quasi-metaphysical principle of social antagonism, which is unhelpful for empirical research. Against these approaches, my research is concerned to keep open questions about the existence and types of systemic conflict, and thus to broaden our understanding of the changes in contemporary societies. The decision to pursue this type of analysis has methodological consequences.

To begin with, the contributions of the political market or strategic behaviour theories to an understanding of social movements can be extremely fruitful. This is because their analysis passes through what might be called a 'sceptical' filter – through a 'disenchanted' framework of analysis that prevents us from wrongly attributing 'general' antagonistic significance to every form of collective action. Many contemporary conflicts, even violent and radical action, are not of this type. They can be explained instead by the theory of political exchange. Collective actors – classes or groups – who demand access to political representation are cases in point. They contain no antagonistic dimension, but instead a demand for inclusion in a system of benefits and rules from which previously they had been denied. If the boundaries of a system are rigid, violent conflict may occur (Tilly 1975, 1978; Shorter and Tilly, 1974), but this does not necessarily mean that it is antagonistic towards the logic of the rules governing the system. Similarly, when an organization experiences a high level of dysfunction, all conflicts could be interpreted as an attempt to re-establish harmonious relations within the organization. Only after these analytical approaches have been explored can any hypothesis concerning antagonistic conflict be proposed.

My methodology, therefore, does not assume the existence of systemic conflicts. It rather attempts to develop this strong theoretical hypothesis by means of an analytical process which reconsiders (and sometimes discards) explanations based on organizational tensions and dysfunctions, competition, and exchange. The point is that the conflict potential of collective action is not a priori, but is uncovered by empirical investigation and by the creation of a theoretical space wherein meaningful questions regarding systemic conflicts can be formulated. In both academic and political circles there has been a tendency to simplify or to avoid such theoretical questions. This tendency is evident in the substitution of many Marxist-oriented analyses, based on models of class and class struggle, by models based on exchange or rational choice. I have reservations about the capacity of both kinds of models to explain the emergent conflicts in complex societies. For this reason it is important to keep open the question of whether or not antagonistic conflicts exist. At the same time, research must concentrate on analysing the 'mode of production' of complex societies in order to elaborate a new model for interpreting the structural changes that currently affect these societies. These changes (exemplified in elusive expressions such as complex, post-industrial, and late capitalist societies) implicitly rest upon assumptions that the contemporary 'mode of production' is qualitatively different from that of industrial or monopoly capitalism.

All too often this assumption hides certain theoretical problems. For instance, the issue of whether or not there are systemic conflicts in contemporary societies raises a fundamental theoretical question: is it still possible to speak of a 'system logic' in highly differentiated societies? Arguably, the spatial metaphors and dualisms (base/superstructure, centre/periphery) characteristic of industrial society are no longer appropriate for describing and explaining contemporary conflicts. New questions therefore emerge: must we abandon all analysis of system level of our societies? Do conflicts of a universal nature still exist? Or can an explanatory model of our systems coexist with the view that our system's dominant logic is deployed on different fronts, thereby broading the range of sites and actors involved in conflict?

'New social movements'?

The debate on the 'new social movements' reinforces the need for theoretical and epistemological speculation. The possibility of determining what is 'new' in contemporary movements

40

depends primarily on an analysis which transcends an empiricist view of collective phenomena and, hence, explains how the integration of many diverse elements produces a collective reality.

This need for theoretical speculation is stimulated by the emergence, during the last twenty-five years, of new forms of collective action in areas previously untouched by social conflicts. New actors have emerged whose organizational models and repertoires of action differ from those of earlier social movements. Observations reveal that:

1 The recent forms of social conflict have a permanent and non-conjunctural nature. They coexist with traditional social groupings (such as classes, interest groups and associations), and though their empirical features vary, they remain a stable and irreversible component of contemporary social systems;

2 Within the new conflicts, the function of socialization and 'submerged' participation is fulfilled by new networks rooted in everyday life, which open new channels for grouping and selecting elites. Hence the traditional mechanisms of political socialization, cultural innovation and institutional modernization are redefined;

3 In complex societies, those who govern have to contend not only with the relationship between institutional systems of representation and decision-making, but also with new forms of action. These new conflicts are not easily adaptable to the existing channels of participation and to traditional forms of political organization, such as political parties. Moreover, the outcome of new conflicts is difficult to predict, and this increases the already high degree of uncertainty in these systems.

Since the 1970s, the sociological significance of these developments has initiated a series of theoretical and empirical studies. The debate about the 'novelty' of these collective phenomena has been dominated by a recurrent question: what is 'new' about the 'new social movements'?

This debate reveals epistemological ambiguities that have consequences for understanding the role collective phenomena play in complex societies. As one of those who introduced the

41

term 'new social movements' to sociological literature (Melucci, 1977, 1980, 1981a), I have noticed the increasing ontologization of this expression, and its subsequent characterization as a 'paradigm'. Many recent contributions utilize a 'paradigm of the new social movements', either to support empirical research or as a way of comparing European and American approaches.[1] The problem of the 'novelty' of the 'new movements' has been discussed extensively and criticized in this literature. However, the debate focuses on a false problem. 'Novelty' is by definition a relative concept, which functions initially to emphasize some comparative differences between classes of phenomena (in this instance between the traditional forms of class conflict and the emergent forms of collective action). But if sociological analysis is incapable of transcending this conventional definition and cannot discern the distinctive features of the 'new' phenomena, the stress on the 'novelty' ends up concealing an underlying conceptual weakness.

To avoid becoming entrapped in an endless debate, social scientists must recognize the relative and transitory nature of the concept of 'new social movements'. Those who are critical of the 'paradigm of the new social movements' base their argument on the similar characteristics of contemporary forms of action and those of earlier historical periods. They dismiss talk of the novelty of contemporary conflicts as merely the effect of that 'myopia of the present' frequently suffered by sociologists when they are involved emotionally with the object of their study.

In its more radical version – the view that 'nothing under the sun is new' – this criticism is based on an ingenuous historicism that assumes an unimpeded, linear flow of historical events. Consequently this view is incapable of identifying the different systemic location – that is, the different significance – of actual events and actions that may reveal genuine parallels and similarities. The softer version of this criticism – 'not everything under the sun is new' – may be empirically justified, but it still lacks validity. Both the supporters and the critics of the paradigm of 'new movements' share the same epistemological limitation: the contemporary phenomena are regarded as a unified empirical object. By assuming this unity, the supporters of the new movements paradigm seek to qualify its novelty, while the critics question or deny it outright. The problem

42

becomes whether 'the women's movement' or 'the peace movement' is new or is not new: some seek to identify the historical differences, others stress the continuity and comparability of old and new social movements.

The shortcomings of the debate are evident. Both sides have failed to recognize that contemporary collective action consists of different relationships and meanings. In order to compare the different forms of action, these diverse components must be distinguished and identified. Otherwise, movements are perceived, illegitimately, as living 'characters' moving and acting upon a stage of history.

When considered from this revised angle, the positive – and unintended – result of the recent debate about the 'new social movements' is that the image of movements as *personnages* seems to have exhausted itself. Discussion about the 'novelty' of contemporary social movements has made possible the recognition of their plurality of meanings and forms of action. It has helped break down global empirical generalizations. It has also prompted us to recognize that contemporary movements combine forms of action that: a) impact upon different levels of the social system; b) contain diverse goals; and c) belong to different phases of development of a system or to different historical systems. Seen in this way, the problem is to understand both the synchronic and diachronic elements of movements, and in turn to explain how their diverse elements are united in organized collective action.

Two questions nevertheless remain: can we speak of the emergence of a new paradigm of collective action in an analytical sense (i.e., in terms of specific levels, elements, and relationships of observed action). Furthermore, are there dimensions of the 'new' forms of collective action in complex societies which are qualitatively different from those in the phase of industrial capitalism?

Critics of the 'new' paradigm reject these questions. This leads them to fall into the trap of political reductionism. If contemporary movements are not seen to be 'new', then the basis of comparison with earlier movements inevitably becomes their impact on the political system; social movements, old and new, are considered only as political actors. This political reductionism dismisses the issue of structural change in

43

complex societies and underestimates the great significance of the social and cultural dimensions of contemporary collective action. The result is a 'myopia of the visible', which leads the analysis to focus all its attention on the measurable aspects of collective action (e.g., confrontation with the political system, and movements' effects on the policies of organizations). It thereby ignores the way in which the visible action of contemporary movements depends upon their production of new cultural codes within submerged networks.[2]

Let us consider the problem of political reductionism in more detail. The action of contemporary movements is frequently described as 'protest', while analysis of these movements is limited to the political system. The use of the concept of protest in this undifferentiated way is a typical example of political reductionism. If the concept of protest were confined explicitly to the political level (i.e., to those forms of collective action which involve a direct confrontation with authority), then it would consciously exclude all other levels of collective action from consideration.[3] But if reductionism is implicit in the concept of protest, then it tends automatically to eliminate from consideration those levels of collective action which are outside the political domain. They are dismissed summarily as uninteresting or unmeasurable, as expressive or as folkloristic.

Political reductionism also affects the observations considered significant by researchers. For example, quantitative research on collective action (Tilly, 1975, 1978; Tarrow, 1988) considers collective events as discrete units of analysis. This is an effective research strategy and provides useful empirical evidence for the study of collective action and social movements. Although this approach privileges empirically observable action (i.e. behavioural events), what is really observed is the *product* of diverse relationships and goals of an underlying structure of action. Particularly when the data sources are newspaper reports and public records, events are the 'objectified' result of constructive social processes which comprise relationships and meanings, which form the basis of the publicly visible action.

A constructivist view of social movements cannot restrict itself to considering action as a visible event. Quantitative studies focus on the outcomes of action, not on how action is itself produced. While the quantitative approach contributes important

44

information about collective action, it requires researchers to recognize its limitations, namely, that collective action is not a 'fact' but a process. The quantitative approach concentrates on those social relationships (such as public activities and confrontations with political authorities) which already form part of a system of order. It therefore fails to examine the network of relationships which constitutes the submerged reality of the movements before, during, and after events.

The conscious emphasis on the visible effects of action can be a legitimate type of analysis in the field of research on social movements. However, it becomes an unhelpful form of reductionism when it neglects the processes of 'production' of collective action – and thus ignores the creation of cultural models and symbolic challenges inherent in the 'new movements'. Since these less visible elements are outside the political domain, their identification requires a different methodological approach.

Individualization

In complex societies material production is increasingly replaced by the production of signs and social relations. Systemic conflicts centre on the ability of groups and individuals to control the conditions of their own action. Complex societies are networks of high-density information and are dependent upon a degree of autonomy for their constituent elements: without the development of formal capacities for learning and action, individuals and groups could not function as terminals capable of self-regulation, that is, of producing, collecting, decoding and exchanging information. At the same time, however, the pronounced differentiation of contemporary societies signals the need for greater integration and intensification of control. Consequently, there is a shift of emphasis from the content to the code of social life, from behaviour to the pre-conditions of action.

In the current period, society's capacity to intervene in the production of meaning extends to those areas which previously escaped control and regulation: areas of self-definition, emotional relationships, sexuality and 'biological' needs. At the same time,

45

there is a parallel demand from below for control over the conditions of personal existence. Even though individuals are implicated in these conditions, they cannot be considered private or individual. Rather they are systemic processes and as such are an integral part of the way in which high-density information societies create the resources necessary for their own reproduction. The simple domination of nature and the transformation of raw materials into commodities is no longer central. Instead, society's capacity to produce information, communications and sociability depends upon an increasing level of self-reflexiveness and upon the self-production of action itself.

In recent years these developments have initiated much debate, especially about the concept of identity (Cohen, 1985). Although I find the concept inadequate, I have used it (Melucci, 1982) when referring to the control of identity – that is, to the reappropriation of the meaning (the conditions and goals) of individual and social action. Yet the term 'identity' is inadequate because it has come to have a variety of meanings. In fact conflicts are always conflicts of identity: actors attempt to push others to recognize something which they themselves recognize; they struggle to affirm what others deny. Every conflict which transgresses a system of shared rules concerning the distribution of material or symbolic resources is a conflict of identity. The central question is why has the theme of identity become such a central issue? The probable reason is that it reflects the capacity of contemporary action to go beyond modifying and transforming the natural environment. Action on 'outer' nature was the binding nucleus of industrial society. It was seen as the foundation of progress or of the development of the forces of production; it was viewed as the path to liberty, the wealth of nations or socialism. Underlying such visions was an awareness of the possibility of expanding the scope of human action on the world. In contemporary systems we find an emerging awareness of the capacity to act upon human action itself – to intervene in our motivational and biological structures. The social and individual potential for action becomes itself the object of action: one acts on the ability to act and plan. Social systems discover their capacities for open, 'plastic' and self-referential action.

46

In the processes of socialization, for example, what was considered as the simple transmission of a society's rules and values comes to mean the potential to redefine and create the 'formal' capacities for learning. In demographic and biogenetic planning, what was considered reproduction of the 'natural' features of a society has become a field for social intervention, and what was once the law of nature is transformed into an object of social action. As Habermas (1976) points out, science develops the self-reflexive capacity to modify 'internal nature', while the systems of relationships in which individuals act are multiplying. Such relations are no longer governed solely by membership; they instead involve an area of choice and, thus, the possibility for individual action.

There are two aspects of this change in human action in complex societies. On the one hand there is an increase in the social capacity of action and the level of intervention on action as it develops; and on the other, the generation of meanings is marked by the need for control and regulation. Paradoxically, individuals perceive the available options for conscious action, but this possibility is blocked by the spread of mechanisms which regulate their biological structure, motivational origins, relationships and forms of communication. In different fields of social life new forms of power are emerging, which control the formation of needs (advertising and marketing), the biological structure of identity (bio-genetics) and the basic motivation of behaviour (neuro-sciences).

A crucial question is why certain groups are more sensitive than others to these systemic processes. The most interesting hypothesis claims that this is due to their differential access to crucial resources (such as cultural markets) and their specific circumstances. Certain groups are therefore more directly affected by the contradictory requirements of the system. They test and utilize the available potential for action, even though they are submitted to forms of power which prevents them from actually enjoying the available options. For example, this hypothesis could be applied fruitfully to specific sectors of young people and women who have found themselves much more exposed to the contradictory requirements of the system. While further empirical investigation is required, these findings have been partly verified by research in the Milano area (Melucci,

1984a). In the light of these findings, the conventional view, which starts from the analysis of a social condition to explain a group's action, must be reversed. The action of a group and the level of the system which it effects must become the basis for analysing the composition of a social condition, which may facilitate the formation of conflictual actors.

This type of explanation of collective action has implications for the concept of identity, which in my view we should replace with consideration of the 'potential for individualization'. For, the process of individualization involves on the one hand, the potential for individual control over the conditions and levels of action; yet, on the other, it entails the expropriation of these self-reflexive and self-productive resources by society itself. Foucault suggests that complex societies are characterized by the homologation of behaviour patterns: by the manipulation of information and of cultural codes which are the basis for consensus and communication. Foucault's arguments over-emphasize the image of a totalizing 'Orwellian' control, yet they point correctly to the diffuse and less visible forms of system integration. Analyses of social health programmes, for instance, suggest that the goal of these programmes is no longer to produce healthy individuals, but to pre-define standards of health and illness. They establish criteria of normality and pathology which are applied preventatively to populations according to the requirements of the system. Again, the outcome is action which shifts control from content to code, from conduct to the pre-conditions of behaviour.

Of course, the process of individualization, which requires self-reflexive action, is in itself a pure 'form' and cannot occur without a symbolic mediation. In contemporary forms of collective mobilization, the appeal to nature, for example, is a species of symbolic mediation. At one and the same time it announces and denies this 'form'. In other words, it is saying that in order to resist pervasive social control we should revive a 'pure' nature, untouched by the human hand; but in a global system where nature is socialized this is no longer possible. Even the possibility of speaking about nature is culturally codified. Paradoxically, the appeal to pure nature draws upon symbolic mediations that deny the cultural and social processes underlying human action, while expressing the need for a reappropriation

48

of the space/time/meaning of life through conscious human action.

A recurrent theme among young people, women, ecologists and peace activists is that action has meaning primarily for the individual: 'if it doesn't make sense to me, I am not participating; but what I do also benefits others'. Participation in collective action is seen to have no value for the individual unless it provides a direct response to personal needs. In a nascent form there is a type of action which conforms to the hypothesis outlined earlier: individuals' control of action is a necessary condition for the formation of collective mobilization and change.

At the empirical level this hypothesis is difficult to test. For example, a group might simply become a site of self-centred, defensive solidarity, protecting individuals from their insecurity and allowing them to express their needs in a convivial environment. Of course there is the second part of the statement: 'what I do also benefits others'. Here the difference between an orientation toward collective goals and a purely defensive enjoyment of the security offered by the group is nebulous. Today's social movements contain marginal counter-cultures and small sects whose goal is the development of the expressive solidarity of the group, but there is also a deeper commitment to the recognition that personal needs are the path to changing the world and to seeking meaningful alternatives.

Factors and actors

Any analysis of the 'novelty' of contemporary movements must consider not only their internal differentiation but also the significant factors which account for their emergence. Most analyses of the factors affecting the formation and social composition of 'new' movements fail to make the important distinction between *structural* and *conjunctural* factors. This distinction refers to the division between elements of a (relatively) permanent and synchronic logic of a given social structure, and elements which emerge as temporary variations of its functioning in a diachronic perspective. The distinction allows one to separate the analysis of the pre-conditions of

x distinction bte structural & conjunctural factors

action from the factors activating specific forms of collective mobilization.

The structural factors identified by the recent literature can be listed as follows (none of them can be considered in isolation and there are overlapping dimensions):

1 *The corporate growth model.*[4] Until the early 1970s, capitalist development, based on private investment decisions governed by profit margins, was centred on economic growth. The path to sustained growth was complemented by a compromise with organized labour in the fields of industrial relations and by the establishment of a permanent welfare system, which enhanced greater income distribution and ensured social security provisions. In addition, decisions about investments and distribution were mediated by forms of 'corporate' representation in the political system. According to the literature, the basic elements of this model – economic growth as an unlimited goal, increased wages and social security measures, highly institutionalized interest organizations and political parties as exclusive means of conflict resolution – produced the following consequences: a) marginalization of unorganized sectors of the labour market; b) extension of the welfare structures and their 'clients'; c) increasing selectivity of political institutions; d) unintended consequences of the system (environmental and urban crisis, fiscal crisis); and e) increasing demands for defence against both international (military policies) and domestic (social control policies) threats.

2 *The production models*[5] stress the changes in the form and content of social production. The advances in information technology and production and the role of world-wide communications are related directly to the formation of a global-village market (of commodities, personnel, ideas, images). These developments affect personal life, work organization, and the definition and perception of time and space.

3 *The educational model.*[6] The educational structures in complex society have dramatically extended their scope and importance. This is evident in the numbers of people they involve (as students and workers) and the time spent within the educational system (the length of educational programmes and the scope of

50

educational activities). Moreover, the modern educational system is expected to encourage general problem-solving abilities instead of transmitting rigid values and moral rules. The outcomes of these processes are viewed as follows: a) the extension of an educated population beyond the opportunities offered by the occupational structure; b) the formation of a large 'uncommitted' youth population, which is increasingly independent of other social structures (such as family, church, the market and politics) and which is also connected directly to the media system and enjoys a position of 'affluent marginality' (in terms of its time allocation, cultural resources and market position); and c) stabilization and development of a highly self-reflexive culture, which is centred on the need for self-realization and made possible by the growing emancipation of individuals from the productive process.

4 *The life-world model.*[7] The increasing autonomy of life-world structures from productive requirements corresponds to a higher level of individual differentiation in everyday life and to a release from traditional family ties. The consequences are seen as follows: a) increasing independence of individuals in affective/family relations (children free from parents, parents from children, spouses or partners from each other); b) increased social mobility at the level of everyday life and the occupational level; and c) multiplication of cultural identities and life-styles, increasingly differentiated by age, territory and cultural traditions, including old cultural patterns which are renewed in a new social context.

The conjunctural factors. Although the literature rarely distinguishes these from structural factors, they refer to two general classes of phenomena: 1) economic factors, and 2) political factors.

1 The first category of events which allegedly influence recent collective mobilizations are sometimes identified in terms of *crisis*: for example, economic crisis generated by domestic and international markets; fiscal problems of the state; urban crisis and, not least, the continual change which affects social structures and therefore widens the gap between central and marginal groups (Offe, 1984; Castells, 1983).

2 The political factors refer to the *unresponsiveness* of political systems to emerging needs and interests. This unresponsiveness has two aspects. In terms of *input* there is an overload of competing interests and demands and the rigidity of gatekeepers, such as political parties, or of institutional procedures. On the *output* side, problems include the inadequacy of authority to respond, both in terms of quality (lack of evaluation, or the use of repression) and timing (time-lags and ineffectiveness of political decisions and planning) (Melucci, 1977, 1981b; Tarrow, 1983, 1988).

A close examination of these two types of conjunctural factors reveals a common feature: in contrast to the structural models, they highlight *the limits of the system*. The economic factors clarify the social costs resulting from technical and economic modernization and from the penetration of these processes into everyday life; and the political factors reveal the inadequacy of the existing mechanisms and the increasing selectivity of political processes.

While the structural factors are essentially *surplus models* (in that they postulate an excess of available resources and possibilities in the system), the conjunctural factors comprise processes which activate and delineate the limits of the system: they specify the clash between different contradictory requirements of the system, between its opportunities and constraints, and between expectations and outcomes within the system.

These structural and conjunctural perspectives help explain the empirical features of contemporary movements. For the most part, comparative empirical research confirms the variety of the actors involved in 'new' social movements. The social composition of these movements derives from three main sectors of the social structure: a) the 'new middle class' or 'human capital class', that is, those who work in the advanced technological sectors based on information, the human service professions and/or the public sector (particularly in education and welfare), and who have achieved a high educational status and enjoy relative economic security; b) those in a marginal position in the labour market (e.g., students, unemployed or 'peripheral' groups such as youth, retired people, middle-class housewives); and c) elements of the independent 'old middle class' (farmers, craftsmen) who are particularly evident in regional and environmental mobilizations. The relative weight of each category is different in different movements and the core group of activists and supporters is to be found in the first group (Offe, 1985).

The three sectoral groups have different structural positions and they participate for different reasons. The 'new middle class' comprises at least two groups of people: new elites who are challenging the established elites, and 'human capital' professionals, who experience both the surplus of opportunities and the constraints of the system. Research has shown that these individuals are well integrated into social activities and institutions such as households, communities, and political and social organizations; that they have participated in more traditional politics and social networks such as voluntary associations, self-help groups and social welfare organizations; and that they are highly educated and relatively young. All these characteristics indicate the central location of these individuals, their identification with modern values and their relationship to the essential structures of society. Their capacity for constructing a collective identity is rooted in the set of resources (such as educational achievement, professional skills, and social abilities) available to them. They can recognize these resources because they are exposed to the information available in society. Given the fluidity (of access to the market, to the professions and to the political system) which is typical of a highly differentiated society, this group can easily shift from a position of conflict to a counter-elite role. For example, environmental groups whose members have the required professional skills can easily become consultant firms working on environmental problems.

The 'peripheral' groups also comprise a variety of actors. Some are 'affluent marginals', for instance students or middle-class women who experience the discrepancy between the surplus of possibilities offered by the system and the actual constraints of their social condition. Still others are marginals in the strict sense (the elderly or the unemployed). Their action has to be explained in different terms: while affluent marginals live in an environment of high-density social networks and available resources of leadership, marginalized groups respond to crisis conditions only when an existing context for mobilization is available, that is, when there exists a high density of active social networks and organizations, and when leadership is available.

The 'old middle-class' groups react to developments that threaten their former social position. Here the populist or *re-actionary orientation is dominant*.

These three sectoral groups have different capacities for building and negotiating their collective identity and therefore have different sets of expectations. Hence individuals become involved in collective action for different reasons. For the 'central' groups and the 'affluent marginals' the likelihood of becoming involved is related to their degree of 'centrality' and to the extent of their exposure to the core information resources of complex society. It is also related to the degree to which the conjunctural contradictory requirements of the system have an impact upon them. For the marginal or deprived groups, by contrast, the degree of exclusion, combined with the pace of development of the crisis processes, is the most important factor.

Finally, the stage at which different individuals become involved in collective action is also variable. For example, those belonging to the first group are more likely to get involved in the early phases of mobilization because they can draw upon the identity resources provided by their educational, professional or social status. By contrast, individuals in the second group tend to use existing waves of mobilization as a channel for their *re-*action and are likely to withdraw sooner.

By examining the contemporary forms of mobilization, we can pinpoint the processes which have exposed certain social groups to the contradictory requirements of the system. With the youth and student movements, for instance, we can see the impact of the diffusion of education, widening areas of autonomy and the extension of resources for self-training and self-determination. We can also observe that these processes are negated by the structure of the labour market and actual employment conditions, which are unable to absorb the inflated possibilities created by education. And we can see that the 'adult' system of labour markets, career structures and professional politics seems incapable of fulfilling the very expectations of flexibility and autonomy which it has nourished through its tolerance of a separate youth culture.

54

Nomads of the present

In complex societies conflicts develop in those areas of the system which are crucial for the production of information and symbolic resources, and which are subject at the same time to the greatest pressure to conform. The actors engaged in these conflicts are affected directly by the contradictory structural and conjunctural processes outlined earlier.

The location of these areas of conflict raises the question of how to identify collective actors. Although patterns of membership in complex societies are differentiated, social conditions are standardized by the creation of and participation in mass markets. Commonly shared social conditions thus tend to converge. Consequently, it is difficult to establish a causal relation between specific social conditions and forms of action. While the field of conflicts is determined by both structural and conjunctural processes, the specific actors and their demands occur within those areas of the system that are gradually influenced by such processes. The first to mobilize, therefore, are those social groups most directly affected by the systemic influences on the formation of meaning.

These groups become the indicators, the symptoms of the structural problems of the system. Through their visible action they publicize existing conflicts, even though their mobilization is limited to a specific time and place. This is fundamentally different from traditional forms of collective action. Conflicts are now played out in the present and as their critics have pointed out, have no programme, and no future. This is true, but not in the sense intended by their critics. Unlike their predecessors, contemporary actors are not guided by a universal plan of history; rather, they resemble 'nomads who dwell within the present'. Expressed in theoretical terms, the *present* is the locus of current conflict.

It is important to realize that the manner in which this conflict is expressed cannot be measured in terms of 'effective' action. The challenge manifests itself by reversing the cultural codes and thus has an essentially 'formal' character. In complex systems, signs become interchangeable: power lies increasingly in the codes that regulate the flow of information. Consequently, the very form of antagonistic collective action, with its organization

55

and solidarity, transmits a message to the rest of society. Instrumental objectives do not disappear from collective action, but its goals are temporary and to a certain extent replaceable. Apart from selecting new elites, these forms of action modernize institutions and at the same time, call into question the implementation of goals which have been decided by an anonymous and impersonal power. In this way, collective actors question the logic of efficiency and effectiveness.

In the women's movement, for example, awareness of inequality and exclusion based on gender has grown among those women affected by the contradictory processes of higher education, political participation and working life, where women's participation is restricted by continuing male prerogatives. But the women's movement involves more than the affirmation of new rights and the demand for equality. It also claims the importance of difference, the need for alternative codes which demand recognition. Women raise the question of difference for the whole of society, and urge that everyone can be recognized as different.

The emerging forms of collective action differ from the conventional models of political organization and operate increasingly outside the established parameters of the political systems. In complex societies collective action creates new spaces which function as a genuine sub-system. These social spaces are the products of different forms of behaviour which the system is unable to integrate, and include not only conflictual action but also deviant behaviour and cultural experimentation.

None of these developments seems necessarily bound up with any specific social condition. The problems raised by collective actors could easily become contentious issues for other social groups, representing different actors and demands. In highly differentiated systems, systemic conflicts neither define an actor's social condition nor establish a fixed identity of a social group. Whether this plurality of actors and problems can be 'effective' depends on society's capacity to transform the questions raised by collective action into negotiated decisions and institutional changes of a political type. However, the existing decision-making processes and institutional arrangements of complex societies are unable to represent fully the interests and demands of the new conflicts. Because collective action questions the system's structural logic it is destined to reproduce itself beyond the forms of mediation that can interpret it.

Notes and references

1 For an extensive comparative discussion of the literature concerning the resource mobilization theory and the 'new movements', see Klandermans (1986); Tarrow (1986); and Cohen (1985). A synthesis of the results of empirical research on the 'new movements' is provided by Offe (1985). Other contributions of a comparative nature are those of Rucht (1984, 1986); Kitschelt (1985); Brand (1985); Nedelman (1984); Roth (1985); and Eder (1985). For a synthesis and comparison see Klandermans, Kriesi and Tarrow (1988). For a critical view see Melucci (1985b, 1986).

2 For a discussion of these aspects, see Melucci (1984a, 1984b, 1985a, 1987).

3 To my knowledge only Tarrow (1983, 1988) has proposed an explicit restriction of the concept of protest to the political level, as a basis for his model of 'cycles of protest'.

4 See, for example, Offe, (1984, 1985); and Castells, (1983).

5 Touraine, (1973, 1978, 1985); and Melucci, (1980, 1985a).

6 Inglehart, (1977); Eckert-Williams, (1984); and Kriesi, (1985a).

7 Habermas, (1981, 1984); see also Cohen, (1982, 1984).

3

Networks of meaning

Action as a symbolic form

The collective mobilizations and conflicts of the last twenty years suggest the emergence of a model of action consistent with the conceptual framework outlined in the previous two chapters. Certain elements of this model were evident in the anti-authoritarian and anti-institutional stance of the student mobilizations of the 1960s. In Italy in 1968, these elements were embryonic, hidden beneath the need to give organized and political form to demands for modernization, i.e., for changes in the working of various social and political institutions, cultural patterns and norms of civil society. It was not until the mid-1970s, with the crisis of the New Left, that there was the first significant development of a new model of collective action. The crisis of the New Left emerged on two fronts: the growth of women's demands from within the Left itself and the 'crisis of militantism', which in turn reflected the steady withdrawal of individuals from Leninist-style politics in the name of self-realization, expressiveness, and affective communication.

This change in the form of collective action was associated with certain disintegrative processes which accelerated the crisis of the political forms of collective action. There were 'dark' or hidden sides to this crisis, the most obvious and extreme example of which was the use of violence and terrorism, the roots of which were to be found in the malfunctions of the political system, against which it tended to be directed (Melucci, 1981b; Wagner-Pacifici, 1986; Della Porta, 1985, 1987; Della Porta and Tarrow, 1986). Especially in the large cities, two other disintegrative phenomena were evident: the proliferation of neo-religious groups and the move towards hard drugs. The case of Milano, covered by the type of research examined in the Appendix, is typical. After 1977 there was a massive switch to the use of heroin, a shift which cannot, of course, be attributed simply to the breakdown of the movements. There were concurrent processes of social disintegration (linked to youth unemployment and to the sharpening urban crisis) as well as the intervention by the international drug rings, who recognized Italy as a potentially lucrative market. What was noticeable in these trends, however, was that the various paths to individual escape were guided by the same motivation. 'There was no longer any room in the organization for personal needs'; 'I felt suffocated by the organization'; 'I was no longer able to conduct my own emotional life or relationships' were oft-repeated remarks among those seeking individuation, and the growth of new religious sects can be understood as a response to these needs. The situation with drug abuse is more complex because it is often triggered by personal crisis, but even here signs of the same search for individuation were evident.

There was also a publicly explicit side to the changing nature of collective action. Towards the end of the 1970s, music occupied a significant place in the emergence of new groups. This was the period of the mega-concerts. These large cultural events seemed to replace symbolically the large political demonstrations of previous years. At a time when the prevailing model of political militancy had already lost much of its appeal the concerts attracted a vast audience of young people, including those who had experienced the last wave of collective youth mobilizations in 1977.

This trend was clearly evident in the history of the few Milano groups that survived after that year. The militants who broke with the organizations of the New Left went on to form 'metropolitan youth centres'. The centres represented a compromise between the different options of expressive solidarity, consciousness-raising groups and a memory of political action. While the ex-militants contributed their experience of past political struggles, the basis of the centres remained young people who wanted to be together, to talk about themselves and to enjoy new relationships. The centres performed a 'unifying' function. Their action extended from the playing of music, smoking marijuana and other expressive activities, to demonstrations and clashes with police, which eventually led to the centres' demise. In the 1980s, the youth centres disappeared and some of them were transformed into more specific and occasionally professionalized forms of aggregation, such as cultural and theatre groups.

These Italian developments exemplify a more general change in the dominant form of collective action. In the 1980s, collective action came to be based on 'movement areas' (Melucci, 1984a). These take the form of networks composed of a multiplicity of groups that are dispersed, fragmented and submerged in everyday life, and which act as cultural laboratories. They require individual investments in the experimentation and practice of new cultural models, forms of relationships and alternative perceptions and meanings of the world. The various groups comprising these networks mobilize only periodically in response to specific issues. The submerged networks function as a system of exchanges, in which individuals and information circulate. Memberships are multiple and involvement is limited and temporary; personal involvement is a condition for participation. The latent movement areas create new cultural codes and enable individuals to put them into practice. When small groups emerge in order to visibly confront the political authorities on specific issues, they indicate to the rest of society the existence of a systemic problem and the possibility of meaningful alternatives.

The research findings on contemporary movements indicate the *self-referential* nature of their organizational forms.[1] The organizational forms of movements are not just 'instrumental' for their goals, they are a goal in themselves. Since collective action is focused on cultural codes, the *form* of the movement is itself a message, a symbolic challenge to the dominant codes. Short-term and reversible commitment, multiple leadership, temporary and *ad hoc* organizational structures are the bases for internal solidarity, but also for a symbolic confrontation with the external system. This confrontation signals the possibility of alternative experiences of time, space, and interpersonal relationships, which in turn challenge the technological rationality of the system.

The organizational form of movements becomes a field of investments, a self-reflexive set of relationships, which can be modelled and remodelled according to the learning process of its acting members. These organizational investments are conditioned by the structural factors (such as education and production) identified in the previous chapter. The excess of available resources and cultural possibilities in the system enables the learning of learning among actors, that is, a self-reflexive action upon action itself. The main actors of the 'new' movements enjoy a privileged access to the resources most suitable for this type of investment; and, at the same time, they are subjected to the most direct impact of the system's contradictory requirements.

Movement networks involve a morphological change which forces us to redefine the categories for analysing collective action. If contemporary conflicts are played out in terms of symbolic resources, then the actors concerned cannot be stable. The reasons are twofold. First, because the means through which personal and symbolic identification is created and distributed socially are continually changing. Second, because the actors who experience and contest the system's contradictory requirements do not do so all their lives and do not belong to a single social category.

Of course, as we have seen, the empirical forms of mobilization contain numerous different dimensions. There are, nevertheless, aspects of the action through which actors signal and expose problems that concern not only their social condition, but also the means of production and distribution of resources of meaning. The actors mobilize to regain control of their own action. They try to reclaim the right to define themselves against the criteria of identification determined by an anonymous power and systems of regulation that penetrate the area of 'internal nature'. This is why the voice of movements, which speak from the particular, are heard with difficulty.

The precarious nature of youth is an example. It poses for society the question of time. Youth has ceased to be a biological condition and has become a symbolic definition. People are not young simply because of their particular age, but because they assume culturally the youthful characteristics of changeability and temporariness. By means of models of juvenile existence, a

61

more general cultural appeal is issued: the right to turn back the clock of life, to question professional and personal decisions, and to measure time in ways that are not governed solely by instrumental rationality.

Women's mobilization, pivoting on a specific biologically and historically determined condition, also raises a question of concern to the whole of society: how to communicate with another person and accept the other's difference without repressing differentiation within the relationship of power so established. Demands for equality and access to the domain of male rights are not the only aspect of women's collective action. Women also call for the right to be recognized as different – even though it is difficult for them to avoid using the dominant language to define this right.

Another example of the symbolic challenge of contemporary movements is the loosely defined area of ecological action that has developed during the last decade. The ecological movement contains certain elements of system modernization – forms of action which produce reforms in the system and have effects on its institutions, both in organizational terms and in the selection of new elites. But environmental action also generates conflicts concerning the logic of the human species' relationship with nature, including each individual's relationship with his or her immediate natural and social surroundings. Thinking in ecological terms poses the problem of how to perceive inner and outer nature. The body, the biological structure and the environment are viewed as limits placed on the destructive potential of technological societies. The question is raised: how far can human intervention extend, and what room remains for the 'nature' which constitutes us and surrounds us?

Complex systems have eliminated from experience all that is not susceptible to verification and measurement; everything, that is, which belonged traditionally to the dimension of the sacred. Yet the contemporary questioning of the meaning of existence now feeds a new search for spiritual experiences or a need for personal development corresponding to external change. The attempt to rationalize all aspects of people's lives has produced a heterogeneous area of social groupings seeking a new consciousness. This social space seems very remote from traditional forms of collective action. Hence are faced not only with transnational corporations which benefit from marketing dreams of salvation, but also by resistance to operational codes, appeals concerning the hidden shadowy side of human experience, and a search for inner unity against the imperatives of efficiency and effectiveness.

In contemporary forms of collective action, then, the challenge to the logic of the system occurs on a symbolic level. The very existence and structure of collective action provides the rest of society with a different way of interpreting individual and collective experiences. Linking personal change with external action, collective action functions as a new media which illuminates the silent and arbitrary elements of the dominant codes as well as publicizes new alternatives.

Building collective identities

Milano, Italy, November 1981. For a number of years, on the outskirts of the city, a self-governed youth centre has made its home in an occupied building. Numerous organized political and cultural activities take place in the centre. The occupation committee, heir of the struggles of the preceding years, seeks to guide the life of the centre based on the political radicalism of the New Left (which is expressed in an extreme manner by the social struggles' commission). The culture commission, including some dissident members of the occupation committee, performs an important intermediary function in the centre. It is responsible for the allocation of rooms (for music, theatre, radio, etc.) to the various groups, and also promotes initiatives of an essentially expressive type (concerts, cinema) that correspond to the cultural needs of a new generation of young people. The policy of the culture commission conflicts with the ideological intransigence and organizational rigidity of the occupation committee and, in particular, of the social struggles' commission. The life of the centre is paralyzed. The culture commission finds itself trapped in an impasse between the new cultural needs and the old models of organization of the centre.

During the same period, in one of the old quarters of Milano, an active group of women convenes. Some of its members have experienced feminism, including the phase of separatism and the struggles for emancipation, divorce and abortion. Others, who are younger, have joined the group either following brief political experiences or to seek answers to personal questions. The group rejects the closed attitudes and the separateness of radical feminism, but also dismisses attempts to reduce the women's movement to claims for emancipation in the professional and political fields. It also refuses the practice of consciousness-raising centred solely on affective experiences. Correspondingly, the group has no intention of transforming itself into a professionalized cultural agency. The work of the group consists in following a path of self-reflection on the differences among women, through the creation of a 'feminine' culture. The group is therefore faced with the problem of relating its internal self-reflection to its external presence in issues of concern to other women and to the movement as a whole.

In the extreme south of the city, where a large working-class district borders on an industrial area which was once a flourishing countryside, a group of young people form a local collective. It deals with the ecological problems of an area particularly degraded in environmental terms. The group consists mainly of ex-activists of the New Left and of young people whose ecological commitment derives from cultural interests. The activity of the group is very pragmatic. It focuses on the everyday problems of the area (the measurement of air and noise pollution, identifying illegal rubbish dumps, and educational initiatives in the local schools). It maintains contacts with similar groups in other districts and participates in common mobilizations on important issues.

Between the end of 1981 and the middle of 1982, these three groups participated in the research programme considered in the Appendix. They were selected after a year of preliminary fieldwork. Each represents, in its own area, the point of convergence of the types of collective action that preliminary investigation revealed as significant. The groups agreed to take part in the research project once a contractual relationship with the researchers, based on the mutual exchange of information, had been established: the researchers provided their services to assist the process of self-reflection, while the groups provided information about their own action.

During the research project the groups consciously activated their own internal relationships and concentrated on the process of constructing their sense of 'we' – which serves as the basis for all collective action. Self-reflection rendered this process visible and contributed new insights into the groups' understanding of their action. In the course of this self-reflection the complex interaction of internal and external relationships, which are characteristic of collective action, also surfaced.

These three research groups were used to mirror situations that express their respective 'movements' as a whole; some individuals within the groups certainly revealed patterns typical of those of the larger movement. By means of this experimental situation, the groups provided material concerning *their action and not their opinions*. They offered the researcher behaviour and meanings simultaneously, i.e. the possibility, which is rare within social movements, of analysing *their action in action*.

Let us consider the first group, the culture commission of the youth centre. Alberto and Pietro come from experiences rooted in the New Left. Even though they ideologically criticize politics, they maintain the goal of universal social change. Pietro rejects any talk of mediation with political institutions, whereas Alberto is more receptive. Adriano, who also experienced the crisis of the New Left, has ended up in expressive marginality, in the sense that spontaneity and individualism are the fundamental reasons for his participation in the group. Gianna's affective feelings of uncertainty find support in collective work, and at the same time affirm her need of self-fulfilment. Carmela sees the group as a convivial space for free and spontaneous communication and for an affectively based collective integration. Camillo, finally, rejects ideology and the subordination of his need for self-fulfilment to the imperatives of political organization. He sees the necessity of a direct confrontation with society. His conflictual drive is expressed as a visible and qualified cultural product that emerges from marginality and can challenge the dominant codes in the market or the professions.

The culture commission group constructs its identity through a system of action which assumes the form sketched in Figure 2. In both the group and the movement three crucial alternatives intersect: changes in the social structure or defiance of the dominant cultural codes; action which either accepts existing political institutions and the market or a marginal radicalism that

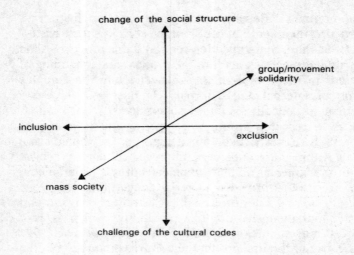

Figure 2

rejects inclusion in institutional practices; and the use and strengthening of resources of affective solidarity within the group or an orientation towards society and the professional resources of a mass cultural market.

Within the group the attempt to integrate these three dimensions struck a defensive balance in the decision by the members to concentrate their energies on affective solidarity and on the development of a marginal culture. The organizational form of the group – open, centred on an intense affective exchange and without strict rules of performance – was the expression of this type of integration. The conflict with the social struggles' commission and the encounter with the researchers confronted this fragile balance with external social reality and with the need to make use of new cultural resources for action.

The group could not reconstruct its collective identity. Its collapse was precipitated by Adriano and Camillo. The former emphasized his spontaneous individual drives, while the latter revealed the group's inability to utilize the cultural resources of the system. The needs of self-fulfilment could have been satisfied by challenging society's cultural codes, but the group was unable to take this step. Mobilization became impossible because a low level of internal resources (such as professional skills and access to the new languages of the media) did not permit the group to take advantage of the opportunities provided by its environment.

If we consider the group as a mirror of the movement and compare the available information on youth groups, it is not difficult to spot elements of the system of action represented in Figure 2. The difficulty of integrating the poles of this system helps explain the particular evolution and the crisis of youth mobilizations in Italy (and western Europe as a whole) in the late 1970s. The Italian youth movement was divided between the political radicalism and the violence of the *Autonomia* groups, the marginalized expressiveness of the counter-culture, the power-seeking of political organizations, and a conflictual approach taking the form of a cultural challenge to the dominant codes. In a social climate which reinforced the 'poverty' of internal resources (unemployment, repression), this final component was not combined successfully with the others. Consequently, the youth 'movement' disappeared in a pure display of signs (the metropolitan 'tribes' defined by their different dress styles), in the professional marketing of innovative cultural resources and, more tragically, in the marginality of drug abuse and mental illness.

In the women's group collective identity emerged from a complex interaction of roles and orientations. Isabella and Luisa, who had passed through all the phases of feminism, considered women's solidarity as the essential condition for individual and professional autonomy. Solidarity was also considered the basis of social action and for expressing the feminine difference. Rossana insisted on the need for a 'new science' founded upon the experiences of women – a different view of reality to modify the perceptions of the dominant male culture. For Pia the women's group provided the support for affective choices. Margherita expressed her personal need of self-fulfilment, but she also recognized the importance of the group as a common space in which the creation of a different culture was possible. These kinds of trends converge in the form of the group. The major investments in this *form* of relationship do not prevent the group from mobilizing externally, but it does make the task of individualization a condition of interventions in the public domain. The group reflects the various tensions of the women's movement: between consciousness-raising groups centred on clarifying internal affective needs and the professional groups committed to establishing a public space for expressing the feminine difference; between groups producing a 'women's culture' for internal consumption (writing, art) and those groups engaged in providing services for women (housing, health, welfare); and between the groups giving priority to research on the self and individual differences and those groups who emphasize sisterhood (Figure 3).

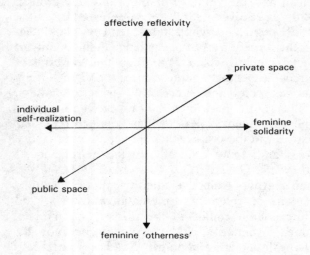

Figure 3

The integration of these various dimensions is made possible by the elasticity and adaptable organizational *form* which is simultaneously *self-reflective* and *productive* of 'feminine' cultural codes. Starting from this identity structure, the mobilization of women is thus possible and assumes a double-level form of visibility and latency: brief and intense public mobilization campaigns are fed by the submerged networks of women's groups and their self-reflective resources.

These various dimensions are also evident in the local environmental group. Massimo, a technician with political experience, sees the need for provocative action which stimulates positive institutional changes in ecological matters. Rosanna, after a brief encounter with naturalism, is conscious of directly experiencing an everyday ecology, including an ecology of the mind which emphasizes the importance of changing one's attitudes towards nature, other living beings and one's own life. Roberto, reflecting his previous New Left activism, places the emphasis on restructuring society as the basis for re-establishing a balanced relationship with nature. Stefano stresses the importance of a daily commitment to register the ecological damage produced locally by pollution. Yet he argues that the main solution to ecological problems rests with initiatives at the level of local and national institutions.

The group displays a variety of approaches which are found in the wider ecological movement. The defence or conservation of nature, and thus an emphasis on the individual/nature relationship, is counterposed to a tendency which views the transformation of the relationship between society and nature as the essential feature of ecological action. Direct action, even of the individual, is viewed as an instrument of change and is juxtaposed with institutional intervention. The resources available for action are seen to be located either in the changing everyday attitudes towards nature and the personality of individual members of the movement, or within the wider social environment itself (Figure 4).

The group and, more generally, the ecological movement demonstrate an ability to successfully integrate these different orientations. The tensions of collective identity are integrated within a very soft, reticulated and multipolar form of organization. Once again the structure of identity facilitates public mobilizations. The integration of defensive and transformative actions of an everyday ecology and a political ecology, and of orientations towards both the individual and the social environment, is accomplished by the maintenance of two levels: intense but temporary mobilizations, and movement networks that produce information, self-reflection and symbolic resources.

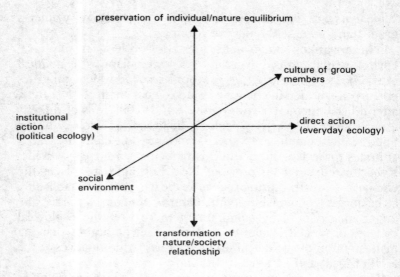

preservation of individual/nature equilibrium

culture of group members

institutional action (political ecology)

direct action (everyday ecology)

social environment

transformation of nature/society relationship

Figure 4

Visibility and latency

In complex societies social movements develop only in limited areas and for limited periods of time. When movements mobilize they reveal the other, complementary face of the submerged networks. The hidden networks become visible whenever collective actors confront or come into conflict with a public policy. Thus, for example, it is difficult to understand the massive peace mobilizations of recent years unless the vitality of the submerged networks of women, young people, ecologists and alternative cultures is taken into account. These networks make possible such mobilizations and from time to time render them *visible*.

Latency and visibility are the two interrelated poles of collective action. Those who view collective action from a professional–political standpoint usually confine their observations to the visible face of mobilization. This view overlooks the fact that collective action is nourished by the daily production of alternative frameworks of meaning, on which the networks

70

themselves are founded and live from day to day. Consequently, there exists a physiological link between the visibility and latency of movements. The actors become visible only where a field of public conflict arises; otherwise they remain in a state of latency. Latency does not mean inactivity. Rather, the potential for resistance or opposition is sewn into the very fabric of daily life. It is located in the molecular experience of the individuals or groups who practice the alternative meanings of everyday life. Within this context, resistance is not expressed in collective forms of conflictual mobilizations. Specific circumstances are necessary for opposition and therefore of mobilizing and making visible this latent potential.

It follows that there is a major difference between mobilization and a movement. In most discussions, references to the movements' political effects and organizational tactics are commonly mistaken for the collective forms of mobilization which develop around specific issues. But movements live in another dimension: in the everyday network of social relations, in the capacity and will to reappropriate space and time, and in the attempt to practice alternative life-styles. This dimension is not marginal or residual. Rather, it is the appropriate response to new forms of control that no longer correspond solely to state action. Resistance and conflict also operate in this molecular dimension as well as bring about important changes. Paradoxically, the latency of a movement is its effective strength.

The latency and visibility of social movements points to the existence of two other paradoxes. First, collective conflicts are increasingly personal and revolve around the capacity of individuals to initiate action and to control the space, time and interpersonal relations that define their social existence. This paradox is already apparent. During the past decade collective action has displayed a tension between the need to publicly declare objectives and the need to practice directly and personally the innovations in daily life. This tension has produced some dramatic splits within the groups.

There is a second paradox: if the basis of contemporary conflicts has shifted towards the production of meaning, then they seemingly have little to do with politics. Instead collective action concerns everyday life, personal relationships, and new conceptions of space and time. Thus collective actors are prone to disperse, fragmented and atomized, into networks which quickly disappear into sects, emotional support circles or therapy groups. While collective action continually faces disintegration, it also poses questions about the production of symbols which transcend politics. As such, collective action can never be wholly represented by political mediation, in decisions (or 'policies') which translate collective efforts into institutional changes. The forms of action I am referring to are at one and the same time prior to and beyond politics: they are *pre-political* because they are rooted in everyday life experiences; and *meta-political* because political forces can never represent them completely. Paradoxically, unless collective action is represented it becomes fragmented and dispersed; at the same time, because it is never fully capable of representation it reappears later on new ground, with changed objectives and altered strategies.

There are numerous examples of this process. The antinuclear struggle, for instance, has been a strong mobilizing force in many countries. Initially, its actions addressed the problem of nuclear power stations, but later it raised more general questions, including the power to make decisions about the equilibrium of the eco-system. No governmental nuclear policy could ever fully incorporate these demands, and this is why particular mobilizations – concerning alternative sources of energy and the risks associated with nuclear power – tend to push conflicts on to different ecological fronts.

The campaigns for abortion provide another example. In Italy, during the 1970s, this area of mobilization had several aspects, including institutional changes at the political level as well as a measure of social acceptance. But there was also a demand for the possibility and right of individuals to make certain fundamental personal decisions, including whether or not to give birth. This demand contains a surprising implication. It is not difficult to see that in a society where pro-abortion opinion guided demographic and family planning policy, anti-abortion campaigns to reclaim the right of the individual to decide, against a system of rationalized biological and emotional life, would be likely. Hence, what has appeared, in the Italian case, as a 'progressive' goal and institutional innovation, could become a future target for new forms of mobilization hostile to state policies favourable to abortion.

72

In complex systems, the visibility and latency of social movements pose a crucial problem: how to represent mobile, reticulating, and apparently atomized demands. It is quite evident that the political systems we have inherited from the liberal tradition are inadequate for representing the present forms of conflict. Contemporary political institutions and procedures nevertheless sometimes have the capacity to produce decisions and rules, and they are therefore indispensable resources for social actors. However, the crux of the problem is *which* forms of representation and *which* types of decision-making are suitable for translating conflictual demands into institutional change. This problem raises important questions. How is it possible to develop democratic public spaces of representation that enable collective action to manifest itself and to be heard without losing its specific character or autonomy? How can institutions respond effectively to specific and discontinuous mobilizations without destroying their symbolic charge? And how can molecular forms of action be prevented from being reduced to marginal forms of expressiveness?

The hidden efficacy of social movements

In order to transcend the current paradigm of new social movements the main characteristics of recent collective action must be identified. Even though I am not in search of *the* central movement of complex society, I maintain that there are forms of antagonistic collective action capable of affecting the logic of complex systems.[2] However, the identification of this type of action requires an analysis that recognizes the plurality of operative factors (opportunities, limits, responses) and does not simply assume that the movement is a metaphysically given 'entity'.

Such general considerations are important when considering what is 'new' about the recent movements. One of their distinctive characteristics is the unstable pattern of their membership. The attributes of the actors are defined almost entirely by the action itself. This means that the energies and resources that actors invest in the construction of their collective identity are an essential part of the action, and not simply an accessory or 'expressive' dimension. The weakness of an exclusively political view centred on the 'instrumental' dimension

73

of action is that it considers as 'expressive' or residual the self-reflective investments of the movements. But these investments in self-reflection are crucial for understanding the effects of movements on the political system. If what movements do to construct a sense of 'we' is not considered accessory or residual, then our understanding of concepts such as efficacy and success is correspondingly modified.

What is new about contemporary movements is first of all that *information resources* are at the centre of collective conflicts. Conflicts shift to the codes, to the formal frameworks of knowledge, and this shift is made possible by the self-reflexive capacity of complex systems. The *self-reflexive form* of action is thus another specific characteristic of recent movements. The decline of movements as 'characters' signifies the dissolution of the 'subject' and an increase in the formal capacity for self-reflection. Finally, the *global interdependence* or the 'planetarization' of action profoundly alters the environmental conditions in which actors are formed and act: the field of opportunities and constraints of action is redefined within a multipolar and transnational system.

These novelties of contemporary movements should be understood not only in the sense that there are now forms of action different from those of the past. Arguments about the novel characteristics of the new movements must also encompass their organizational form. In contemporary collective action, the organization has acquired a different status. It is no longer considered as a means to an end, and it therefore cannot be assessed only in terms of its instrumental rationality. The organization has a self-reflexive character and its form expresses the meaning (or goals) of the action itself. It is also the laboratory in which actors test their capacity to challenge the dominant cultural codes. Finally, the organization directly governs the visible forms of mobilization; the present movements' pursuit of an external objective is no longer separate from their internal forms.

Given the changed nature of the 'new' movements, is it still possible to speak of the efficacy of this type of collective action? If so, how are we to assess its success or failure? The concepts of efficacy or success could be considered, strictly speaking, as unimportant when considering this type of collective action, because the conflicts within the realm of collective action take place principally on symbolic grounds. They challenge and overturn the dominant codes upon which social relationships are founded. These symbolic challenges are a method of unmasking the dominant codes, a different way of perceiving and naming the world.

This certainly does not mean that collective action has no visible effects. Contemporary forms of collective action produce 'measurable' effects on at least three levels. First, they initiate *institutional change* through political reforms or the redefinition of organizational practices. A second effect is the *selection of new elites*. In many western countries during the 1970s, for example, collective action produced certain changes in the left-wing or progressive political organizations (such as political parties and trade unions). More importantly, collective action resulted in the emergence of a new generation of skilled personnel in the key comunications media, advertising and marketing sector of the 'information society'. (A survey of young managers within these sectors, especially in metropolitan areas, could throw significant light on the relationship between the new elites and their prior experiences within 'movements' or alternative cultures.) The third effect of collective action is *cultural innovation.* This refers to the development of models of behaviour and social relationships that enter into everyday life and the market. Here changes in language, sexual customs, affective relationships, dress and eating habits modify the functioning of the social order.

Nevertheless, the significance of collective action is not confined to these effects, even though they are often the focus for determining the political efficacy or success of contemporary movements. To limit social analysis to these effects is to overlook a fundamental dimension of contemporary conflicts: the movements no longer operate as characters but as *signs*, in the sense that they translate their action into symbolic challenges that overturn the dominant cultural codes. Movements also reveal the irrationality and bias of cultural codes by operating at the same levels (of information and communication) as the new forms of technocratic power.

We can identify three main forms of symbolic challenge. The first is *prophecy*: the act of announcing, based on personal experiences, that alternative frameworks of meaning are possible, and that the operational logic of power apparatuses is not the only possible 'rationality'. However, prophecy contains an insurmountable contradiction. Prophets proclaim something other than themselves, while at the same time holding themselves up as a model. For example, women speak of a right to differ which goes beyond the female condition, but they must also base themselves on the particularity of their biological and historical condition. Similarly, young people talk of possible alternatives in the definition and use of time, but they speak against the backdrop of their marginal and precarious condition. And ecologists' call for a 'pure' nature depends upon a resourceful and developed society. Under pressure from this contradiction collective actors are frequently torn between their prophetic role and their activity as *particular* social actors.

Paradox is a second form of challenge: the reversal of the dominant codes by means of their exaggeration, which in turn reveals their irrationality and their inherent dimensions of silence and violence. By exaggerating or pushing to the limit the dominant discourse of power, the movements expose the self-contradictory nature of its 'rationality' or, conversely, they show that what is labelled as 'irrational' by the dominant apparatuses is perhaps dramatically true.

The third type of challenge is that of *representation*: collective actors' capacity to isolate form from content permits, as in a play of mirrors, the retransmission to the system of its own contradictions. It is no accident that the use of expressive languages, theatre, video and images of various kinds constitutes one of the central practices of the everyday networks of contemporary movements.

These three forms of symbolic challenge produce *systemic effects*, which should not be confused with modernization and institutional changes, the circulation of elites or processes of cultural innovation. The systemic effects consist mainly in *rendering power visible*. The function of contemporary conflicts is to render visible the power that hides behind the rationality of administrative or organizational procedures or the 'show-business' aspects of politics. While visible power disappears from complex societies, it expands and is dispersed throughout the whole society. Even though power comes to play a crucial role in shaping all social relationships, it is difficult to pinpoint it within individuals or institutions.

Under these circumstances, not only the movements but power itself ceases to be a 'character'. Power is transformed into a set of signs which are frequently concealed, interwoven with procedures, or crystallized in the patterns of mass consumption of an expanding media market. In complex systems, no one appears to be responsible for the goals of social life. Hence, one of the fundamental roles of collective action is precisely that of rendering explicit these ends by creating public spaces in which power becomes visible. Power which is recognizable is also negotiable, since it can be confronted, and because it is forced to take differences into account. Collective action makes possible the negotiation and establishment of public agreements which, although increasingly transitory, nevertheless serve as a condition of a political democracy capable of protecting the community against the increasing risks of an arbitrary exercise of power or violence (see Chapter 8). Since power is neutralized behind the formal rationality of procedures, it cannot be controlled unless it is rendered visible. However, in complex systems the available spaces for reaching agreements are limited and temporary. They have to be redefined continually and rapidly, because the differences change, the conflicts shift, the agreements cease to satisfy and because new forms of domination are constantly emerging.

But in what sense can we still speak of change? Collective action produces two types of change. There is, first, a molecular change which is cultural in the anthropological sense: an alteration of daily life, of ways of living and forms of social and personal relationships. Second, there are the effects on the institutions and political systems (Tarrow, 1986). If in the 1960s collective action accelerated the advent of post-industrial capitalism (Tarrow, 1984), in the 1970s it encouraged an overhaul of the ideas and personnel of political organizations and the market. There is no doubt that the movement areas of the 1980s have been responsible for the alteration of public attitudes and the greater acceptance of difference. The private radio stations, for instance, have established a style in radio broadcasting, and have created a generation of professional figures (who subjectively see themselves as belonging to the movement, but who in reality are professional communicators with innovative market-orientated roles).

Conflicts no longer have winners, but they may produce innovation, modernization, and reform. Even when viewed from the standpoint of the individual, this type of mobilization represents an important break with the past. The 'militant for life' figure was tied to an objective condition and a specific class culture. The contemporary commitment to movement areas, by contrast, is of limited duration. Actors are mobilized for a definite period of time and only for certain issues of concern to them; they take part simultaneously in several activities which they see as compatible; and following their period of mobilization, they are drawn into other channels, towards the market or other institutions.

In more general terms, what are the implications of this shift to commitments of limited duration? Of fundamental significance is the fact that change always occurs according to a 'regional' schema, that is, within particular areas of the system but never within the whole of the system. The problem of explaining change thus concerns the relation between different levels of change, which may proceed together and in part converge, but which also remain distinct. The traditional political structures which brought together excluded interests, supplying representation to those social groups arguing for the extension of citizenship, are no longer capable of interpreting emergent conflicts. The movements require much more flexible and provisional forms of representation, which could themselves converge with more permanent and longer lasting political forms.

Two general points emerge from these considerations. First, it is necessary to distinguish between *the mobilizing and latency phases of collective action*. While mobilization may occur for very important objectives, it is still of a limited duration. 'Political entrepreneurs' therefore cannot hope to represent the mobilized forces beyond the realization of the particular goal in question. And as a result of the mobilization, there is no reason to expect any necessary increase in the organizational or electoral strength of the 'representatives'. Mobilization is directed primarily at obtaining clearly defined results, through which, in turn, it can gather solid support and produce change. The remaining question is how the political system can give continuity and effectiveness to these sporadic and discontinuous mobilizations. In response, it is perhaps necessary to draw a sharper distinction than in the past between policy formation and established interest-based organizations such as political parties and trade unions. It might also be suggested that the point of contact between movements and political systems is increasingly found in policies rather than in organizations. We could consider the ability to wrest policy formation from the almost exclusive control of professional and institutionalized political bodies as both a measure of the effectiveness of the movements and an indicator of the degree of openness of the political system.

Second, there is a need for *public spheres of representation* (for example the media, the universities, the social services) in which it is possible to express the conflicts and demands that develop in civil society. These public spheres would provide social actors with the opportunity to appear and to make themselves heard, without losing their particular character or autonomy. Through these channels, the questions raised by collective action could become the subject of policy-making negotiations, thereby having effects on the social system as a whole, without institutionalizing the actors of movements. In these intermediate areas specific forms of provisional and *ad hoc* representation could operate. Within these areas, umbrella organizations, distinct from the institutional actors of the political system, could play a fundamental role in the mobilization phase of movements (as happens, for example, in the peace and ecological mobilizations; see Diani and Lodi, 1986).

Rather than reaffirm the Leninist model, which assigned movements the fate of either taking state power or failing completely (e.g. in trade unionism), it becomes possible to prefigure other roles for collective action: the movements produce reforms, provide new elites for the political system and the market, while at the same time serving to locate and reveal relations of power. In this way, the movements enable society to address and face the larger questions affecting human life in complex societies – issues which are often disguised behind themes of redistribution and exchange or neutralized by the allegedly 'technical' nature of decision-making procedures.

Notes and references

1 See Nedelmann (1984); Gundelach (1984); Beywl and Nelles (1983); and Donati (1984). For an evaluation of the effects of movements of the 1960s and 1970s in the United States see Stein (1985), Breines (1982), Freeman (1983). On the role of popular music see Chambers (1985).

2 While acknowledging my debt to Alain Touraine's theoretical work, my analysis has progressively taken me a critical distance away from his hypothesis that in 'post-industrial' society *a* central movement is likely to replace the working-class movement (Touraine, 1973, 1984, 1985; Touraine *et al.*, 1978, 1980, 1981, 1982, 1984).

4

Challenges on the void

The challenge of peace

The conceptual framework outlined in previous chapters can be applied to the unexpected wave of mobilizations for peace which have made their presence felt in all western countries since the early 1980s. These massive and unprecedented demonstrations crossing the main capitals of the western world raise two general questions: what produces these forms of mobilization? and what is the meaning of this individual and collective action?

The answers to both questions might seem obvious. Mobilization is a reaction to the changing political and military situation, a response to the further deployment of nuclear weapons in Europe. And peace is the goal, a universal good threatened by the nuclear arms race and by the risk of total warfare. These answers are as obvious as they are incomplete: they apply the same simplified description of the 'peace movement' as that already applied to other recent collective mobilizations in complex societies.

Rather than using the term 'peace movement', however, I use the term peace *mobilization* because, as I argued earlier, the 'peace movement' is not a unified entity. The collective actions of recent years are multi-dimensional realities which converge, only in a specific conjuncture, on the ground staked out by peace mobilizations.

The changes in military policies provide the conjunctural conditions for the emergence and crystallization of different elements of collective action into peace mobilizations:

This reaction has two key dimensions:

a) the *mobilization of political actors* (in the broad sense of parties, unions, pressure groups, associations). Here the logic of action can be explained almost entirely within the framework of national political systems. Inner dynamics, already operating in these systems, are activated by new international circumstances: the residual political 'New Left' of the 1970s in West Germany, or the Community Party in Italy, finds in the peace issue an opportunity for political action.

b) the *collective fear* of an irreversible catastrophe. This reaction can be analysed, following classical analyses of crowd or aggregative behaviour (Smelser, 1963; Alberoni, 1981a), as the sum of the atomized behaviour of individuals.

1) There is, first, a *reaction* to the changes in military policies.

2) Second, peace mobilizations also display a form of *moral utopianism*. This is not just a contemporary phenomena. Every social system contains a certain number of moral and totalizing expectations for happiness, justice, and truth. These claims do not reside in specific social groups, and they do not involve specific interests or practical–historical projects. They live on the fringes of great religions or great cultural and political trends, in the form of small sects, heretical cults and theological circles. The great collective processes, such as the emergence of new social or cultural patterns, provide a channel for expressing this moral utopianism, which otherwise would survive only in marginal enclaves.

In recent years, the peace issue has provided a ground for expressing these totalizing aspirations, which become visible periodically in cyclical waves. The contemporary international conjuncture provides a social and cultural opportunity for a form of collective action which has only casual links with the precipitating military situation.

3) Third, in this respect, peace mobilizations are not only a reaction to recent military policies. Political actors have only a minor role in mobilization. The fear of the bomb does not explain the patterns of solidarity, organization and identity of recent collective action. These patterns of collective action are

very different from aggregative behaviour such as a panic. Moral
utopianism would remain marginalized if it were not effected by
collective processes which have their roots elsewhere.

My argument is that peace mobilizations also express conflicts
peculiar to complex societies. As a result, there is, in many
countries, a certain qualitative gap between recent mobilizations
and the pacifism of the 1950s. There is, however, a continuity
with other mobilizations of the 1970s and early 1980s (youth,
women, and ecological mobilizations) (Lodi, 1985). An understanding of peace mobilizations of the 1980s therefore requires
a consideration not only of the threat of nuclear war, but of the
whole planetary system in which this possibility occurs.

Information has become a central resource and complex
systems depend on it for their survival and development. In the
last two decades the capability of collecting, processing, and
transferring information has been developed to an extent
unsurpassed in all of human history. That increases the *artificial*
or constructed characteristics of social life; large parts of our
experiences occur in a socially produced environment. The
media represent and reflect our actions, and individuals
incorporate and reproduce these messages in a type of self-
reinforcing spiral. Where are 'nature' and 'reality' outside the
cultural representations and images we receive from and
produce for our social world?

This central role of information means that complex societies
develop forms of cultural production not connected directly to
the needs for survival or for reproduction: they are 'post-
material' societies and they produce a 'cultural surplus', that is,
a widening of choices available to individuals and groups far
beyond their possibility of actually experiencing them. Since
information cannot be separated from the human capacity to
perceive it, social intervention increasingly affects human beings
themselves. Large investments in biological, motivational and
brain research and recent developments in the neurosciences
show that the deepest bases of human behaviour become a field
of exploration and intervention. The biological and motivational
structure of humans thus becomes a valuable resource.

A society based on information redefines *space* and *time.*
Space loses its physical limits. It can be extended or contracted

to a degree that was inconceivable only a few years ago. A whole library can be stocked in a space smaller than a book, but the symbolic space everybody can experience encompasses the whole planet and beyond to extra-terrestrial space.

The time required to produce and process information has been reduced to such an extent that we can already perceive the dramatic gap regarding other human time experiences. The gap between the time a computer needs to process information and the time for human analysis of the output is still very large, although the growing research on artificial intelligence is reducing this lag. But the most dramatic is the gap concerning other moments of our everyday experience: the sense of inner time, the time of feelings and emotions, of questions without answers and the times for unifying the fragments of personal identity.

Control over the production, accumulation and circulation of information depends on codes which organize and make information understandable. In complex societies power consists increasingly of operational codes, formal rules and 'knowledge organizers' (for example, the power found in the languages of computing machines or the increasingly coded languages of organizational science or electronic media techniques). In the operational logic of complex societies, information is not a shared resource, but an empty sign, the key to which is controlled by only a few people. Access to knowledge becomes a new kind of power and conflict. Moreover, the possibility of integrating individual experience above and beyond the standards of operational rationality becomes more and more difficult: there is no place for questions concerning individual destiny and choices to do with life, birth, death and love.

The nuclear situation, which entails the possibility of total destruction, has to be considered within the framework just outlined.

1 The nuclear problem is an extreme and paradoxical example of the social capacity to intervene on society itself. It is the ultimate expression of an 'artifical', or socially constructed self-reflexive social life. Complex societies produce themselves to a degree that includes the possibility of finally exterminating themselves.

2 For the first time in human history, this situation transforms peace and war into a *global social problem*. While war, from the point of view of technology, becomes more and more a specialist's field, its meaning is paradoxically reversed and becomes a general social issue which concerns everybody.

3 War and peace, for the first time in history, acquire a planetary dimension. They break the limits of relations among states which until now have maintained a monopoly over them. Complex societies acquire the power of self-destruction, while at the same time they have the power for survival and development. 'The social' becomes the field of power, risk and responsibility.

4 The nuclear problem brings the threat of war to the field of information, particularly to a symbolic ground. An actual war would mean the disappearance of war and humankind. So the confrontation within the limits of global survival is necessarily a symbolic battle for controlling information. The concept of deterrence, a key concept in contemporary political and military international relations, operates mainly on symbolic ground. It intervenes in the information and representations of opponents by creating a mirror game in which every player tries to influence the other and to take advantage of the enemy's misperception.

The nuclear issue contains two paradoxes. First, if society produces the power of self-destruction it shows both the highest level of self-reflection, of action on itself, *and* the potential destruction of this capacity. Second, the nuclear problem is the product of a complex society based on information and, as such, it is no longer reversible. It is virtually impossible for information about the production of the nuclear bomb to disappear; a return to a pre-nuclear society is therefore also impossible. One has to imagine, in Orwellian terms, a situation in which there is the total control over information, the systematic erasing of facts, and the rewriting of history. Otherwise the bomb has an irreversible presence in human society: it is both a result of the widening of choices and opportunities produced by material and cultural evolution, and an irreversible risk, which we can therefore only understand and confront.

85

The nuclear situation is analogous with other contemporary forms of society's intervention on itself. For example, genetic engineering, in fact all forms of voluntary action on the biological bases of behaviour from reproduction to life itself, are as radical interventions on human destiny as the nuclear threat. The difference lies not in the irreversibility of the nuclear threat (which could also be true for genetic manipulation or ecological disasters), but its specific characteristics – *time* (destruction would be almost instantaneous) and *space* (destruction would be global) – which make nuclear war incomparable to any other intervention in the future of humanity.

What is at stake in contemporary movements, and particularly in peace mobilizations, is *the self-production of the human species* at the individual and collective level. What is at stake is the production and quality of human existence – the possibility for people as individuals and as a species to control not only the production, but the cultural and social (and increasingly the biological) quality of human existence.

This concern with the fate of human existence is found in peace mobilizations. The struggle against military policies also reveals the *transnational* nature of contemporary problems and conflicts (Hegedus, 1983), and the *global interdependence* of the planetary system. Collective action challenges not only the cultural shape of international relations but the logic governing them. The world system is, formally speaking, a set of relations among sovereign states, but in fact is dominated by the logic of the two blocs and by the imbalances between north and south. Within the two empires, technocratic and military apparatuses control the resources of information and decision-making for their survival. They are also responsible for the unequal exchange among different areas of the planet. The decline of the nation-state system is perhaps the fundamental message of contemporary pacifism, even if many 'national' questions remain unsolved (Melucci and Diani, 1983). Peace mobilizations issue an appeal to give society the power of deciding and controlling its own existence, in a new set of relations among its diverse constituents (groups, interests, cultures, 'nations'). A new *trans-societal* order is not a utopia, but a great aim of our planetary situation in which nation-states are extinguishing themselves. The decline of the nation-state is not due to socialism (the myth of the abolition of the state), but because nation-states are losing their authority: from above, a global, multinational political and economic interdependence moves the centre of actual decision-making elsewhere; from below, the multiplication of autonomous centres of decision-making gives 'civil societies' a power they never had during the development of modern states.

The task of politically managing this new situation is not easy. But the planetary system has to begin with the *social* transformation of its nature, if it wants to find new *political* means for its survival. Peace mobilizations also point out the increasing role of *decision-making* in the contemporary situation. Society and its destiny are constructed. They are a result of decisions and choices, a product of social relationships and not of the apparently fatalistic logic of apparatuses which pretend to have a monopoly of 'rationality'.

Collective action for peace reveals, finally, the *contractual* nature of social life in complex systems. The survival of the species depends on the capacity of negotiating ends. Discussion about ends disappears from the scene of collective debates, nullified by the operational criteria of effectiveness and efficiency or by the pure consumption of signs. By contrast, collective action proclaims that the ends must be visible, negotiable and subject to control.

The acceptance of the contractual nature of contemporary society requires recognition of the fact that the heterogeneity of interests and conflict cannot be eliminated in complex systems. It also requires recognition of the necessity of limits, i.e., rules of the game, which can be established and changed only by negotiation. Furthermore, there is the acknowledgement that power is one of these limits and that its negotiability depends on its *visibility*. Finally, there is the recognition of *risk*, i.e., the open-ended and temporary nature of every decision-making process bent on reducing uncertainty. Risk, which in ethical terms implies responsibility and freedom, is an irreversible component of the contemporary problem. The level of risk is no greater in the nuclear issue than it is in the other possibilities of destruction (biological, chemical, ecological) connected to the increasing intervention of society on itself. In each case, the risks involved indicate that human destiny has been put into human hands.

We can now apply these general considerations to peace mobilizations, as well as understand why they cannot be dismissed as ineffective reactions to military policies. Those observers who stress the lack of efficacy of contemporary forms of collective action not only fail to grasp their symbolic antagonism, but also underestimate the political impact of these mobilizations.

For instance, the peace mobilizations have fundamental *transnational effects*: for the first time action, which is also located in a specific national context, has effects at the planetary level and on the present system of international relations. The lack of mobilization in the countries of central and eastern Europe is paradoxically a part of the same scene: it reveals the authoritarian structure of these societies and the degree of repressiveness of the power used to control them.

Collective action also functions as a *symbolic multiplier*: since its aim is not efficiency, it challenges the operational logic of technocratic–military apparatuses and questions the bases of their power. It forces apparatuses to justify themselves. It pushes them to reveal their own logic and the weakness of their own 'reasons'. It makes power *visible*. In systems where power becomes increasingly anonymous and neutral, and where it is incorporated in formal procedures, forcing it to become visible is a fundamental political achievement. It is the condition for negotiating the rules and for making social decisions more transparent.

What peace mobilizations propose to the collective consciousness is that the survival of societies is not assured any more by a meta-social order or by historical laws (based on progress or revolution). For the first time societies become radically aware of their contingency; they realize they 'are thrown in the world' (Heidegger). They discover their existence is not a necessity and that therefore they have no choice but to take responsibility for their own destiny. Catastrophe, suffering and freedom all come to belong to the future. They are not viewed as fatal events. Nor is collective well-being assured as a final solution. It has to be renewed by decisions, negotiations and actions within the *polis*.

The voice of the roots

During the phase of industrial capitalism there was a close correspondence between the position occupied within productive relations and the cultures of the various social groups. These cultures were clearly characterized as 'class cultures' and, paradoxically, in this context the subordinate classes enjoyed a certain autonomy. That is, they were able to develop practices and forms of communication qualitatively different from those of the dominant culture.

The modernization of complex societies has a direct influence on these areas, throwing them into the great machine of mass culture. The multiplication of contacts and the constant flow of messages destroys the homogeneity of the individual cultures: the media transmits standardized models, while migration and mass tourism encourage the extinction of cultural practices bound up with specific territorial or social circumstances. The growing differentiation of roles breaks up the unity of individual groups and forces their members into networks of functional and atomized relations. Consequently, basic social functions are entrusted to bureaucratic organizations that intervene in the definition and regulation of social behaviour.

But the highly differentiated relations typical of complex societies are unable to provide forms of membership and identification to meet individuals' needs for self-realization, communicative interaction and recognition. The bureaucratic and impersonal nature of complex organizations makes them ill-suited to achieving these goals. On the other hand the safeguarding or revival of declining traditional ties may offer new channels of solidarity and identification.

Ethnic identity is one of these channels. A revival of ethnicity is not necessarily related to open discrimination but is a response to a need for collective identity which transcends the general status of the group and tends to be stronger precisely where an ethnic group's position is relatively strong. Parsons has suggested the term 'de-differentiation' to explain this need for a collective identity among particular groups (Parsons, 1975). He argues that there is a growing plurality of social roles in which the individual is called upon to act. Yet none of these roles is able adequately to offer the individual a stable identity. Selective mechanisms of de-differentiation thus come into being to provide identity via a return to primary memberships. Thus, ethnicity is revived as a source of identity because it responds to a collective need which assumes a particular importance in complex societies.

Theories of 'ethnic dislocation' (see, for example, Lijphart, 1977) which view the revival of ethnicity as a reappearance of a type of solidarity 'dislocated' from that of class by industrialization, tend to ignore this fundamental change. Ethno-national conflict is rooted in the past and testifies to the continuity of historic questions and ancient solidarities, but within this legacy it also introduces discontinuous elements, associated with the transformation of complex societies. Without such roots the ethno-national struggle would lose its social foundation and disappear into merely symbolic demands. But without the new themes introduced by emergent collective needs it would be reduced to a form of resistance which is archaic, utopian and regressive (Melucci and Diani, 1982).

The ethno-national question must be seen, therefore, as containing a plurality of meanings that cannot be reduced to a single core. It contains ethnic identity, which is a weapon of revenge against centuries of discrimination and new forms of exploitation; it serves as an instrument for applying pressure in the political market; and it is a response to needs for personal and collective identity in highly complex societies.

Meanwhile, analyses of the various historical circumstances of different nation-states contain two long-standing political issues: inter-group relations in segregated societies; and pluralism and international relations among multi-racial states. Here the protagonists are the state and the international system. We thus pass from a structural and synchronic analysis of ethno-national collective action to a diachronic and conjunctural reconstruction of its motives, development and outcomes. The ethno-national movements are also historical actors and their main fields of action, from this point of view, are states and relations among states. Thus, while these movements expose problems related to the structure of complex societies, they are also rooted in history and the actual workings of nation-states and international relations.

If we are to grasp the meaning of the movements' action, we

must avoid conflating the analysis of these historical and structural aspects. Unless we link their appearance with the transformation of complex societies they become simple historical by-products of the process of nation-building or incidental events in the narrative of international relations. If on the other hand we ignore their origins in 'national questions' and in their conflict with the states, we risk reducing them to mere cultural appeals in the name of diversity.

Many ethno-national movements develop their action on cultural groups, to ensure the protection and renewed vitality of group culture. This activity can be regressive and strongly conservative, or it can develop historical traditions in the context of a changing society. The reference to cultural traditions is valuable in creating new symbolic systems. Past codes and languages are used by these movements to express demands and conflicts unique to complex societies: in particular, the need for the autonomous self-determination of identity finds fertile soil in ethnic cultures.

The ethno-national struggle also affects the distribution of resources and social opportunities, revealing old and new inequalities: those crystallized by centuries of historical conflict and those resulting from processes of modernization and related developments.

At the political level the ethno-national movements bring to light two problems central to complex societies: first, they raise questions about the need for new rights for all members of the community, particularly the right to be different; and, second, they claim the right to autonomy, to control a specific living space (which in this case is also a geographic territory). In terms of political action this means fighting for new channels of representation, access for excluded interests to the political system, and the reform of the decision-making processes and the rules of the political game. It is not only a struggle against the historical legacy of the nation state, but also against the fundamentally changed state apparatuses. We must not forget that the need to reduce the complexity of highly differentiated systems and to make change predictable feeds new policies of rationalization that usually result in the normalization of everyday life. In some cases the ethno-national movements have managed to throw into question the overall logic of this

91

development and to regain a form of control that takes into account the needs of the individuals and groups involved.

Rapidly accelerating processes of development have accentuated differentiation and multiplied communications. Even peripheral areas find themselves exposed to the demands of the models of the 'centre'. Meanwhile statutory constraints are weakened and traditional social structures are no longer able to ensure the cohesion of groups. They consequently suffer disintegration. As supra-national systems of exchange broaden the economic and political markets, dependence and the threat of desegregation become evident – along with the potential for the autonomy of the marginal regions.

The ethno-national movements offer a response to these processes. They both continue and break with historical nationalism. They are the final outcome of nation-building and represent one of the most striking cases of persistent exclusion from citizenship. On this particular battlefield ethno-national movements exert a massive presence. But they are not only the product of a system of international relations that have not yet come to terms with the gulf between political and cultural processes. As other criteria of group membership (such as class) weaken or recede, ethnic solidarity also responds to a need for identity of an eminently symbolic nature. It gives roots, based on a language, a culture and an ancient history, to demands that transcend the specific condition of the ethnic group. The 'innovative' component of ethno-national movements, albeit a minority issue bound up with their struggle against discrimination and for political rights, also has a predominantly cultural character. The ethnic appeal launches its challenge to complex society on such fundamental questions as the goals of change and the production of identity and meaning. The conflicts affecting the 'centre' of complex systems transpose themselves to the 'periphery', where they express themselves through the social relations and symbols supplied by the 'ethnic nation'. Difference is thereby given a voice which speaks of problems which transverse the whole of society.

A possible difference

In the 1970s, women broke publicly, and in a massive way, from a condition that confined them to a narrow domestic identity. At the same time they introduced into the political arena ideas and actions which were incompatible with the established logic of interests and the calculation of means and ends. This massive entry of women into the political arena meant not only that they became part of it; they also presented the political system with a challenge.

The emergence of women's collective action was related to the development of social policies that provided the institutional resources and motivations for their active participation. Women's public mobilization also had its own influence on social policies and in turn was influenced by them. This reciprocal influence precipitated an institutional redefinition of the movement's issues and objectives. Although this appeared to dissipate the conflictual force of the women's movement, in reality it took on a widespread cultural presence throughout society.

The well-known voyage within the women's movement through separatist radical feminism and self-consciousness brought out its specific form of solidarity. For example, the awareness of difference broadened out from the initial stance against a male-dominated world to the recognition of plurality within the actual female subject herself. The attempt, evident in other types of collective action, to create a specific unifying myth of origins – the idea of an essential female subject – served to concentrate women's attention on the female condition and the history of women, but it spread quickly to cultural models regulating social exchange, including questions of role-division and gender identity.

Social policies intervened in this process to produce or accelerate a 'disintegrative revolution'.[1] Through new policies on education, work and social services, women found themselves increasingly present in public spheres from which they were previously excluded. New resources of aggregation, communication and organization became available through these channels, but social policies nevertheless continued to display forms of discrimination against women. Ironically, in schools, the labour market and public services, social policies worked to

93

promote women's integration into public life, while at the same time perpetuating their subordination. In this way the conditions emerged for the formation and recognition of female collective action and conflictual mobilization. The presence of political actors with previous experiences of mobilization, such as the New Left organizations and former activists from the student, anti-war and civil rights movements, accelerated the process of women's politicization. They accomplished this by supplying organizational and communicative resources and by deepening, through their own actions, the crisis in the system, thereby opening up the political market to traditionally excluded subjects.

The wave of feminist mobilizations, fed by social policy, displayed both integrative and destructive forces. Through the benefits handed out by the political system – representation, the setting up of special agencies, the legitimization of movement-specific issues such as abortion, divorce, health care and family policies – women increased their influence on the political market. On the other hand, precisely because many of their demands were met, women saw their conflictual demands diluted and undermined. The multiplication of institutional channels and filters, the formation of new elites through struggle, and the creation of institutions incorporating the issues and practices of the movement all contributed to the institutionalization of action. But the growth of female representation in the political arena was also accompanied by the growth of grass roots initiatives by women. Indeed, the process of institutionalization did not touch the women's movement as such; rather, it affected its issues and demands for equality and citizenship. Over and above the pressures for emancipation, the idea of difference, which remained outside this process, shifted from the political arena to everyday life, nourishing an underground process of cultural production. The cycle of struggles of the 1970s fostered a distinction between feminism and the women's movement. Feminism principally concerns that generation of women who in the earlier years of the decade were the first to utilize the public arena and who later flowed into numerous feminist institutions (such as the research centres concerned with issues of gender, the campaigns for political representation and committees for equal rights) born out of the struggle and later diffused throughout society.

The women's movement, as recent empirical studies show,[2] comprises a much more articulated variety of submerged phenomena, in which the cultural dimension predominates over direct confrontations with political institutions. In terms of mobilization, current analyses concentrate primarily on the political arena and inevitably neglect the richness of this submerged cultural production. It is within these submerged networks that the female difference becomes the basis for the elaboration of alternative symbolic codes at odds with the dominant cultural and political codes.

It is important to stress, even after the collapse of publicly visible mobilizations of women, both the ambivalent role of public policies and the continuing presence of women's collective action at the level of everyday life. The end of mobilization set in motion at least three different processes. First, there was the integration of feminist issues in the political market and in the market as a whole. Second, there was the formation of feminist institutions, the selection of new elites which reasserted the issues of the movement in the public arena. Finally, there was the creation of a 'women's culture', which was submerged and woven into the fabric of daily life, and which sustained and nourished women's mobilizations. But this conflict has moved away from the strictly political spheres, in which it intervenes occasionally on single issues, and operates instead predominantly in the sphere of symbolic codes. In this way, the women's movement supplies alternative definitions of otherness and communication, and transmits to the rest of society the message of a possible difference.

Living with the planet

In present-day complex societies ecological questions are the constant focus of attention in the media, in daily conversation and in politics at the local, national and international level.

Why have ecological issues assumed such importance? The answer does not lie only in increasing pollution or the gradual worsening of environmental decay. The real reason is that we are beginning to perceive reality in different terms; our definition of individual and collective needs is changing. The ecological problem reflects and expresses a profound change in cultural models and social relations. If we fail to take into account this qualitative change, the questions and answers surrounding the ecological issue will be falsified and thrown off course. To discuss these problems as if the society in which we live and the culture that nourishes our social relations were unchanged; as if we were living in the heyday of industrialization and witnessing the rape of nature; as if the mainspring of our action were still the acquisitive needs that formed the basis of the industrial mode of production and social organization – to assume all this is to shut our eyes to what is occurring around us. The gathering concern around the ecological question is a sympton of changes that go far beyond mere environmental issues.

First, the ecological discussion reveals a _systemic problem_. It highlights the worldwide interdependence of complex societies. This means that it is impossible to deal with individual problems without taking into account the interrelated networks that bind them together. The planetary interdependence of today's world alters the frontiers of knowledge and action. Linear causality is at an end; single-cause explanations, forms of 'determination in the last instance' have had their day. We live in systems where the circularity of causes demands the renewal of our cognitive models and expectations of reality.

Second, the ecological debate highlights the _cultural dimension_ of human experience. We are emerging from a model of society in which the economy was seen to determine all aspects of social life. We are living through a transitional phase in which politics, decisions and exchanges appear to become fundamental. However, the ecological problem demonstrates that the basis of survival is no longer the system of means (i.e. goal-oriented rationality and calculations of political exchange), but rather ends themselves. The ends here refer to the cultural models that guide action and structure daily life, modes of production, exchange and consumption. Culture, in its capacity to give meaning to things and relations, to 'create' a human environment, is the ultimate, insuperable horizon in which demands on humankind's destiny can be placed. It is impossible to imagine a future worth living without taking into account the unprecedented 'cultural' intervention – on social relations, symbolic systems, and on the circulation of information – of the new technologies (such as electronics, bio-technologies, communication techno-logies and artificial intelligence) on the 'material' environment. The fears that appear to preoccupy those responsible for making decisions in today's complex systems are expressed in technical terms (lack of resources, the high costs of environmental policies, etc.), and this exemplifies the contemporary risk of tunnel vision, or short-sightedness. To change things today involves operating on the symbolic codes; 'material effects' depend on cultural models that structure everyday social relations, political systems and forms of production and consumption.

The ecological question has a third component: ecological problems not only affect individuals in so far as they belong to a group, a class or a nation; they also affect *individuals as such*. The protection of the species that can be assured only by a new equilibrium between individuals and nature is a problem that today affects the lives of everyone. Thus change is not separable from individual action; direct and personal investment becomes a necessary condition and resource for systemic intervention.

Finally, the ecological question signals that *conflict* is a 'physiological' dimension of complex systems. The differentiation of interests and social positions, the uncertainty of human action on the environment and on society itself inevitably create a whole series of conflicts. Industrial culture saw conflict as a necessary result of exploitation or as a pathology related to dysfunctions in the social order. The recognition that we cannot avoid but can only contain conflict means that we must redefine our criteria of coexistence. Only by an effort to render transparent and negotiable the differences, possibilities and constraints of associated life, can a new solidarity be founded, both in micro-relations and in macro-systems.

We can now look more closely at ecological mobilization and its related movements. The Greens' recent electoral successes are evidently related to processes internal to the electoral market in the various countries. (And here students of the polls may advance their explanations.) But it is undeniable that these electoral successes cannot be understood properly without reference to the vast ecological networks whose forms of organization, cultural orientations and historical evolution have become subjects of recent study.[3] Empirical research reveals that these networks are not a unified phenomenon, but contain a plurality of different actors. A variety of motives, interests and objectives converge around the concern to protect the environment or to promote a better quality of life. There are forms of mobilization and protest reflecting the local interests of communities threatened by environmentally damaging development. There are also voluntary associations that act as pressure groups at a national level, and which have been encouraged by Green electoral successes to step up their environmental lobbying. The ecological area also indicates emergent elites who legitimize innovative technical and cultural skills, through which in turn they acquire a place in the market, the media or the political system. Finally, there is a molecular environmentalism, which is expressed through micro-networks of solidarity which alter personal life-styles and experiment with alternative practices.

Various studies show that the actors involved in ecological mobilization fall into three social categories. The literature on 'new movements' has amply described them as the 'new middle class', and 'affluent marginals' and the 'old middle class' (see Chapter 2). Beyond these characteristics there is a more general distinction to be drawn between two types of action and actors involved in ecological mobilization. This mobilization includes both conflictual and defensive forms, which correspond to two different ways of confronting the systemic changes expressed by the ecological question. Actors exposed to the central processes of ecological and institutional change, who therefore use its resources and live its contradictions, are more likely to adopt a 'progressive' or conflictual approach. On the other hand, those who must bear the full brunt of change but lack resources can only see it as a threat and therefore adopt a 'regressive' position. The conflictual approach tends to be in the forefront of public mobilizations, while the defensive form takes advantage of the slipstream created for their own defensive action and tends to withdraw more quickly from participation.

In some countries, Italy and the Federal Republic of Germany for example, the specific risk of ecological action is that it will recycle outmoded politics and former elites into new environmental issues. This danger is reinforced by the competition triggered off in the political system as traditional politicians discover the electoral capital to be gained by espousing ecological concerns. An elite with specific skills and experience in the political market, acquired during previous phases of commitment, is probably better able to compete effectively than militants recruited directly through mobilization on single issues. But it can also cut institutional action adrift from the grass roots networks, thereby robbing the mobilization of its cultural subsoil.

Notes and references

1 The expression is used by Y. Ergas (1986) in his analysis of the relationship between movements and social policies.

2 See especially Bianchi and Mormino (1984) and Calabrò and Grasso (1985).

3 See especially Biorcio and Lodi (1987) and Diani (1987).

II

COMPLEX
SOCIETIES AND
EVERYDAY LIFE

5

The boundaries of
everyday life

The construction of time and space

Although everyday experiences appear to be far removed from
visible collective action and the major social changes taking
place in contemporary societies, they are in fact crucial for
understanding contemporary conflicts and movements. Consider
our experience of time, which originates in an earlier model of
society, that of industrial capitalism. In this system, the
experience of time has two fundamental reference points. The
first is the machine. The time that modern society knows is
measured by machines (clocks are machines *par excellence*). The
machine also creates a new dimension of time: it is no longer
'natural' (that is, marked only by the cycles of day and night, the
seasons, birth and death) and no longer 'subjective' (that is, tied
to the perception and experience of actors). The time of the
machine is an artificial product that has the objectivity of a thing.
It is also a universal measure which permits the comparison and
exchange, by means of money and the market, of performances
and rewards. Time is a measurable quantity: in the everyday
rhythms of work, in the annual balance-sheets of companies
and, in fact, in every calculation which is based upon instrumental
rationality, the machine establishes a continuum between
individual time and social time.[1]

The second characteristic of the modern experience of time is
a finalistic cultural orientation. Time has a direction and its
meaning derives from a final point, however this is established.
The very idea of a course of history, evident in the emphasis
placed by industrial society on history as a project, derives from

a model of time which rests upon a teleology, such as progress, revolution, the wealth of nations or the salvation of humanity (a linear time which moves towards an end is the last secularized inheritance of Christian time). There is thus a unity and an orientation of time, and the experience individuals have of it acquires sense only in relation to the final point: all the intermediate passages are measured in relation to the end of time.[2]

In the present situation we perceive our distance from these two reference points because our experiences of time are increasingly differentiated. The times we experience differ greatly, to the point where they sometimes seem to us to be antithetical. While there are times which are very difficult to measure, there are also diluted times and greatly accelerated times. One has only to think of the multiplicity of times that images from television, graphics and advertising introduce into our everyday life. And now there are also divisions and discontinuities between the different times that we live which are much more perceptible than in the relatively homogeneous social structures of the past.

In particular there are definite divisions between the interior times (the times that each individual lives in his or her inner experience, affections and emotions) and the exterior times, marked by different rhythms and regulated by the multiple memberships of each individual. The presence of these differences of temporal experience is not entirely new; but in a rural society or even in the industrial society of the nineteenth century there was a certain integration, a certain proximity of subjective experiences and social times, and of the various levels of social times. In highly differentiated complex systems, by contrast, a gap between these dimensions becomes part of our habitual experience.[3]

It is no accident that there exist today widespread tendencies to extend artificially the subjective dimensions of time by means of particular stimuli or constructed situations. There is for example the recourse to experiences and artificially dilated inner time, such as those produced by drugs. Drugs have an important place in traditional societies, but in the interior of a ritual order which assigned them a specific function. There was no separation, for example, between the role of the ritual drug of the American Indians in the social life and the inner life of individuals. This permitted ritual 'fracture', this dilation of subjective time induced by the drug, formed part of a sacred order and contributed to the reaffirmation of a balance between social life and the space given to the individual within the group.

In our societies, by contrast, the extreme example of drugs is a dramatic sign, the most significant symptom of a difference between outer and inner times. But there is also, though on a less dramatic scale, an increase of artificially constructed opportunities – from exotic tourism or the 'liberation' of the body in cathartic group experiences, to the totalitarian paradises of the neo-mystical sects – to live and experience emotions free from the bonds of social time. The ambivalence of these phenomena, in which deep individual needs are transformed mostly into market commodities, cannot be ignored. They are cited here as signs of an unresolved tension between the multiple times of everyday experience.

The differentiation of time produces several new problems. It increases the difficulty of reducing different times to a homogeneous, generalized measure. At the same time there is a heightened need to integrate these differences both at the collective level and, above all, within the unity of an individual biography and a 'subject' of action (Fraser, 1978; Gorz, 1983).

Furthermore, a differentiated time is increasingly a time without a story or, better, a time of many relatively independent stories. Time therefore loses its *telos*; the present becomes the inestimable measure of the sense of things. Finally, this multiple and discontinuous time comes to be seen as something 'constructed' as an unmistakably cultural product. The industrial factory cancelled the natural cycle of day and night. Now all the other times given by nature are dissolving. The experience of the seasons melts on our dining-room tables, where foods lose all reference to seasonal cycles; or in our holidays, which offer us tropical sun or snow at all times of the year. Even birth and death, quintessentially events of natural time, are losing their necessary character and becoming, as we shall see later, products of medical and social intervention.

Connected closely to these changes in the sense of time are alterations of the common experience of space. We are confronted by a radical alteration of the traditional measure of

105

space. Space is a 'measurable' reality, the perception of which is constructed through references to known dimensions and by means of accumulated experiences and comparisons. But our everyday experience is now losing its spatial bearings because of two contrary developments. We find our experience of space undergoing both unlimited dilation and an apparently unlimited restriction – a paradoxical development which is not connected with the physical dimensions of objects.[4]

To understand this paradox it is enough to think of the extent to which the resource of information modifies our spatial relationships. Industrial societies were based on the accumulation of material goods. They had to take space into account as a physical resource because things have a dimension. Whether it is the accumulation of human beings, goods or machines, it is necessary to allocate space for them since their transfer or exchange is tied to spatial relationships. Today a radical change is taking place because information can be stored in an infinitesimal space. In the last twenty years this has occurred at an astounding rate. There is no longer a significant ratio between the quantity of information and the space required to contain it, and because enormous quantities of information can be collected in minimal spaces, their transfer or exchange no longer has a direct relationship with physical dimensions.[5]

At the same time we are coming into contact with spaces which are no longer based on our direct physical experience. Today, planetary dimensions have become an everyday fact of life and gradually, in the last few years, we have even come to refer to spaces outside the planet. In these ways, stable spatial references, measurable in physical terms, disintegrate. Space becomes multiple and discontinuous, a cultural construction and a symbolic reference point.

Inner rhythms, social rhythms

In the modern world, social time, the time of collective events and experience,[6] is *linear* time. It is characterized by the *continuity* and *uniqueness* of events, which follow one another in a single direction, and are therefore viewed as *irreversible*. Thus we can speak of a before and an after. We can even establish a relation of *cause* and *effect* between the before and after: previous events are seen to give rise to or produce the events that follow.

Social time is *measurable*. It is broken up into rhythms or units of measurement that we all recognize, though these differ for each class of event: long and short periods of time, routine daily activities or more irregular events. The fact that time is measurable means it can be used as a resource in market-based production. This kind of time is *predictable*, because different periods of time can be compared and the past helps us to forecast the future more or less accurately. Finally, social time is *uniform*: for each type of event there is a particular scansion, a set rhythm on which social experience is structured and expectations are founded.

Inner time – deeply personal, individual time – has contrasting characteristics.[7] As with sacred or mythical time it is *multiple* and *discontinuous*. Different times exist together in inner experience; they succeed, intersect with and overlap one another.

To begin with, there is *cyclical time*, which resembles myth: in the body, in sensations, and in dreams, events recur and repeat themselves in nearly identical form. Inner time is also *simultaneous* time. Many times exist simultaneously (yesterday and today; my time and that of the other; here and there). I can be an adult and a child, black and white, in the before and in the after. The simultaneity of inner time abolishes non-contradiction. Inner time is, therefore, also *multidirectional*: we can establish the relations between events running forwards and backwards through time, but also upwards and downwards (and hence passing into other times). We can move through inner time both successively and simultaneously. It is therefore constantly *reversible*: what happens to me now changes my past; what happens to another changes my time; the effect which is produced may be cancelled out; and so on.

In inner experience, time is *immeasurable*, since the perception of time varies from one moment to another and from situation to situation. Above all, inner time can *stand still*; it can cease to pass. This may occur through a rapid blur of repeated events (moments, sensations, images) so fleeting that they no longer constitute a cycle, but create the experience of immobility; alternatively, it may result from the absence of events and thoughts which are experienced as emptiness. In either case, time ceases to be sequential and instead becomes a fixed motionless point. The passage between different inner times is *discontinuous* and marked by *interruption*. Inner times are *unpredictable*; they can suddenly irrupt into each other as an event that interrupts routine.

Inner rhythms are therefore variable and not assignable once and for all to a particular category. A minute can 'last an hour', while a day passes in an instant; exactly the same sensation is rapid at times and deadly slow at others. Hence the opposition between inner time and social time could not be more marked. Of course, societies generate mechanisms for controlling this tension – such as art, play and myths. Individuals, too, have resources for reconciling contrasting times – sleep, imagination and love are a few examples. In society, however, the contradiction comes to the fore whenever there is a more direct clash between inner rhythms and the constraints of social regulation, such as in the relationship between adult and child, the treatment of madness, and in social definitions of diversity. In the life of an individual, illness is the clearest sign of opposition between inner and social time.

The passage from one time to another, their fluid, if not quite harmonious, cohabitation is one of the principal conditions of personal equilibrium as well as a critical factor for social life as a whole.

Metamorphosis

In complex societies knowledge is increasingly reflexive. It is no longer merely a question of learning, but of learning to learn, i.e. of exercising control over cognitive and motivational processes and adapting them to new problems.

Individuals find themselves involved in a plurality of member-ships arising from the multiplication of social positions, associative networks, and reference groups. Entry to and exit from these different systems of membership is much quicker and more frequent than before, and the amount of time invested in each of them is reduced.[8]

Meanwhile the quantity of information that each individual emits or receives is growing at an unprecedented rate. The media, the working environment, interpersonal relations and leisure time continue to generate information for individuals, who receive, analyse and commit it to memory and sometimes respond with more information (Klapp, 1977).

The pace of social change, the plurality of memberships, and the abundance of possibilities and messages thrust upon the individual all serve to weaken the traditional points of reference (church, party, race, class) on which identity is based. The possibility that an individual will say with conviction and continuity 'I am x, y, or z' becomes increasingly uncertain. The need to re-establish continually *who I am* and what it is that assures the continuity of my biography becomes stronger. A 'homelessness' of personal identity (Berger, Berger and Kellner, 1979) is created, such that the individual must build and rebuild constantly his or her 'home' in the face of changing situations and events.

The experience of time, as I have argued, becomes multiple and discontinuous, since it involves the passage from one membership to another, the overlapping of symbolic codes and a multiplicity of reference points. Time also ceases to be uniform. The rapid processing and circulation of information reduces the duration of many experiences and alters the rhythm and perception of other human times.

In complex societies we find ourselves living increasingly in a framework of time which is wholly secularized and 'profane'. The cyclical nature of sacred or mythical time has been weakened along with Christianity. Christianized linear time still had a *telos*, an end. Human history marched towards salvation and events assumed meaning in the light of this ultimate goal. Philosophies of history, the myths of progress or revolution shored up this temporal structure. The meaning of the present was found in the final destination of history.

Today, as the great narratives and myths of salvation dim and fade, time loses this finality and catastrophe becomes a possibility. But it is precisely this development which reveals clearly for the first time the uniqueness of individual experience. Inner time, and each moment within it, is unrepeatable. Not only does it not return in an endlessly repeating cycle, but it no longer carries within itself another sense, another end besides that which the individual him- or herself is able to produce.

The need to give unity to rapidly changing and multifaceted social experiences triggers a search for a point of reference for individual identity. *Metamorphosis* appears as the best response to this need for continuity through change (Baumgartner, 1983). In other words, the unity and continuity of individual experience cannot be found in a fixed identification with a definite model, group or culture. It must instead be based on an inner capacity to 'change form', to redefine itself repeatedly in the present, to reverse decisions and alliances. But it also means cherishing the present as a unique, unrepeatable experience within which the individual realizes him- or herself.

At the point of intersection between numerous circuits of information the individual can only preserve his or her own unity by being able to 'open and close', to participate and withdraw from the flow of messages (Klapp, 1977). It therefore becomes vital to discover a rhythm of entry and exit that allows the individual to communicate meaningfully without nullifying him- or herself as a subject of communication.

To live the discontinuity and variability of time and space we must find a way to unify experience other than by means of instrumental rationality. The passing from one time to another, fragmentation and unpredictability, escape the clutches of cause and effect, criteria of efficiency and the logic of rational calculation. Instead, they demand the use of the more immediate perceptions, intuitive awareness and imagination that were the patrimony of traditional cultures. The current interest in Eastern philosophy, besides being a transient fashion, is also a significant symptom of individuals' need to unify experience on a plane which is beyond mere rational and instrumental thought.

Existence as a choice

In complex societies, the meaning of fundamental aspects of the human experience of birth and death is changing. It reveals dimensions of human existence which had been inconceivable until quite recently. For the first time birth has ceased to be a matter of fate. Techniques of fertility control and of intervention in the physiological phenomena of pregnancy and birth have profoundly modified a fact that has characterized societies for thousands of years, namely, that the reproduction of the social system depends primarily on its biological basis and on the fact that the population reproduces itself. This reproduction may have varied according to environmental conditions and genetic and evolutionary factors, but it was still a quasi-natural fact which depended only to a very small degree on human intervention.

Deliberate intervention into the possibility of conception and the conditions of birth has profoundly modified this apparently unchangeable biological fact, subjecting it to choice. Certainly this is not true for every one on a planetary scale, but the seed of this change is present and could be sown universally. Birth, in short, is ceasing to be a fate and becoming a choice.[9]

At the opposite extreme, one could say that death is ceasing to be a natural necessity and is becoming increasingly a social fact. The possibilities of intervening in and controlling death are expanding. Not only do people on average now live longer than in the past, but the ability to prolong life by means of ever more sophisticated bio-medical techniques is increasing. At the same time, however, death is becoming something to banish from the social scene and to confine to specialized sectors controlled by the 'power of white coats', the aseptic rationality of medical structures. In traditional societies death was a natural fact. It was a feared and exorcised fatality, but it was also cultivated by means of rites which made it a friend of sorts, or at least not extraneous to the human experience. In modern societies, by contrast, death is highly socialized but also increasingly neutralized. It is regulated by technical, medical and pharmacological circuits that seem to annul the individual experience of dying.[10]

In a deliberately selective phenomenology of the fragments of everyday life, such as the one presented here, birth and death cannot but be associated with the experience of health and illness. Here two main facts can be observed. Our societies have freed themselves progressively from illness as a 'scourge', as a mass catastrophe. The great epidemics have diminished or disappeared, and the dangers of infectious diseases and infant mortality have been greatly reduced. At the same time, however, there has been a great increase of a new class of pathologies associated with social life: disorders caused by stress, neoplastic degenerations, immunity deficiency, diseases caused by pollution and disorders caused by the administration and indiscriminate consumption of drugs. Our everyday imagination is haunted by the menacing ghosts of new monsters produced by the hyper-socialization of the systems in which we live.[11]

This paradoxical growth of pathologies is accompanied by another paradox. The general improvement of hygienic, nutritional and living conditions and the increase of education and health information have improved the ability of the individual to perceive and define his or her state of health. The autonomy of the individual and personal responsibility for health have thus increased. But at the same time there has been an extension of the powers of social intervention into the health field, which leads increasingly to externally enforced definitions of pathology and health.

Prevention policies are geared to entire social categories without regard for individual differences. The possibilities of detecting pathologies and preventive treatment have extended to infancy and even intra-uterine life. Belonging to a 'category at risk', to a sector of the population predetermined by administrative decisions, may make us sick by decree and thus render us liable to health treatment.[12] In the field of infancy, the definition of mental health, pregnancy and childbirth, and in the sexological field, these tendencies are already part of our everyday experience.

Otherness and communication

A final observation can be made about the forms of relationship among individuals in everyday life. There is frequent talk of the atomization or disintegration of social life in the great metropolitan areas. In the 1950s, Riesman's famous book, *The Lonely Crowd*, pointed out the factors capable of affecting the feelings and imagination of individuals: the metropolises create 'lonely crowds', isolated individuals who do not communicate and for this reason are susceptible to anomie and manipulation. There is certainly some truth in this image of atomization, but it seems to me that today it is possible to interpret this phenomenon differently. I prefer to speak of individuation, of the extension of

112

the individual dimensions of action and of an increasing awareness of the meanings that each individual attributes to what he or she does.

In contemporary societies there is an increase in the level of resources at the disposal of individuals, enabling them to assert and to recognize themselves as individuals. It is enough to bear in mind two major processes that have been a feature of the history of industrial societies for over a century: mass education, and the creation of a mass political market by means of the extension of rights of citizenship and political participation to the entire population. Both processes have often been interpreted in terms of the increasing integration of the subordinate classes into the dominant cultural models and the rules of the political game controlled by elites. This view, however, tends to underestimate or overlook one fundamental fact: these processes also signal the possibility of individuals' access to resources of knowledge and action, from which previously they were excluded. Their inclusion in universalistic codes of communication and their (potential) exercise of decisions extend the range of action of these individuals and increase their independence.

In modern complex systems, individual social actors have the chance of becoming individuals, that is, of defining themselves as distinct subjects of action irrespective of their group memberships, their situations or their heritage. Ties based on place, language and religion gave way slowly in industrial society to new 'elective' identities linked to new roles and institutions: the individual came to be defined by his or her membership of a profession, a party, a state or a class. These references still hold, but a new question seems to have come to the fore. It relates exclusively to the single individual: 'Who am I?'.[13]

This question is of limited importance in traditional societies, where in any case it finds a response within the social order and its rites. Pierre Clastres provides a significant example in his discussion of the Guayaki Indians of the Amazonian forest (Clastres, 1974). For these small groups of nomadic hunters struggling against a hostile environment, the primary imperative is to enable the group to survive by means of intense exchanges among individuals divided into sex groupings. There is no room for individual difference: the social bond has to be maintained at all costs by checking any threat to solidarity. It is only in the

113

ritual song of the male hunters, round the fire in the evening, that the question, 'who am I?' can make its appearance. In celebrating his hunting achievements each may speak of himself as a distinct individual, within a symbolic space which is circumscribed and therefore does not threaten the life of the whole group.

This example of a culture so distant from ours can serve as a mirror for modern experience. The question 'who am I?' today occupies a large part of our individual lives and at a social level involves our culture as a whole. Individuals invest time and energy in finding an answer; the system itself supplies opportunities and resources for this purpose. The form of interpersonal relationships is consequently modified. The society of the Guayaki hunters again serves as a mirror: in the group there is a taboo against the hunter eating the meat of the animals he has personally killed. The survival of the group is thus tied to the maintenance of exchange and the strength of the social bond. Each exists because he depends on others.

In the modern systems, on the other hand, the process of individualization tends to transform the quality of the relationships among individuals from a bond towards a choice. Relationships with the other are the condition of possibility of choosing and recognizing the difference among individuals. A relationship exists if and when what distinguishes one individual from another is accepted and becomes the basis for communication. To communicate thus signifies the need to depend on what is common in order to discover and affirm difference. The possibility of choice introduces contingency and risk into relationships and makes them a field of emotional commitment and self-reflection.

Boundaries

Changes in everyday experience not only generate but also reflect new needs in the lives of individuals. Identity must be rooted in the present to deal with the fluctuations and metamorphoses. The individual must be able to open and close his or her own channels of communication with the outside world in order to keep alive his or her relationships, without at the same time being swamped by the vast quantity of available information. In addition, to embrace a widening field of experience that cannot be confined within the rigid limits of rationalist thought, each person must develop new capacities for immediate and intuitive contacts with reality. These requirements shift the boundaries between inner and outer and stress the need for self-reflection, greater awareness and responsibility for one's own choices. This self-reflective orientation leads the individual to search for closer contact with his or her inner experience.

Consciousness of one's own existence as a living psycho-physical being highlights, more dramatically than ever before, the problem of establishing a relationship between inner and social time. Only self-awareness can assure the unity and continuity of personal identity through changing external circumstances. An inner world of sensations, perceptions and representations persists in the face of changes in the perceptive signals received from the outside, or from one's own receptor organs. This 'container' of self-awareness, which can assume different forms at different moments, is open to perceptions in the here and now, and can serve to unify differing and contradictory experiences. The presence of each individual as 'body, mind and spirit' is the thread linking together the fragments of his or her own life.

The body is the primary medium of all communication. The 'opening' and 'closing' of the individual to the external environment can be achieved by activating and dis-activating the senses of contact with the outside world. The body sends and receives the basic messages (visual, audile, proprioceptive, cenesthesic) that give sense to communication. Switching off, turning away from the world and terminating communication in no way cancel the presence of the person to him- or herself. The inner continues to be perceived, assuring both continuity and the possibility of new openings to the individual. Contact with the inside also permits direct and intuitive perception, as a form of knowledge which is different from 'instrumental' rationality, and which allows the discrete fragments, times and discontinuities of experience to be synthesized. A consciousness that includes bodily information, and which can tune itself on 'feelings' as well as 'thoughts', serves to further extend the field of knowledge. The body has faculties and resources connected to its biological energy (such as breathing and the sensory systems), which operate naturally to regulate vital biological functions, such as adaptation to the environment or the functioning of the immune system. The conscious activation of these faculties and resources brings individuals' entire perceptual experience within the bounds of the conscious and broadens the range of possibilities open to that individual in relation to him- or herself and the outer world.

A consciousness capable of juggling the widest possible spectrum of information without being swamped – which is capable of 'seeing' without being dazzled – facilitates the passage from the inner to the outer, from inner time to social time and vice versa. A fluid communication between these two dimensions of experience is essential to individual integrity. Conversely, the difficulty in passing from one to the other is a sure sign of some form of unease or pathology. Obstructed access to the inner world leaves one stranded in an empty and monotonous play of social masks. The inability to escape from the incommunicable sphere of inner experience locks away the individual in a prison of silence.

The definition and recognition of these boundaries is the key to movement in either direction: towards communication with the outside and compliance with the rules of social time; or towards an inner voice that speaks to the individual in its 'secret' language. This oscillation between two worlds follows no causal path from the depths to the surface or vice versa; there is no place here for the familiar determinism of nineteenth-century thought, which supposed that individual consciousness is determined either by the obscure domain of instinct or by the social order. Instead, relations are circular in a process that can be described as dynamic. Inner experience and social experience have a mutual influence on each other, but not through the spontaneous irruption of the inner (instincts, impulses) in to the normality of daily life. Instead, the inner is constantly being redefined: elements gathered continually by the individual via social experience and the acquisition of cultural data alter his or her inner perception and awareness. In this way a cycle of opening and closing is established, a permanent oscillation between the two levels and times of experience. The individual becomes increasingly the arbiter and regulator of this oscillation. He or she becomes the only one able to set the rhythm and the pace. Such passages mark the dynamic evolution, the meta-morphoses of personal life.

The fragile hinge between inner and outer is the meeting point between the internal and external signals that the individual must decode in order to situate him- or herself in relation to changes within that individual and in his or her interactions with the world. As the range of possibilities become too wide compared to the actual opportunities for action and experience, the question of boundaries becomes the fundamental problem of individual and collective life. This problem of choice, uncertainty and risk in the hyper-technological scenario of complex society reminds everybody of the human experience of limits. And of freedom.

Notes and references

1 On the measurement of time in the modern age see Cipolla, (1981); Davies, (1977); and Landes, (1984).

2 Sociological and historical reflections on time have given rise to a large number of studies during the last ten years. Among the more significant are Fraser, Lawrence and Park, (1978); Parkes and Thrift (1976); Carlstein, Parkes and Thrift (1978); and Zerubavel (1981).

3 On temporal experience in different models of society see Zerubavel (1981); Fraser, Lawrence and Park (1978). The differentiation of the times of experience has been analysed by Fraser (1978); and Parkes and Thrift (1976). On the difference between inner times and social times see also Melucci (1984c).

4 On the modern definition of space and on the time-space relationship, see Davies (1977); and Carlstein, Parkes and Thrift (1978).

5 For an analysis of the 'micro-electronic revolution' and its social implications see Dizard (1983); Forester (1982); and Friedrichs (1982).

6 On social time see Pomian (1977); Agamben (1978); Felson (1980); and De Santillana and von Dechend (1977).

7 On inner time, see Giovannelli and Mucciarelli (1978); Sabbadini (1979); Matte Blanco (1975), Reali (1982); and Fachinelli (1979, 1983).

8 My main references on this development have been Ricolfi and Sciolla

(1980, 1981); Saraceno (1984, 1987); Cavalli (1985); Gallino (1982); Alberoni (1981a); Baumgartner (1983); Sciolla (1983a, 1983b); Crespi (1982); and Rositi (1983).

9 On the evolution of childbirth and its social representation, see Pizzini (1981). More general studies of the possible development of genetic intervention include Cherfas (1982); and on artificial reproduction see Snowden, Mitchell and Snowden (1984).

10 The attention paid to the theme of death has increased considerably in the last ten years. See in particular Vovelle (1974); Thomas (1978); and Baudrillard (1979).

11 See especially Attali (1979); Krause (1977); and Illich (1975).

12 Policies of prevention are discussed by Castel (1981); and Donzelot (1984).

13 This aspect has been emphasized in mainly negative terms by Lasch (1978) and Sennet (1976). The ambivalence of this question is emphasized more strongly in the analyses of Berger, Berger and Kellner (1973) and Alberoni (1981b).

6

The culture of
individual needs

Nature versus society?

In all human groupings, even those most exposed to natural constraints, individual needs have always been bound up with a system of social relations and the capacity for symbolic representation. Needs are inevitably the result of cultural perception, of a process of symbolic mediation that permits their definition and representation, on the basis of biological and environmental conditions. In complex societies the perception of *needs as a cultural product* has grown out of all comparison with past societies. Nevertheless, the definition of needs still appears to be polarized between an appeal to nature and a model of hypersocialization. Needs are seen either as an expression of a 'nature' which resists or rebels against the social, or as a reflex of the system of relations in which individuals find themselves.

It is tempting to link the first model (naturalism) with emergent movements, and the second (hypersocialization) with the growth of technocracy. In the former case, the spontaneity of primary needs comes up against omnipresent social control; here we recognize certain ideological traits of the feminist, ecological and youth movements. In the latter case, the 'relational' view of needs is the ideological basis of modern pedagogic theory, and it is evident in the emphasis upon communicative processes and in the group-based processes of psycho-pedagogic and psychiatric services. An individual dimension in behaviour or pathology is excluded; everything is reduced to and resolved by communicative processes. The individual can only be educated, cared for, informed, within the context of a group, i.e., integrated in a relational code of normality.

However, equating these two extreme models with dominant and oppositional ideologies may be misleading. In reality we are faced with a system of cultural representations that cuts across the whole of society and which different social groups make use of in diverging ways. The appeal to nature in fact functions as an appeal to integration diffused and propagated by the media; it sustains new markets by generating life-styles and patterns of consumption and in effect it creates a new conformity. Analogously, the 'sociality of needs' model legitimates the mobilization of opposition groups against the processes of social marginalization, individualism and the welfare system's atomization of social demands.

In modern society the symbolic terrain can never be divided neatly into the clear-cut symmetry of good and bad, as in a Hollywood western. Instead it presents a complex web of contradiction, ambivalence and plurality of meaning which various actors try to utilize in order to give sense to their action.

Having said that, it has to be recognized that the appeal to nature has played a crucial role in the formation of new conflictual demands. Nature appears as that which resists external pressures, because it lies beyond instrumental rationality. It has the inestimable weight of a 'given entity' in opposition to the enforced 'socialization' of identity by the new forms of domination.

But this appeal is also based on the intuition that natural existence is potentially a field for human action, a goal to be attained rather than a given condition. The body, desire, biological identity, and sexuality are all cultural – in the sense of socially generated – representations of the incipient awareness that 'human nature' can be produced and transformed by social action – that it can be used for ends other than those imposed by the dominant system.

Here lies the root of all ambiguity in collective action. Contemporary movements centred on the spontaneity, purity and immediacy of 'natural' needs stand in opposition to the tendency of 'the social' to reduce individual differences to systemic normality. But at the same time nature becomes an ideological phantom that nourishes the delusion of escaping from the constraints of social relations. The retreat to naturalism in marginal counter-cultures thereby becomes a pathological denial of the problems involved in *all* forms of sociality – scarcity of resources, the need for efficient and effective action, the distribution of work and power.

Hence the urge for liberation results in the exaltation of an illusory 'spontaneity', the veneration of immediate experience over and above reflective thought. In this way actors nullify and disguise the essential character of the human need for identity, i.e. for belonging to nature *and* to society, for simultaneously experiencing each as a possibility and a limit. Through this experience, the 'nature' within and around us ceases to be the realm of obscure forces and lays itself open to conscious human action; but none the less it remains the 'limit' of this action. In turn, society 'delimits' nature by means of rules and codes, by turning natural human energy into information.

This point is obscured by appeals to 'spontaneous' nature, which can justify every act of submission. Meanwhile, in highly developed societies the systems of control are being restructured to integrate the alleged 'naturalness' of needs in support of the new models of conformity promoted, for example, by advertising campaigns based on the mythology of a 'pure' body and a 'natural' and 'healthy' environment. This trend can be resisted only by keeping open the tension between 'natural' needs and the constraints of social existence. That in turn requires the recognition that the 'nature' we are beginning to discover within us, and which expresses itself as a site of deeply felt needs and resistance to external pressures, is in reality inseparable from the rules and rituals of social life.

An analogous ambivalence is evident in the appeal to the social character of needs. This appeal becomes ideological when it is instrumental in the diffusion of social control, and especially when it is used to justify the integration of the individual into networks that impose conformity and reduce individual problems to those of the group. But at the same time this appeal testifies to the presence of communicative needs that atomized, mass society tends to deny. It underlines the social origins of welfare demands and the political character of collective needs. And it resists the reduction of needs to processes of bureaucratic/ administrative specialization, and to the fragmentation produced by the welfare system.

The rise and fall of the body

The body is invading the social sphere. Through a widespread process of medicalization, clinics and centres devoted to the 'care' of the body are institutionalized; within a vast network of services, experts lay down the criteria of health and sickness. Meanwhile interest in physical well-being is growing. Exercise and fitness training reappear in new expressive forms, while oriental disciplines like yoga have never been more popular. Although these are informal, uncoordinated, activities and apparently individual, they signal the emergence of new collective needs and a new culture of the body.[1]

The discovery of human beings' natural dimension is one component of this trend. The human being is one natural system among many. Our society's past is marked by principles of transcendence, such as God or the laws of history, which are situated beyond everyday social relations. In the face of such principles, the body could not but be seen as a limit, as the product of a fall, as degraded nature in opposition to the spirit. With the death of the gods and the demise of their most recent incarnation – history as a process with an ultimate destination – the way was opened to the discovery of humanity's naturalness.

The new areas of knowledge opened up recently by sciences such as biology, anthropology and genetic psychology locate human beings as an integral part of the natural world, at the same time as providing the opportunity for conscious intervention in nature, to inspect or change it. Knowledge of the body testifies to the discovery of humanity's membership of nature and its potential emancipation (or, as we shall see, renewed dependence). Thanks to these new sciences, it becomes evident that society is a product of humanity, a result of collective action, as well as the field of encounter and conflict between two areas of human belonging: the nature of which we are constituted, and the social relations which are created by us and which allow us to intervene in the natural process.

A second component of the new culture of the body has to do with awareness of the body as a subject of needs. The body is accepted as the centre of impulses and desires, as a source of energy that is no longer considered a foreign or alien force possessed by mysterious demons. Whether one talks of libido or

122

biological energy, the new body culture reveals a human dimension which is neither reducible to instrumental rationality nor stamped with the sign of darkness or perversion. Desire, impulse, energy and emotions all become dimensions of experience, recognized and accepted as one measure of humanity among many. At the same time they create problems for a society which is structured around instrumental effectiveness and which tends to deny or denigrate whatever does not conform to its logic.

A third element of the body culture is the discovery of relations with the other. As a symbol and instrument of communication, the body is the channel for affects which refuse to be wholly neutralized in the rituals of social interchange. Sexuality is no longer relegated to the obscure level of instinct. Instead, it becomes an essentially human form of communication, one that opens up a broader range of relational possibilities. 'Passion' loses its negative connotations and is synonymous with a 'feeling' rooted in the body. Emotions regain their earthly character, nourished as they are by moods, sounds, odours and vibrations. Fear and joy, tenderness and pain are not merely ideas, but tears, breath, warmth, cold and trembling. The human encounter reveals itself as an encounter of bodies and of words.

Finally, the return to the body initiates a new search for identity. The body appears as a secret domain, to which only the individual holds the key, and to which he or she can return to seek a self-definition unfettered by the rules and expectations of society. Nowadays the social attribution of identity invades all areas traditionally protected by the barrier of 'private space'. Consumption, sexuality, and affective relations are all fields of 'public' intervention; they are subject to a growing pressure from socially imposed behaviour models aimed at obtaining the productive and social performance necessary for growth, as well as mass consensus for policies of rationalization. Faced with this expanding control, it is as if the body is mobilizing the resources of 'nature' to safeguard a non-manipulated identity; as if our deepest impulses and needs belonged to us and defined us, as if they were inscribed in the body that is ours, or better, the body that we are.

I do not intend here to revive the old nature–society

dichotomy. I simply wish to indicate the form that the cultural definition of identity is assuming in contemporary society. The natural environment is being discovered, and this poses drastic limits on the production/destruction of resources. The human being is being revealed as energy, eros and aggressiveness, thereby posing limits on the production/manipulation of social relations. The body is seen as unique and inalienable 'property' which is capable of resisting and opposing the pressures of social order. For these reasons, we should not underestimate the conflict potential of the search for identity based on the body: it carries an enormous charge of cultural innovation and social transformation.

However, it is also important to appreciate fully that there exists a deep ambiguity in the 'liberation' of the body. The body is becoming an object of consumption and an instrument of control. It sustains many (and important) sectors of the market as a well-packaged good. It induces consumption through the appeal of *sex-symbols*,[2] and the basis of numerous businesses, from cosmetics and fashion to erotic publications and pharmaceuticals. Such market manipulation is matched by a growing exploitation of the body as a resource of social control. Advanced capitalism balances its books with puritanical rigour while placing a high price on pleasure. Bodily satisfaction is an effective guarantee of social order. Each day, more and more invitations are extended to erotic gratification; and manuals on lovemaking, guides to healthy living and recipes for making better use of the body's charge of eros and desire become ever more available.[3]

Besides this more obvious – but also cruder – manipulation, there is a subtler phenomenon whose ambiguity is more difficult to grasp. The drive towards liberation exalts an illusory 'spontaneity' of the body and thereby effectively exercises deeper control than the manipulation of consumers' choices by the market. Promising unlimited 'expression', it submits the individual to a new dependence. The body is in reality the indispensable meeting point of needs and constraints, impulses and limits. A 'liberation' of the body – the actualization of the human capacity for expressiveness and communication – cannot be achieved by evading the tension that binds the body's two poles; it can be effected only if it permits the individual to express his or her deepest needs within the limits of his or her social existence.

Awareness of these limits imposes an intimate rapport with reality; it is the necessary condition of any transformation. As the site of profound demands and of resistance to external pressures, the body, like language, is also the medium of social interchange. As such, it never fully escapes the rules and rituals governing social intercourse, even though it is never absorbed entirely by them. Any body politics aimed at emancipation must inevitably fall within this dialectic. It must facilitate a return to the body of needs and impulses, but it must also help individuals locate themselves within the constraints of their social existence. It cannot but express the tension between full 'liberation' and total 'repression' and thus, between the discovery of limits and the search for the possible.

Current talk about the body masks the dramatic terms of this dialectic and disguises, with promises of easy liberation, the steady diffusion of manipulation. The process of manipulation occurs through medicalization, mentioned above, through the delegation of care and treatment to organs of control which resemble manufacturers of well-being, and also through the individual's rush to procure those means of 'liberation' which break down inhibitions and defences. Given the impossibility of living each moment of one's day-to-day existence in the orgasmic illusion of a body released from all repression, separate societies are formed in which the elimination of inhibitions becomes the guiding rule. Hence we see a flourishing of sects which offer an easy paradise through an all-embracing communal experience.[4] These sects deny the tension between the body and society described above. They project the fleeting image, illusory and fragile, of a world of unlimited expression and creativity. But their mirage cannot stand the test of reality. Consequently, it often leaves those attracted by it defenceless in the face of external social pressures.

This development of a culture of the body prompts the conclusion that at the very moment that we are witnessing the triumph of the body, it is ceasing to exist as an object with a single, unequivocal shared social meaning. The notion of the body itself dissolves into a plurality of meanings, which in turn stimulate further discussion and practice focused on 'the body'.

The body no longer possesses the harmonious geometry attributed to it by the natural sciences, since organs, functions and systems are once again put into question by the widespread experience of the links between 'nature', affectivity and social relations. Moreover, the body no longer retains its symbolic and ritual meanings, since it is increasingly difficult to separate them from the biological dimension, now exposed in all its complexity. The body is no longer an object. It has become a field of action on which social and cultural contradictions are delineated. From this body spring demands for scientific consideration and social practice on many fronts.

Normality and pathology

Another topic of central concern in complex society is the definition of normality and pathology. This is a theme that runs not only throughout medicine and psychiatry, but also cuts right across the whole spectrum of social behaviour. This theme raises the problem of what makes an individual an autonomous subject or prevents him or her from being recognized as such. I do not intend to tackle this problem in its broadest form. Instead I shall use the limited example of madness to answer a more general question: how can health and sickness, normality and pathology be defined in societies that increasingly act directly upon the subject's 'inner nature'?

Madness raises more questions for contemporary society than ever before. Today we have reached a turning point in both the history of madness and the response to its disturbing presence. I first want to quickly survey the stages that have led to the present situation[5] before considering the meaning of madness in relation to more general problems of identity.

The transition from the prison to the asylum historically marked the birth of 'mental illness' as a distinct entity subject to the observation and treatment of a body of specialists. 'Illness', which medicine distinguished from criminality and isolated within the guilt-ridden misery of *les classes dangereuses*, was handed over to a specific sector. Essentially this process involved safeguarding bourgeois reason from the 'dangers' of the poorer classes, who were seen to require separate treatment.

126

By defining a norm consistent with the criteria of bourgeois rationality, psychiatry constructed the 'scientific' edifice that framed and classified 'sickness', segregating it in its 'caring' institutions.

Of course the history of psychiatry does not fully coincide with the function of protecting bourgeois reason, nor can it be wholly identified with the asylum. Psychoanalysis lent important corrections to the psychiatric view, while progress in neurology clarified certain organic aspects of illness. Yet it remains the case that until the 1940s the asylum model, with all that that implied in theory and practice, was the keystone of both society's treatment of madness and the definition of psychiatry as the 'scientific' discipline entrusted with that task.

From the 1930s onwards, and especially after the Second World War, the establishment of a welfare state in most capitalist countries involved a crucial change in the treatment of madness and numerous other 'social problems' (such as unemployment, sickness, old age and crime). There was a reorganization of social 'assistance' to deal with such problems. The institutions of segregation and repression were replaced to tackle 'deviance' by inserting the single case back into the social fabric. Pathological behaviour was no longer seen as an individual problem; intervention was transferred to the network of social relations that created the pathology. It has been shown that this change corresponded to a theoretical redefinition of deviance:[6] the accent was shifted from intrapersonal causes to the social and relational mechanisms producing deviant behaviour.

Once the 'public' character of social problems and the 'social' nature of their causes are established, they fall within the jurisdiction of the welfare system. The psychiatric institution, and social services in general, expand and fragment, penetrating every sphere of daily life. The individual escapes the violence of segregation only to be integrated, as a user of services, into the 'circuit of welfare dependence'.[7] The welfare system's area of administrative responsibility spreads throughout the fabric of personal life. Deviance is dealt with through administrative channels that also help reduce 'social problems' to a myriad of 'practices' handled by a web of specialized bodies.[8]

In the midst of these changes there developed a current of psychiatric thought which initiated a critique of the psychiatric institution and sought, in both theory and practice, to give shape to an alternative psychiatry. In Italy this process of 'depsychiatrization' has been pushed further than in other countries, challenging the scientific and institutional basis of mental illness.

In an atmosphere of closed, rigid and archaic thinking about the role of the asylum, anti-institutional forces denounced the inhuman character of the psychiatric institution, the poverty of the hospital system, the connection between illness and societal organization, and the complicity of medicine and economic interests. The heightening of awareness, discussion and mobilization around these questions has had a fundamental modernizing effect. It has resulted in legislation in the field of psychiatry which, for all its limitations, is one of the most advanced in the world.

De-institutionalization initiated a process of restoring former inmates' civil rights and returning them to social life through legislative reform and widespread changes in the treatment structure. The subsequent abandonment of the asylums not only meant potential independence for inmates, but the search for new professional skills for those who had worked in the asylums. The treatment of personal suffering thus became integral to, and contemporaneous with, the process of restoring the individual's autonomy in society. The intention was to distance illness from the psychiatric system's codified definition of it, to make it possible to consider the 'sick person' in his or her entirety.[9] The changes tested in the struggle against the institutions anticipated and promoted legislative reform.

With this and the subsequent reform of the health service, the psychiatric institution was returned in full to the welfare system, where it has come to share all the latter's contradictions. The broad tendency in complex societies is to absorb individuals' difficulties of adaptation into a nexus of social relations, and to entrust their remedy to an articulated network of agencies that specialize in dealing with 'pathology'. The result is a process of medicalization and codified treatment that neglects both the social dimension of behaviour and the individual's suffering. Left untreated are the really crucial problems entailed in the transformation of contemporary welfare/health services: the relation between madness and individual autonomy and responsibility; the right to dispose of one's own body against a medical practice that reifies it; and the meaning of the instruments of treatment in a society that tends to 'cure' any diversity.[10]

In the wake of the struggle against segregation more profound needs and demands have surfaced. While modernization continues, despite numerous obstacles, alternative psychiatry tends to redirect its critique on to the structures and functions of health and welfare systems in complex societies. It attempts to give form to the new scientific and therapeutic contents of the process of deinstitutionalization. The problem today is to promote discussion about this matter so that the social conditions of pathology are not separated from the individual's difficulties in generating an identity.

The conscious production of one's own identity – self-identification – is a necessary condition for enabling the individual to establish social bonds, and to locate him- or herself as one of the poles in a relationship of solidarity or conflict. There are profound personal obstacles to self-identification which prevent the subject from making contact with reality. The social causes of mental suffering (marginality, lack of socialization, stigmatization, etc.) in turn act as obstacles to self-identification. The consequent breakdown of interaction isolates the individual in a fantasy world of the individual's own making, since he or she receives no recognition from others. This absence of reciprocal identification (I recognize myself and I am recognized/ I recognize myself and I recognize the other) is therefore always a consequence.

The madness which we speak of ordinarily is thus a multiple phenomenon, the resultant of individual and social impediments. On one side there are individual obstacles to assuming one's own identity: numerous hypotheses can be adduced to explain the origin of these obstacles and much current research in psychology, biology, neurophysiology and embriology is devoted to this theme. On the other side pathology is imposed by social relations, through the processes of marginalization, through societal labelling of every difference. One can think of two extreme situations in which the individual is completely unable to assume an identity and society's absolute imposition of a stigma upon socially unacceptable conduct. True cases of 'mental illness', of psychic suffering, are always located some-where between these two extremes.

Viewed from this angle, all 'therapeutic functions' are located within an irreducible dialectic between emancipation and control. Every 'therapy' responds to individual needs within a particular context of social relations. It aims to relieve individual suffering by applying, more or less loosely, a socially generated code of normality. Ambivalence in the status of therapy is therefore unavoidable. To opt for the emancipation of 'the patient' (the user/sick person/deviant) does not mean one escapes entirely from the logic of social control. The chances of maintaining the ambivalence without neutralizing it depends on the theory and practice of the chosen 'therapy'. The more violent and heteronomous the treatment, the greater will be the exercise of control and repression, and the more explicit the 'normalization' of the subject in terms of a social code (even when there is ideological talk of 'liberation').

Any 'therapeutic' intervention that is not founded upon respect for 'the patient' and upon his or her responsibility, becomes an orthopaedics of social relations, an adaptation of the individual to the norm. Respect for the individual, combined with the responsibility of the subject for his or her own progress, may facilitate a process of autonomization. Psychiatry is today faced with practical choices that directly touch on these issues. One possible road leads towards increased use of neuroleptic drugs, the direct or indirect manipulation of the cerebral cortex, and the more or less explicit conditioning of behaviour; another route leads to the search for new therapeutic instruments capable of restoring the subject's responsibility for his or her emergence from suffering and the reconquest of his or her identity. These choices are crucial, for the problems posed by madness are paradigmatic for numerous other sectors of the welfare system which serve needs and employ instruments of 'normalization'.

The ambivalence at the heart of 'therapy' brings us back to the definition of *rationality* (and therefore of normality and pathology) in post-industrial society.[11] Sickness and treatment, emancipation and repression, reason and madness are in reality reciprocal definitions of the same terrain: human beings' capacity to give meaning to their action. 'Reason' (or normality) means, at one and the same time, normative control imposed by the dominant social relations and the autonomous capacity to produce and recognize the meaning of human action. 'Madness' indicates a refusal/loss of 'meaning', but it also reveals a possible distance from the dominant 'reason'. Similarly, 'normality' is the responsible assumption of capacity for action, but it is also dependence on the rules of social integration. Perhaps for this reason, to speak of madness is always to speak of ourselves and our ambivalence.

The limits of therapeutic intervention

The welfare services, in particular those dealing explicitly with health care, and therefore utilizing some definition of pathology and normality, remain locked in the emancipation/control dialectic to which I have referred. Dealing with needs, whether individual or collective, within the constraints exercised by system integration, necessarily implies applying some criterion of normality and a social definition of pathology. Opting for the emancipation of the 'user' can never be divorced entirely from control. Denying the ambivalence, squeezing it into one of the two poles (which in the end always turns out to be control, regardless of ideological intentions) means masking its structural character. The capacity to hold open and to render visible the dialectic of emancipation and control depends on the quality and content of the 'services' offered, and on the room these allow for autonomous demands. Choices are never definitive; they always involve decisions that favour demands for the reappropriation of identity or the orthopaedics of social relations.

I have discussed above the historical transition from segregation to the welfare system. Pathology was redefined in social and interpersonal terms. We are no longer involved with curing the individual. Control over the individual is now achieved by acting on the system of relations to which he or she belongs. The psychiatric institution, once a geographically separate institution, breaks up and spreads out into a diffuse network of social and geographical bodies, articulated in various specializations.

Through this process, which penetrates everyday life, the likelihood of pathology being given a social attribution increases.

But so also does the potential demand for emancipation. As medicalization intervenes in the daily life of 'normal' people, the individual and collective demand for direct control grows. The institution (social services, psychiatric clinic, hospital) creates its users, but at the same time arouses latent needs and demands activated by contact with these services: greater self-awareness, responsibility for one's body, one's health, one's emotional needs, one's birth and death. The identity resources made available by the services do not work solely for integration; they also stimulate the identification and appropriation of every aspect of personal existence.

The instruments and techniques employed, the methods of personnel training, the patterns of organization and decision-making, and the therapeutic content, are all indicators of the extent to which the processes of transformation of the welfare services may be held open or, alternatively, made to coincide with the requirements of administrative rationalization. In such circumstances, the welfare system must inevitably become a field of ambivalence and conflict. Demands for 'treatment' or demands for the reappropriation of identity; the administrative definition of needs and responses or institutional openness to new collective identities and individual growth: this is the complex terrain which defines the possibilities and limits of collective action within the welfare system.

Outside the welfare system the trend towards therapeutic intervention appears to extend into many other areas of ordinary life. Our daily existence is becoming a focus of attention and a zone of intervention for a growing number of specialists who identify problems and propose solutions.

Welfare policies are the first to feed this process. The experts signal a change in the theoretical and epistemological status of 'social problems', especially health problems, caused by the development of *prevention* policies.[12] Prevention policy operates by initially classifying the population into groups on the basis of specific social, geographical and epidemiological indicators. Membership of a certain population group and entry into one of the channels designed to deal with the problem (defined as either illness or risk of illness) then becomes the key criterion for identifying each individual and marking his or her subsequent passage through the system.

This scenario promotes the transformation of social relations into 'problems' or pathologies. It also promotes the diffusion of 'therapeutic' intervention in various fields, from sexual relations to the family, parental education and schooling. In each of these areas of daily life the alarm signals multiply along with the interventions aimed at solving problems heightened by the alarm signals themselves.

The field of sexual relations and the couple is a significant example of this process. 'The relationship' is seen as a problem; difficulties in attaining behavioural standards proposed as models are pinpointed; and emphasis is given to the need to continually compare one's actual experience against the images established by the various social agencies: all this serves to increase the individuals' area of uncertainty and to expose some form of pathology. Individuals thus discover problems of which they were previously unaware. Even before entering the treatment circuit, they begin to apply diagnostic criteria originating in the social processes I have described – a genuine *self-labelling* mechanism is set in motion. Hence intervention is called for by specialists, experts and counsellors, who try to identify and if possible 'solve' the problems in question.

Other examples of therapeutic intervention are clearly evident. In the family and at school the tendency to transform the educational relationship into a therapeutic one is well advanced. Difficulties in learning or communication are regarded as a psychological or social handicap, and this triggers a treatment process that is usually just the beginning of a whole series of interventions. In a different area, therapeutic intervention is also evident in the massive expansion of the market for self-administered drugs. In response to the bombardment of health warnings, individuals' perception of health and illness alters; they have recourse to patented medicines as one way of checking the continually widening area of uncertainty about themselves and their bodies.

To summarize: the therapeutic interventions described here contain several processes:

1 The growth of preventive medicine through the classification of illnesses and social groups increases the pressure to label individuals. Moreover, the emphasis on the diagnostic function

extends the length of the journey the 'case' must take through the system: the problem is passed from one specialist to another and frequently results in an unnecessarily lengthy process of diagnosis in the search for greater and greater precision, without the patient receiving effective treatment;

2 The pressure of the media and other information broadcasting agencies broadens the perception of pathology and induces people to measure their behaviour and relationships against standards of normality and well-being;

3 The agencies and professionals designed to 'solve' the problems so identified increase this pressure by setting in motion a process of diagnosis–treatment–new diagnosis that perpetuates the individual's dependence on expert intervention;

4 The above processes tend to broaden the practice of *self-labelling*, through which the individual internalizes the external definition of his or her condition, thereby reinforcing the circle of dependence;

5 In the continual diffusion and penetration of therapy into daily life there exists a certain ambivalence. A demand for reappropriating and controlling one's living space is making confused headway. Increased information plays a role in broadcasting individuals' knowledge about themselves and their capacity for action. In the most direct experiences of everyday life (affective relations, illness, the body) what once appeared as given facts now become an area open to modification and individual intervention. Individuals learn to recognize a field of action that concerns them directly and about which they can make their own choices. This is not enough to counter the strong and widespread pressures towards dependence. But it ought to sharpen our awareness of signs of potential resistance and molecular change, which the system triggers in ordinary daily life, but which it cannot entirely control. This nearly invisible level of change must be considered carefully if the contemporary sources of collective action are to be grasped.

Healing practices

Every complex society has in recent years witnessed the appearance and diffusion of therapeutic techniques that differ from those recognized by orthodox medicine.

Traditionally, there has always existed a distance, an area of diversity, between institutionalized medicine and healing techniques and practices of a non-institutional form. Today, as unorthodox forms of therapy are being widely re-evaluated, popular medicine is enjoying something of a rediscovery. Traditional medicine and a range of healing techniques related to magic or religion have always, in fact, played a role parallel and in part complementary to institutionalized practice. Any discussion of the present-day relationship between orthodox and alternative healing practices must therefore recognize their coexistence and complementarity as a feature of various systems throughout history, and not as something unique to our times.

A corollary of this point is that the extent to which a society tends to institutionalize its healing practices always falls short of actual demand. From this standpoint of the social and psychological processes underlying therapeutic practice, this is a crucial point. It indicates that the needs related to the demand for medicine are never clearly apparent, never expressed fully. Otherwise one would be led to believe that whatever a society institutionalizes – its orthodox medicine – necessarily represents an adequate response to the illness which exists. But the mere fact that non-institutionalized healing practices continue to exist, and that they often address a sizeable portion of the demand, indicates that this cannot be the case. Some of the demand for medicine contains other, latent meanings to which orthodox medicine fails to respond, whereas parallel practices offer, if not effective results, then certainly the possibility of symbolically interpreting these demands.

If the existence of parallel healing practices is nothing new, there is nevertheless something different about their role in the current situation. Research shows that the spread of alternative medicine is related to other cultural innovations, movements and changes in customs and culture that began to appear in complex societies from the 1960s onwards (Wolpe, 1985a). The popularity of unorthodox medicine is a mass phenomenon linked with other processes of collective transformation.

This link is reinforced by the retrieval of the discarded cultural baggage of society (which had been abandoned in society's cultural 'attic', so to speak). For example, social movements, during their formative stage, generally adopt languages, ideologies, expressions and patterns of organization which are inherited from the past, but which are ill-suited to their actual content. They sometimes find it necessary to rummage through society's cultural chest to find the languages, practices and symbols needed to give voice to needs which they are as yet poorly equipped to name.

During the nineteenth century, the worker's movement continued for years to use the language of the French Revolution – a bourgeois revolution occurring almost a century before and under completely different historical circumstances. Only in the last quarter of the nineteenth century did Marxism come to dominate the language and organization of the socialist movement. The same process can be seen in the series of mobilizations that swept through complex societies in the 1960s and 1970s. The youth and student movements and, for a certain period, the women's movement all began by taking on board the entire cultural baggage of the socialist tradition; this language, as well as the forms of organization and slogans of the movement in reality had little to do with actual content of the emergent conflicts. This process is a constant feature of cultural innovation: social actors gather together a ragbag of pre-existing cultural elements to express new contents for which an adequate grammar has yet to be developed. Exactly the same process is evident in our daily lives, whenever we find ourselves confronted with a new and unexpected situation for which we are unprepared. Faced with an unknown quantity for which we have no name, our immediate strategy is to apply familiar language from the past, until such time as the new forms of reality crystallize and we are obliged to create or to discover more appropriate cultural codes.

The reviving interest in traditional medicine must be seen
___ this framework. Before examining its therapeutic merits
___ recognize this as a process through which new
___ essed: it is a recycling of elements from among
___ ultural material in order to give form, in a rough

and intuitive way, to meanings strived for in the new situation. How else can we explain the recent diffusion on a mass scale of practices that have existed, some for centuries, others for millennia, and which all along have been readily available in society? Certainly, it is legitimate to ask if indeed they are valid therapeutic alternatives. But if we concentrate solely on their content and effectiveness, we will lose sight of their sociologically most important aspect: that they are triggered at a particular historical moment and that they have similar characteristics to other, parallel forms of cultural innovation.

The present revival of non-institutional medicines responds to several types of innovation in complex societies. Processes of individuation are among the most important of these innovations. In complex society, individual autonomy increases because people have the resources to invest in their own self-realization and development. This potential for individuation makes individuals more attentive and sensitive to their conditions of existence and encourages them to assume a more direct responsibility for their own health. Thus the creation of a 'demand for health' is related to new individual needs.

A second type of innovation is linked with the changing meanings of health and sickness. Sickness is ceasing to be an inevitable fate, an event that belongs to the natural order like the weather. Disease is no longer the scourge of the masses. The evolution of western society is marked by a steadily growing control over epidemic disease, thanks largely to progress in medical science and the discovery of antibiotics. Epidemic outbreaks were the characteristic manifestation of disease in traditional society; they were inevitable and uncontrollable events, before which society could only surrender or seek protection through rituals of exorcism, magic or religion. In contemporary society there is a general improvement in the hygiene/sanitary conditions of the population. At the same time, however, sickness also assumes a 'social' dimension; new forms of pathology related directly to well-being and the conditions of urban life begin to appear.

Third, in the face of these new forms of 'epidemic' – which necessarily imply the radical undermining of the immune system, the organism's basic defence mechanisms – the limits of orthodox medicine are becoming increasingly evident. The development of modern medicine is founded on a model of linear causality: the symptom indicates a cause; the elimination or removal of the cause produces recovery. The internal specialization of orthodox medicine has led it to view the human body as a collection of interacting organs and apparatuses, which are considered individually or in their functional inter-relations. Dysfunctions are supposed to consist in the pathological phenomenon to be treated either in their symptoms or by tracing them back to connected organs and apparatuses. Symptoms are seen as an impediment to be eradicated or removed to allow the body to return to its proper working order.

Given the more obvious limitations of this approach, a new systemic model is today taking root gradually in the scientific world itself.[13] This new model offers a profoundly different perception of the process underlying sickness and recovery. Symptoms are not a target of elimination but the sign of a chain of related causes, the point of departure in a circular process whose endangered equilibrium must be restored. This new vision of the body appears to renew, among the scientifically disenchanted, the traditional wisdom that has always seen disease as a loss of harmony, the blockage of a cosmic process. Today this traditional wisdom reappears as a systemic view. It reminds us that dysfunctions are never of the organ alone, but of the individual as a whole, and that symptoms are often the only signal a person can produce to express his or her unease or suffering.

The practices of non-institutional medicine are located within this social and cultural framework and contribute to its evolution. They appear to be capable of supplying, at least temporarily, adequate cultural responses to new needs. In particular, through their system of humanist and spiritualist values they serve to stimulate and enhance the patient's individual responsibility for his or her sickness, thus meeting the 'demand for health' to which I referred above. Moreover, the energetic conceptual framework, which is common to much traditional medicine and tends to emphasize the continuity of humanity, community and cosmos, draws attention to the 'environmental' dimensions (ecological and social) of sickness and health. In this sense, paradoxically, traditional medicine appears more modern than its hyper-specialized orthodox

138

counterpart, as well as better equipped culturally to tackle the social and environmental causes of the new pathologies. Finally, the holistic model, and the concept of global interdependence that typify all traditional healing practices, appear to meet the need for a new systemic model which is emerging today in the contemporary sciences. This emerging scientific paradigm emphasizes components such as interdependence, the circularity of causal processes, holism and ecological concerns.

Non-institutional healing practices thus seem culturally adapted to provide a symbolic response to today's needs. They are not only a perceived alternative to orthodox medicine; they also frequently gather momentum precisely from the latter's failures and shortcomings. This trend is surely temporary and the prelude to a process of refining the contents and practices of traditional medicine within the framework of a general redefinition of the model of medical theory and practice. In the meantime, the question is how the institutional system is likely to react.

Here we see something similar to what happens in other areas when a process of innovation is set in motion. The established institutions adopt one of three responses: rejection, in this case a cultural rejection expressed, for instance, through sworn silence and the monopolization of information; co-optation, the gradual absorption and integration of new elites into the existing institutions; and reform, progressive change or adaptation of the institution as a whole.

All three processes are already under way in the field of medicine. The first is evident in the limited diffusion of information concerning not so much the bases of traditional medicines, but the possibility of interpreting differently the available scientific data, or of explaining the failures of medical structures with vast resources. The second process is taking place in the sense that certain elites of 'alternative' medicine are becoming institutions, which have their own share of the market, participate in professional and scientific organizations and enter into dialogue with the orthodox elites. The third process seems the slowest to get off the ground, especially in Italy. It is more evident in other countries where, for example, homeopathy or acupuncture wards are an integral part of ordinary hospitals and where traditional doctors are invited to operate within the orthodox institutions. In Italy institutional reform is becoming increasingly difficult; the Italian system's greatest sticking point appears to be in translating cultural innovation into institutional change. The more likely outcome is therefore the creation of institutional counter-elites, not reform.

But whatever the difficulties, the processes under way are preparing for the birth of a new model of the definition of health and sickness, and of the role and instruments of medicine. This change is accelerated by the non-institutional practices themselves, encouraging the emergence of a differentiated medical model that recognizes a plurality of levels and techniques.

Diagnostic skills, for example, represent one of the most solid contributions of modern medicine. They comprise highly sophisticated tools that permit accurate and in some cases extremely precise diagnoses. The problem is that very often the process stops there, at the diagnostic stage, leaving the patient tragically helpless to cope with his or her illness, or otherwise setting him or her off on an endless chain of symptomatic examinations, with the harrowing and often avoidable final option of undergoing surgery. Here there is clearly room for a new relationship between the instrument of diagnosis and therapeutic practice that respects individuals and their responsibility for their own health.

Another of modern medicine's strong points is evident in emergencies, in its power to cure pathology, either epidemic or traumatic, in its limit state. The targeted use of antibiotics, the progress of surgical techniques and re-animation systems are good examples of this capacity for effective action. But here again what is required is a marriage of this capacity with ordinary practices able to assure recovery, or at least relief, from the numerous chronic illnesses which afflict the daily lives of men and women in the technological age. The ancient medical maxim *primum non nocere* has a particularly modern ring in a world where iatrogenic disease, that caused by medical treatment or the misuse of drugs, is becoming alarmingly more common.

A form of medicine capable of reconciling various polarities – between precise diagnosis and patient's responsibility, between effectiveness in emergency and everyday care – requires a new, quite different model. We must be willing to recognize various levels of intervention, to use different keys to open different doors. For this purpose, the emerging model of sickness and health is crucial. It is formed through controversies about the crucial points that mark the passage from the old to the new. In this way it contributes to a plurality of therapeutic languages and instruments. Non-institutional practices thus contribute to changes in motion not only or mainly by what they offer, but even more by the alternatives they help us to imagine.

Medicine for the soul

The expanding demand for psychotherapy is another symptom of the growth in complex societies of the need for identity and self-realization. Greater resources in terms of education, knowledge, and time are now available to individuals to enable them to conceive of themselves and their situations as individuals. They begin to think of their lives as a choice between various possibilities, and as a process of growth, discovery and realization of their potential.

There is a second reason for the new demand for psychotherapy: the growth of individual dissatisfaction and pathology related in particular to the conditions of urban life and the mounting complexity of everyday experience. The vast differentiation of modern life, the multiplication of roles and social masks each person is called upon to assume, and the burdens of making choices quickly create enormous psychological tensions in addition to traditional pathogenic factors.

Finally, the extension and penetration of welfare services, which tend increasingly to medicalize social and personal problems, pressure individuals into consciously assuming responsibility for their own health, while at the same time generating suffering and anxiety, whose causes can be traced back to the same circuits of institutional 'care'. On the one hand the services offered by the health and social welfare systems tend to stimulate the need for awareness, emotional balance and self-realization in personal and sexual life, and in relations between parents and children. On the other hand, welfare policies are also a source of new psychic distress in at least three ways. First, sickness prevention policy works to classify people into greater or lesser 'risk' categories, institutionally defined; thus individuals find themselves 'sick' irrespective of their own subjective perception of their condition. This labelling by preventive policy and mass screening cannot but disturb the psychic and emotional equilibrium of the individuals involved. Second, the simple utilization of health and social services by individuals frequently has the perverse effect of feeding their need for psychological support (due, for example, to the effects of hospitalization or of a traumatic gynaecological operation). Last, health and social workers are themselves subject to a high degree of 'wear and tear; in turn, they require psychotherapeutic support. The phenomeon of 'burn-out' among welfare workers, which is caused by the extreme emotional burdens of their job, is assuming alarming proportions in all developed societies (Cherniss, 1980).

In the face of this widespread demand for psychological treatment and assistance we are witnessing a growth and differentiation of available therapies. Their growth is due to the increasing variety of demands as well as to the expansion of research, theoretical discussion and clinical experience.

A plurality of psychotherapeutic approaches – including not only psychoanalysis but also new family therapies, body therapy – is now a permanent feature of the social and cultural framework of complex society. Such pluralism leads inevitably to comparisons of the arguments and validity of the various orientations. Their theoretical rivalry at times masks their real competition in the market-place, where the need to differentiate the product tends to accentuate distinctions among the competitors. The bulk of research and clinical data nevertheless indicates a strong similarity of the factors influencing the success or failure of therapies, irrespective of their specific techniques.[14] This convergence is reinforced by critical revisionism among the better established schools. This not only results in new frames of reference for a continually evolving clinical practice, but also stimulates a need for comparison of and communication among the different psychotherapeutic approaches.

Of course, what therapists actually do in their immediate relationship with the person wanting help can sometimes be very different from what their theory advocates. The psychotherapeutic situation is one of listening and accommodation. It provides space and time in which suffering is recognized and not denied.

142

It encourages the expression of psychic anxiety or unrest, although for the therapist it is difficult to listen without falling prey to the theory and to the desire to change the patient. Psychotherapy involves a relationship created between two consenting individuals: a person who chooses to undergo the therapy, and a therapist who is guided by his or her objectives, expectations and fears. Without this contractual freedom and presence there is no therapeutic situation.

In psychotherapy one can 'recover' in many different and even mysterious ways. It is not always clear to the sufferer, or indeed to the therapist him- or herself, why one feels better or why suffering ceases. However, what appears to happen in every case is that for the person undergoing therapy the process is a path towards an altered awareness, a recognition of his or her existence and an assumption of responsibility for his or her place in the physical, affective, mental and spiritual dimensions of reality. This is also how traditional cultures define sickness and health. In these cultures, the individual is seen to occupy a definite position in relation to a physio-biological, social and cosmic-spiritual order. 'Sickness' signals an interruption of this relationship, while 'healing' is seen to be possible only by re-establishing equilibrium and by repairing the circuit that binds the individual to the cosmos. But for this to be achieved there must be a change in the person's perception and definition of his or her situation which is the root of suffering. It is this restructuring that the modern therapeutic situation tries to bring about.

A mutually agreed consensus underpins the therapy relationship. There is thus a clear difference between psychotherapy defined in contractual terms and psychiatric care defined in terms of external medical intervention. The social and organizational distinctions between private and institutional practice are well known; there are also evident difficulties in applying therapy in institutional settings when the nature and treatment of the suffering are defined by others (the family, the institution or social context). Institutional constraints are certainly an obstacle to a consensual relationship, but as certain innovative forms of psychiatry have shown, the institution can also offer some advantages. Within the institution everything can be therapeutic if the actual context is suitably structured, and if the sick person has the chance to be heard, welcomed, and to be autonomous.[15]

This requirement goes further than the institutional situation itself. In general we can say that the 'healing' process extends and develops beyond the period of actual therapy: the relationship serves to trigger processes that unfold elsewhere. Therapeutic events merge with ordinary life but only become recognizable as such thanks to the therapeutic relationship. Here again, there is rediscovery of elements of traditional culture, such as the idea that healing is in every case a choral event, a ritual that involves the community as a whole. 'Illness' is cured through rituals that re-establish the link between the individual, the group and the cosmos, that is, between the individual and life itself.

Studies of the effectiveness of psychotherapy are rarely conclusive in absolute terms. However, they point very explicitly to *the relationship* as a vital key to the healing process. Research has shown that the factors influencing the success of psychotherapy are related intimately to the quality of this relationship. On the therapists's side the significant factors appear to be their authenticity (we might say their closeness to themselves, their consciousness of their needs and objectives); their capacity to accept the other (i.e. without an omnipotent desire to take the other's place); their ability to listen (which is nothing more than allowing the voice of the 'illness' space and time in which to speak). On the patients' side therapeutic success depends on their capacity to face their own weakness and to recognize change as possible and desirable; this 'strength in weakness', this ability to trust the other, while at the same time relying on oneself, seems to be the decisive factor in a successful therapeutic outcome.

Aside from terminological differences – which appear to spring more from the various theoretical contexts rather than the actual clinical practice – the psychotherapeutic process produces a change of perspective in the sufferer which enables him or her to take a different view of him- or herself and the world. This new horizon, with its ensuing cognitive and affective consequences, is not generated in a vacuum but inside a very special relationship. It is therapeutic precisely because it offers a specific time and space in which the two poles of the relationship may coexist in their difference and at the same time communicate. Otherness and communication, openness and closure, closeness and distance, if chosen freely and not imposed from without, make possible a wholly new outlook.

The magic circle

In the traditional world illness has a foreign presence; it is the irruption of an obscure force into the cosmic order. It is related to death, but can be approached and tamed, like a wild animal, through the mediation of the sacred and of rites. Ritual brings the illness back within the sacral order, using its strengths to produce a new equilibrium in the individual, the community and the cosmos.

The contemporary world lives the paradox of an apparent victory over illness: just as we feel we can control the obscure natural forces underlying illness, new scourges appear. The inevitability of illness produced by contemporary civilization creates a double sense of alienation: that of the individual towards his or her suffering and that due to the control over illness being wholly entrusted to external and impersonal structures. In the experience of the individual, illness once again becomes a deeply alien and uncontrollable fact, though without ritual to create that link with the sacred order, as in traditional society.

What contact can be re-established between humans and their illness in a society that challenges death with the power of its technology? The sacred and the ritual are no longer able to provide this bridge. The link can be built only as a cultural process, as humans' capacity to measure themselves against the finite and against possible death. There are no longer gods to protect humans from suffering, but suffering and the release from suffering can be human experiences to which everyone can give sense (Natoli, 1986).

A therapy that establishes a specific relationship between a person who 'suffers' and one who 'cures' has a role to play in this context. The therapeutic relationship has several paradoxical dimensions. First, the relationship is in itself founded on a paradox: it is only possible to cure through the self-assumed responsibility of the 'patient', and if at the same time the 'healer' assumes responsibility for the ill person. The patient on the other hand can be cured only if he or she trusts the other, even though he or she is the only one who can decide whether or not to trust.

The second paradox concerns therapeutic space. Therapy is grounded in the 'real life' space of everyday life and at the same time another, different space: a magic place, where unique and unrepeatable contact is established between the individual and his or her limit, and where the surpassing or transformation of this limit becomes possible.

Last, the sense of time within therapy is also marked by paradox: it is both a biographical time and a 'timeless time', in which events do not succeed one another in the normal chronological way, but in the unpredictable unfolding of the sick person's biological and psychological experience.

How can the two sides of these paradoxes be reconciled in a disenchanted world in which the sacred no longer reconciles human beings with that uneasy experience that places them in contact with the finite and the inevitability of death? How can one count on the sufferer to assume responsibility and at the same time take responsibility for his or her recovery? How can we ensure the coexistence of real and magic space? How can we pass from the time of the clock and calendar to the time of inner experience? There are no simple answers to these questions. And yet through them we measure our definitions of health, sickness and therapy in contemporary society.

Despite the enormously powerful means deployed, illness has not disappeared from the scene. 'Technological man' can still picture 'himself' as a sacrificial victim, selected by fate to suffer the consequences of a chance event, while leaving the job of defining it to others. Or else 'he' can draw nearer to it, just as traditional cultures approached the experience of the sacred, but this time with a disenchanted consciousness. In making contact with their limit, contemporary human beings can no longer avoid the risks associated with a decision that may jeopardize their capacity to give sense to their action, to suffer or to die. They can no longer avoid existing as individuals.

Therapeutic practice, in whatever form, is faced with the same alternative. It can act as an instrument of external control or regulation, blinded by a mistaken belief in its own omnipotence. Or it can lead the sufferer towards the hazardous confrontation with his or her limit. For the two individuals involved, 'the sufferer' and 'the healer', the experience of illness can turn into a furious struggle against an invisible enemy. Or else it can represent the way through the magic circle to the recognition of the human limit and the unavoidable striving for freedom.

Notes and References

1 On the significance of this new culture compare Foucault (1975b, 1976); Chombart De Lauwe (1975); Maisonneuve (1976); Bourdieu (1979, 1982); and Gorz (1977).

2 For an analysis of the advertising of the body, especially women's, see Goffman (1979).

3 The changing meaning of sexuality is analysed by Foucault (1976). On the rationalization of sexuality in contemporary society see Wolton (1974, 1976); Bejin and Pollak (1977); and Bruckner and Finkielkraut (1977).

4 On communal, neo-religious and pseudo-therapeutic sects see Marx and Seldin (1973a, 1973b); Marx and Holzner (1975); Baffoy (1978); Seguy (1978) and Hall (1978).

5 The history of psychiatry is traced in Foucault (1961, 1975a); Castel (1976), Dörner (1975); and Jervis (1975).

6 See De Leonardis (1980). Labelling theory is a particularly important example of this change; among the classic works on this theory are Lemert (1974) and Kitsuse (1975).

7 For an analysis of this process see especially De Leonardis and Mauri (1980).

8 Compare Castel *et al.* (1979) and De Leonardis and Mauri (1980).

9 On innovative psychiatry in Italy see Manacorda and Montella (1977); Micheli (1982); De Leonardis (1982) and Mauri (1983).

10 On the power of medicine and the growing medicalization of social problems, compare Attali (1979); Conrad (1979) and Krause (1977).

11 In contrast to the so-called primitive societies, the relationship between normality and pathology in complex societies exercises great control over their structures (as Devereux, 1976 indicates).

12 On prevention policies see in particular Castel *et al.* (1979); Castel (1981). Their position within the overall field of social policies is discussed by Donzelot (1981).

147

13 On the demise of the dominant model of western medicine, see Attali (1979); Krause (1977); and Wolpe (1985b). The emergence of a new systemic model is analysed in Capra (1982) and Ferguson (1980).

14 See, for example, Smith and Glass (1977) and Frank (1979).

15 For an analysis and discussion of the change produced by innovations in psychiatry, see Mauri (1983).

7

Reproduction, eros, communication

Production of reproduction?

The biological basis of human behaviour is becoming a target of social intervention and manipulation. The reproductive sphere is one of these target areas. Reproduction ceases to be a destiny and becomes a field of action, decision, and choice. But whose choice? The individuals who are responsible for their own existence, and who thus are capable of desiring or not desiring? Or scientific, medical and social bodies which establish codes of behaviour and the canons of normality and pathology?

The end of reproduction as a fate gives rise to a new and radical ambivalence. While the increase of information, greater control over pathologies, and the modification of morality and sexual customs create new opportunities for individual choice and responsibility in the reproductive sphere, there is also an increasing possibility of externally regulating behaviour, not primarily by means of the visible action of repressive institutions and authoritarian rules, but by means of the symbolic codes that guide behaviour and manipulate the bio-psychic bases of human action.

In complex societies the reproduction of the human species has ceased to be a natural fact. Situated between biology and culture, the reproductive sphere has always been the point of encounter between the biology of the species and our capacity to produce social significations and relationships. Even people's adaptation to their environment, a key determinant for our reproductive fortunes, has always been a compromise between nature and culture.

But on the threshold of the third millennium reproduction seems already to have been detached from its natural roots and to belong entirely to the area of social production. If reproduction primarily ensures the biological continuity of the species, the final alteration of its 'natural' status is symbolized by two phenomena which have radically modified the 'naturalness' of human evolution: the nuclear threat and the manipulation of the genetic code. Both phenomena represent an irreversible break in the evolutionary continuum of the species: they imply that survival no longer depends only on its reproductive capacity but on the choices – to destroy, to conserve or to transform – that it makes for itself and for other living species. And since these phenomena concern the entire planet, there remains nothing 'natural' in the evolutionary destiny of the human species and the planet that does not depend in some way on social intervention.

In the reproductive area the most evident sign of this change is the process of separating sexuality from reproduction. In the history of the species the difference between these two aspects has played an important cultural role. What men and women have written, imagined and practiced in matters of love testifies to this possibility of symbolically elaborating the separation of eros from reproductive necessity.

However, this possibility was never more than exceptional or the privilege of small social groups. Only during the past decades has the separation of sexuality and reproduction become a mass phenomenon and a definitive cultural acquisition. Two processes have decisively contributed to this. Rapid progress in the fields of scientific discovery, pharmacological experimentation and medical techniques have rendered possible interventions in the human reproductive mechanism. And cultural transformations have considerably modified both the household and reproductive roles of women as well as the sexuality of young people.

The development of a youth culture independent of the institutions of the adult world has modified the sexual behaviour of young people. Sexual experience, anticipated in time and signifying much more than reproduction, represents a stage of youthful initiation and means of access to peer group culture. Within these sexual experiences, dimensions of communication

150

and socialization prevail, while the goal of reproduction is virtually abandoned.

In a different way the new women's culture has also contributed to profound changes in the representation of sexuality. Female sexuality which was traditionally denied or confined to the functions of maternity, has also acquired an independence of its own because of the development of a new feminine awareness (Shorter, 1975). When women begin to refuse subordination and the rigid family roles that determine their fate as wives and mothers, there arises the possibility, especially for the younger generations, of perceiving sexuality as a choice: as a source of pleasure and an instrument of communication, an eros without reproductive purpose.

Cognitive and technical resources, changes in cultural models and forms of relationship thus contribute irreversibly to the separation of sexuality and reproduction. Symbolically and practically this separation is evident in contraception and artificial fertilization: in the possibility of *sexuality without reproduction* and of *reproduction without sexuality*. When contraception becomes a mass cultural practice, it finally uncouples the sexual act from its reproductive purpose: human sexuality becomes a field of experience open to every possibility. It becomes an area of symbolic investment and production of meaning controlled by the participants themselves. The techniques of artificial fertilization developed in recent decades represent the other half of this equation: the possibility of changing the 'natural' dictates of reproduction or its impossibility means that for the first time successful reproduction no longer depends on the sexual encounter of the partners.[1]

Whether we interpret the necessary link between sexuality and nature in the evolution of the species as devices of nature or divine design, it is difficult not to be bewildered by their irreversible separation. The future of the species (reproduction) and of human relationships of love (sexuality) seem to lose the certainty assured to each by the complementary presence of the other. Who will be able to guarantee the continuity of the species? How will this continuity be possible if reproduction becomes one option among many? And once the 'natural' limit of sexuality has been broken, which of the many possibilities of reproduction will be chosen? And what will be the consequences of an eros released from the chains of reproduction, free from limitations, threats, but also from the responsibilities of its 'natural' function? How and where can we make room for the erotic 'creation' that replaces procreation?

Such questions already trouble moralists of every persuasion. More fundamentally, they delimit an ethical field which still has to be constructed. This ethical field must be capable of guiding collective life in systems which have an increasingly radical effect on the nature of the species. It must be capable of directing human action when it is no longer dominated by natural fate and is therefore exposed to a more radical destiny: the destiny of choice and responsibility.

Reproduction as a choice

In the sexual and reproductive spheres, as in other areas of human life, the range of possibilities is increasing. These spheres come to resemble an enormous laboratory in which numerous cultural models are adopted and tested. The technically and culturally available options allow the individual to decide and to act. In a field freed from the unequivocality and linearity of the 'natural' processes, sexual and reproductive choices become *individual*; they lack the regularity of a general model.

This pluralization affects above all the relationship between partners. In addition to the model of the heterosexual and monogamous couple, who are the foundation of the family institution and guarantee of the continuity of the reproductive process, new choices become possible. These parallel models, which are capable of coexisting with the heterosexual model and even of becoming institutionalized, include homosexuality, singles, and a range of mobile and temporary couples living outside a stable matrimonial relationship.

In the area of reproduction there is for the first time the possibility of reversing and even rendering interchangeable the poles of reproductive destiny: fertility and sterility. A paradoxical feature of contemporary life is the parallel progress of research, experiments and campaigns concerned with contraception and sterilization, on the one hand, and the development of increasingly sophisticated techniques of artificial insemination on the other. Contraception and sterilization, and artificial insemination, deprive fertility and sterility of their 'naturally' given character. The individual can thereby make choices, whereas previously fertility and sterility appeared to be the necessary opposites of an irreversible condition.

As choice comes to embrace the whole field of human experiences connected with sexuality and reproduction, so too does the power of intervention. These two aspects of modern life are inseparable. The individualization of sexual and reproductive choices would be incomprehensible without analysing the forms of social intervention which are transforming, with exceptional rapidity, the reproductive sphere and all the areas traditionally connected with it. This social intervention moves in three directions, relating to *sexuality, reproduction* and *birth*.

In the field of sexuality forms of intervention are mainly evident in the medicalization of sexuality and the control of fertility. Sexuality, now an important subject of study and scientific elaboration, has finally entered the medical circuit. Sexual practice is the subject of new codes of behaviour, while the media propagate systems of medical–scientific interpretation. A whole branch of medicine and psychotherapy, sexology, has been formed. At the same time contraceptive and sterilization practices extend to large numbers of the population, while abortion becomes a stable institutionalized form of reducing the birth-rate.

In the field of reproduction, techniques of artificial fertilization now encompass a wide range of interventions of two types: artificial insemination and *in vitro* fertilization. These interventions facilitate combinations of all the variables involved in the reproductive event: maternal ovule/ovule of donor; paternal sperm/sperm of donor; sterile mother/sterile father; and a maternal uterus which is able/unable to complete pregnancy.

Social intervention is also increasing in the field of birth. The medicalization of birth seems to be an irreversible fact. Even demands for its humanization, expressed above all by the women's movements, do not appear to question the guarantee of safety and control by the hospital system in cases of emergency. Hospital births therefore continue to increase while at the same time parents are better informed and prepared for birth and infant-care. Another line of social intervention relates to the foetus, with the advances of embryological and perinatal research and the possibility of very early intra-uterine interventions.

These processes, which often reinforce each other, open a new and unprecedented chapter in the history of human society: reproduction becomes subject to choice. But whose choice?

On the one hand choice enables individuals to become better informed about themselves, their bodies, their sexuality; more independent in their choice of partner and reproductive decisions; better protected against the risks (unforeseen events, pathologies, emergencies) connected with the 'natural' aspect of sexuality and reproduction and, finally, more capable of recognizing the plurality of options, including ethical options, to which the separation of eros and reproductive functions gives rise.

On the other hand, choice also becomes the prerogative of organizations and institutions which intervene in the sphere of sexuality and reproduction by means of technical decisions and 'neutral' procedures, upon which the symbolic control of this sphere nevertheless depends. The monopoly of information and the manipulation of relationships are realized by means of *counselling*, systems of *expertise* to which individuals are obliged to resort, and the monitoring of large sections of the population for particular purposes, such as prevention policies and identifying populations at risk.

Reproduction is thus becoming a choice, but it is also profoundly ambivalent, exposed to the insecurity and risk of unforeseen effects, new powers and new conflicts. In particular, the techniques of artificial insemination prefigure the end of paternity and maternity as biological events. These techniques have undermined even the fundamental certainty, the *mater certa*, of 'natural' affiliation. The possibility of using the ovule or the uterus of a donor has already compromised this principle. The road leading towards the no longer science-fiction possibility of an extra-corporeal gestation is thus opened, thereby complementing the extra-corporeal conception achieved already by techniques of artificial insemination and *in vitro* fertilization.

Such changes would deprive paternity and maternity of every 'natural' connotation and would make the birth and nurturing of children an entirely cultural choice, open to many meanings. The problems raised by this development make it possible to foresee types of social regulation extending to the motivations and interior life of individuals. Policies concerning reproduction cannot avoid defining standards relevant to the deeper dimensions of individuals' affective lives. For this reason the ambiguity of the processes of choice enlargement should not be hidden. They should be rendered socially more visible and subjected to open debate.

Technological fate

There is often a tendency to ignore the fact that 'progressive' aspects of the emancipation of sexuality and the possibility of controlling the reproductive biology of the species also produce unexpected, negative counter-effects. In a world in which natural events seem ever more subject to the control of effective techniques, 'fate' appears as that which eludes the control of society. It reappears in the form of limited technologies which fail to fulfil their promise; as new pathologies and sufferings, which touch the deeper levels of human affections and relationships; and as the unforeseen effects of emancipatory social processes. To recognize this ambivalent development is also to recognize the shadow which restricts and calls into question the capacity of the human species to manipulate both the world and itself.

Consider the following examples of this new fate. Changes in the sexual and reproductive spheres are certainly among the factors contributing to a fall in the birth-rate in all complex societies, in which the average birth-rate is now 1.5 children per woman, with small variations from country to country. In demographic terms two children per woman represents a population growth of zero, which means that the population decreases of the 'central' countries will become more pronounced, while the populations of the 'peripheral' countries will continue to increase rapidly, thereby exerting a drastic pressure on the more privileged areas. (It is forecast that at the end of this century the countries of the Third World will account for 80 per cent of the world population; within fifty years the inhabitants of the United States who are of African, Asiatic and South American origin will outnumber those of European origin).

This enormous transformation will involve major changes and conflicts among cultures and regions, which cannot but modify the relationships between states at the planetary level as well as ethnic relationships within various countries.

At a level of experience closer to the individual, the demographic fact of falling birth-rates in complex societies is accompanied by the clinical fact of an alarming increase in the number of sterile couples. The World Health Organization estimates that in the advanced countries about 30 per cent of couples are sterile. This trend seems destined to strengthen. Researchers have shown that in the great majority of cases sterility has functional causes connected with stress, pollution and industrialized food. In this respect sterility represents a sort of silence of the body, a silence imposed by the 'noise' of civilization. These evident psychogenic and environmental roots of sterility must be considered alarming: the affluent societies are beginning to damage their reproduction basis at the very moment that they celebrate their research triumphs and technical achievements in the reproductive sphere.

The culture of sexual liberation is not extraneous to this increase of sterility. The mass circulation of medical and scientific information about sexuality give rise to performance models and establish standards of behaviour which generate anxiety. In the cultural models propagated by the media and the market, the body often becomes a machine for sexual performances devoid of eros. Sexuality which is exhibited but de-eroticized favours sterility and adds to the impact of environmental factors. Individuals find themselves exposed to an excess of stimuli – especially visual stimuli – of a sexual nature, but the over-abundance and unlimited exhibition of the messages deprives sex of its erotic content and confines it to the genital level.[2] At the same time individuals compare themselves with the performance models proposed in medical–scientific pronouncements, which tend to establish the criteria for a 'satisfying sexual life'.

Individual attitudes and behaviour are deeply affected by these pressures, which also create cultural patterns. On the psychological plane, increased sexual anxiety and insecurity result, while the erotic tension which is the mainspring of the sexual relationship is reduced. This fragility of the psychic structure is exacerbated by the stress factors present in the environment: competition and conflicts in the field of employment, urban rhythms and pollution, dietetic imbalances and chemically treated foods.

Another phenomenon which complex societies seem unable to control is the re-emergence of sexually transmitted diseases, of which AIDS is the most striking and dangerous example. Before the AIDS controversy erupted in public and attracted the attention of the media and of governments, epidemiological research had already revealed an alarming increase of sexually transmitted diseases. In addition to the more traditional pathologies, there has been an increase of infections, which were once marginal but which seem to have become unusually vigorous.

The threats posed by the AIDS epidemic encouraged moralists to see the signs of divine punishment or the revenge of nature against the Promethean pride of technological civilization. Such reactions satisfied the need to dramatize in a society of spectacles. They were also grist for the mills of the media. But they are of little help in understanding how such phenomena come about and, above all, how they should be treated.

The public concern with AIDS has concentrated above all on the perception of the disease in the collective imagination, and on its impact on everyday life, particularly on sexual habits. But in addition to these more visible effects of the phenomenon there are also hidden processes which radically affect the functioning of modern systems.

Among these effects are systemic perturbations which are capable of triggering off a series of chain reactions in various sub-systems (examples include the obligatory reorganization of the health system and the effects of screening policies on schools and households).[3] There are also processes of discrimination against whole social categories, such as homo-sexuals, who see their recently acquired autonomous social spaces threatened by a stigma which disallows appeals, and drug addicts, especially those living within the margins of large metropolises, whose already dire situation risks further deterior-ation.

157

The less visible effects of the AIDS phenomenon also include processes of cultural codification and definition of standards. A key example is the definition of categories at risk. Present definitions of this kind are in fact culturally coded. They translate into policies the uncertain findings of epidemiological research, even though the specification of categories at risk may have serious consequences for both the judicial system and the resulting forms of social control. These definitions of categories at risk are based in any case on a fundamental ambiguity, which only a few people have begun to expose. The available knowledge about AIDS, though it remains inadequate, points to the fact that the danger of infection is tied essentially to *risk behaviour*, that is, to a series of mainly individual variables. Prevention and control take very different forms depending on whether the target is individual behaviour or entire social categories, to which such behaviour is attributed officially, in a process of administrative codification which is illogical and invalid, but which undoubtably enhances the power of administrative procedures.

Finally, there is the subjective experience of those who suffer the disease directly, and those who live with its visible signs and alarming risks: the victims, their friends and families, the positively diagnosed, and the social and health workers, all of whom are exposed in different ways to the dramatic confrontation with death and to the limitations of the available knowledge and means of intervention.

To be present and to listen, to be a companion to the sufferer and to respect in silence the drama of the individual's encounter with an inevitable death, requires qualities which have become rare in the disenchanted culture of the modern metropolis – qualities which are at odds with the rhythms, sounds and signs of the urban universe. And yet, as always, these qualities are vital for all those, victims and witnesses, who are faced with an uncontrollable event and who personally experience the fear and vertigo of impotence in the face of death.

Eros and reciprocity

The relationship of love between human beings, no longer guaranteed solely by the biological necessities of reproduction, is becoming a field of choice, and thus subject to insecurity and risk. It also becomes an area of communication, of freely chosen encounters among different people who are potentially responsible, that is, who are capable of 'responding' to the other and to their own selves.

Sexuality which has been detached from reproduction may in fact resemble an encounter mediated by the body and tending towards the liberation of the most intimate spiritual energies. Oriental culture, Tantric and Taoist, traditionally proposed this as a possibility, although restricted it to those elites who accepted its superior knowledge. In societies which intervene in their own reproduction this same possibility becomes a (potentially) universal cultural possibility. However, the experience of sexuality as a gift, as a voluntary search for the self and for the other, is an option which must compete with certain opposite tendencies.

As has been pointed out already, sexuality which is separated from reproduction may also become a sexuality without eros. The performance culture, depriving sex of its erotic content, reduces it to a gymnastics of orgasm. This is a prevailing characteristic and extreme of masculinist culture, which was manifested in its most extreme and paradoxical form in the early phase of gay culture, especially in the United States. Here the rapid multiplication of anonymous and casual relationships was seen as a sign of liberation. But in so doing it hastened the reduction of sex to the genital level and revealed the poverty of an exclusively male sexuality without eros.

By contrast, the experience of love as a voluntary given, mutually recognized gift can be extended to embrace the relationship with children. When biological parentage is exposed to choice and contingency and escapes the compulsions of nature, the parent–child relationship may also be founded solely on reciprocity and choice. This implies a profound change in the adult–child relationship. The child is no longer only someone to be brought up, a vessel in which to pour the values and standards of society. He or she becomes an individual endowed with personal autonomy and a partner in a love relationship – a partner from whom the adult can learn to play and wonder.

The emphasis on reciprocity and choice highlights the creative aspect of eros, which extends beyond interpersonal relationships to the relationship between human beings and the cosmos. In such relationships, eros freed from reproductive obligations can be a force which contributes to processes of creation, innovation and transformation which are unbridled by calculation.

But far from prefiguring a transparent society of expressive creativity and pure communication, this possibility accentuates the ambivalence of human action, whether individual or collective. Unforced eros implies the acceptance of insecurity and risk. It requires assuming responsibility towards the self and towards the other, in a situation in which external guarantees of the relationship itself are lacking.

The freely chosen and incalculable testifies to the irreducibility of the individual to his or her relationship. If in the relationship between individuals not everything is calculable and exhausted by the exchange, then the irreducible otherness that characterizes the experience of each individual can become the acknowledged foundation of personal autonomy and of a risk-laden commitment to the relationship.[4]

But this potential does not eliminate the hesitations and deviations of relationships based almost entirely on choice. It weakens the foundations of solidarity, making the social bond precarious. The risk of disaggregation and of self-destructive individualism cannot be ignored. But it is this very fact of self-conscious fragility that can alter the ethical orientations upon which social life is founded. Communication and solidarity can be assured only by a situational ethic, one which does not evade the risks of choice and which is capable of meta-communication about choices themselves. A situational ethic is necessarily an ethic of responsibility. When the survival of the human species is no longer guaranteed by divine will or laws of evolution, and when the foundations of relationships and communication itself depends mainly on actors themselves, the choice to exist and to exist with – of living and living together – is left solely to the responsibility of each individual.

Responsible choice of this kind could reunify all the threads that tie the individual to the species, to the living and to the cosmos itself. Each individual could then acknowledge his or her responsibility for the destiny of the human species and for future generations. But the individual could also renew his or her respect for the other living species and for the universe of which the human species is only one part. This insight, which is central to the wisdom of all traditional cultures, has been bequeathed to the 'technological man' of complex societies. This bequest amounts to a single fundamental possibility: the continuing amazement about what exists. Amazement, in a disenchanted modern culture, could perhaps be the most profound index of potential freedom, the sign of a freedom in motion.

Notes and references

1 Useful contributions to the discussion about artificial reproduction and its psychological and social aspects include Sbisa (1985); Arditti *et al.* (1984); and Snowden *et al.* (1983).

2 On the distinction between genitality and the cultural elaboration of sexuality, see Fornari (1975).

3 The systemic effects of AIDS have been described in terms of 'cultural disaster' by Stella (1987).

4 The myth of a potentially transparent communication is implicit in the otherwise impressive work of the later Habermas (1987).

III

RETHINKING DEMOCRACY

8

The democratization
of everyday life

The end of politics?

In complex systems politics has not become simply a residue of
the past. On the contrary, political relationships have never been
so important. Never before has it been so necessary to regulate
complexity by means of decisions, choices and 'policies', the
frequency and diffusion of which must be ensured if the
uncertainty of systems subject to exceptionally rapid change is to
be reduced. Complexity and change produce the need for
decisions. They also create an unprecedented plurality of
variable interests; the multiplicity and changeability of interests
results in a multiplicity and changeability of problems to be
solved. Hence the need for decisions, and for decisions which
are subject continually to verification and to the limitations and
risks of consensus in conditions of rapid change.

I define a political relationship as one which permits the
reduction of uncertainty and the mediation of opposing interests
by means of decisions. I consider political relationships in this
sense to be fundamental to the functioning of complex societies.
In societies of this type we are, in fact, witnessing a process of
multiplication and diffusion of political instances. In different
areas of social life, and within institutions and organizations of
many kinds, there is taking place a process of transformation of
authoritarian regulations into political relationships. This process
of 'transforming the authoritarian into the political' entails the
introduction of systems of exchanges and procedures of
negotiation which, by means of confrontation and the mediation
of interests, produce decisions, whereas before there were only
mechanisms for authoritatively transmitting regulations by
means of power.

This 'political level' of relationships is to be found not only in national political systems, but also within numerous productive, educational, administrative, and regional institutions, as well as in areas of society in which, often after a struggle, new instances of political decision, interest representation and negotiation are brought into being. This process of 'politicization' is linked to the complexity of contemporary systems, to their need to cope with a changeable environment and to the multiplication of requirements of balance within the system itself. The importance of the political level of relationships is evident not only within present-day western parliamentary political systems. The problem of politics confronts every complex system, whatever type of political organization may be envisaged for it. Any project of democratization in an advanced society cannot ignore this problem, even though the intellectual and practical tradition of opposition movements is scarcely adequate for its resolution. For too long it was assumed that the specificity and autonomous logic of decision-making processes and mechanisms of representation could be annulled by means of the cathartic power of mass struggles. Today, it is evident instead that these problems remain entirely unresolved.

This does not mean that the quality of the interests entering into a decision-making process is irrelevant, or that all these interests carry the same weight, or that a given system automatically ensures equal access to each interest. It does mean, however, that the decision-making and representation process is a specific and necessary condition of the functioning of complex systems.

This problem of decision-making processes, which function by means of representation, was underestimated or ignored outright by the Marxist intellectual tradition, which reduced representation to its 'bourgeois' forms and to parliamentary institutions, and in so doing annulled the problem of how to mediate and represent a plurality of interests. The problem of representation is tied to complexity and it therefore cannot be annulled, whatever model of political organization is envisaged. Representation involves an inevitable difference between representatives and those whom they represent, between the interests of each and between their concurrent or divergent logic of action. Any process of democratic transformation must

166

necessarily take into account this difference between the structures of representation and the demands or interests of the represented; a project of democratization intended to be 'progressive' or 'radical' is forced to imagine the social and political means of controlling this difference. A necessary condition of democratization is the refusal to deny this problem ideologically: only if and when it is acknowledged does it become possible to look for ways of controlling and reducing the distance separating power from social demands.

To return to the initial problem of political relationships: these considerations serve to allocate politics its proper dimension, by both recognizing its specificity and defining its limits. A definition of politics as all-embracing is replaced by a recognition of its specific function and its 'necessity'. For the radical tradition, this recognition involves the difficult journey through 'disenchantment' that always accompanies processes of desacralization and laicization of social life.

Politics guarantees the possibility of mediating interests in order to produce decisions. There are two different reasons why politics in this sense is not the whole of social life:

1 There are structures and interests which precede, delimit and condition politics. Even if they are subsequently mediated by politics, these structures and interests exist irrespective of every ideological illusion of pluralism and official pretensions of representing society as if it were a spontaneous and open plurality of demands and needs. The political game never takes place on an open field with equal chances. In order to understand the unequal distribution of political chances and political power, it is therefore necessary to consider the *limits* of the political game and, thus, the manner in which the social power underlying political institutions is formed.

2 There are dimensions of social phenomena – affective or symbolic relationships, for instance – which cannot be considered as political because they function according to a different logic, which it is therefore necessary to respect and not to violate.

These considerations suggest that we are not faced with the end of politics but, rather, with its radical redefinition. One indication of this transformation of the significance and meaning of politics is the increasing difficulty of utilizing the classic distinction between 'right' and 'left' political traditions. The analytical vacuity of the term 'left' is now evident. While its sole function is that of empirically defining political agents linked to the western historical tradition, it no longer indicates anything about either the new conflicts and actors, or about the direction of contemporary social and political transformations.

Traditionally, the 'right' displayed an orientation towards the past, whereas the 'left' displayed an orientation towards the future. But the appearance of contemporary social movements has impressed upon collective consciousness that we live in a society without a certain future, not only because the future is threatened by the possibility of a global catastrophe, but because the central problem of complex systems is the maintenance of equilibrium. The allegedly 'anti-modern' character of movements in fact consists in their proclamation of the end of linear progress and their affirmation of the sense of fighting for the present, upon which our future also depends.

Change in complex societies becomes discontinuous, articulated, differentiated. These systems never change at the same time, and in the same way at their various levels. The political system, by means of decisions, can reduce the uncertainty and increase the transformation potential produced by conflicts. But this involves a separation of the agents of change from those who manage the transformation. The actors who produce changes and those who manage, i.e. institutionalize, the transformation are not identical.

In my view, the idea of a movement transforming itself into political power while maintaining the transparency of its own expressed demands was revealed as an illusion the day after the October Revolution. But now we know the theoretical reasons why this idea was illusory from the beginning. Changes within a complex system are always changes of an adaptive type; while they may also entail ruptures, these changes always pertain to the overall systemic balance. We know that power is necessary for the regulation of the complexity of any system, and that it is structurally distinct from conflicts. The significance of conflicts is that they can prevent the system from closing in upon itself by obliging the ruling groups to innovate, to permit changes among elites, to admit what was previously excluded from the decision-making arena, and to expose the shadowy zones of invisible power and silence which a system and its dominant interests inevitably tend to create. These possible consequences of conflict appear to be a fundamental function of social movements: the new conflicts can render power visible, even the new forms of power arising from 'progressive' social struggles. In other words, these conflicts can counteract the tendency of any form of power to reproduce itself.

The dilemmas of 'post-industrial' democracy

In recent years, a considerable number of studies have been concerned with the crisis of the welfare state and with the problems of governability, pluralism and political exchange in neo-corporatist systems. At the same time, considerable attention has been given to the political effects of complexity.[1] In relation to the problems discussed above, this extensive debate has brought to light what can be called the dilemmas of post-industrial democracy.

The dilemma of *surplus variability* consists in the necessity of constant change while at the same time maintaining a stable framework of norms and procedures. In complex systems, it is necessary, on the one hand, to take into account changeable interests, a wide distribution of social actors and the variability of their aggregated interests while, on the other hand, guaranteeing systems of rules and norms which ensure a certain predictability of behaviour and procedure.

A second dilemma is that of the *undecidability of ultimate ends*. Complex systems display a great fragmentation of power. There is an increase in the number of groups capable of organizing themselves, representing their interests and extracting advantages from processes of political exchange. There is also a fragmentation of political decision-making structures, giving rise to numerous partial governments that are difficult to co-ordinate. At the same time, there is a consolidation of uncontrolled and invisible organizations within which decisions about ends are made. The circles in which the sense of collective activity is determined become invisible and impermeable. Hence the dilemma of the undecidability of ultimate ends: while the quantity of decisions grows, it becomes increasingly difficult to decide what is essential.

Finally, there is the dilemma of *dependent participation*. In western pluralist systems, there is an extension of citizenship and participation taking place, together with an increasing need for the planning of society as a whole by means of bureaucratic–administrative organizations. The extension of the sphere of individual and collective rights necessitates planning, in order to co-ordinate the plurality of interests and decisions and to protect the corresponding rights of representation and decision-making. But each episode of planning necessitates a technocratic decision-making centre, which inevitably curtails participation and effective rights.

These dilemmas are linked to profound transformations within complex social systems. An exclusively political interpretation, one that is tied to the logic of decision-making and interest representation, fails to take into account the transformations of social production and the modification of social needs and interests through processes that precede the political system and subsequently enter it in the form of demands. Exclusively political interpretations of this kind are today prominent in the theories of 'rational choice' and political exchange, which evidently substitute the economistic approaches of the past with a new reduction of social relationships to political relationships. Politically reductionist approaches fail to appreciate that the understanding of the above-mentioned dilemmas, and possibly their solution, depends rather on the capacity to supplement what can be observed at the political level with an understanding of transformations in the structural logic and new structural contradictions of complex systems.

These complex systems are forced to mobilize individual action resources in order to enable their high-density and highly differentiated organizational, informational and decision-making networks to function. At the same time, however, individual action acquires an 'elective' character, because individuals are provided with increasing possibilities of controlling and defining the conditions of their personal and social experience. The process of individualization – the attribution of a sense of social action to potentially every individual – is thus two-edged: while there is an extension of social control by means of an increase of 'socializing' pressures on the motivational and cognitive structures

170

of individuals, there is also a demand for the appropriation of space–time–sense of life by these same individuals who are provided with broader possibilities of meaningful action.

The dilemmas of 'post-industrial' democracy are linked to this structural tension pervading the complex systems. If both the pressures for integration and the needs for identity-building are not taken into account, the essential components of the dilemmas mentioned above will escape analysis: variability and predictability, fragmentation and concentration, participation and planning represent, in the political sphere, two sides of a more general systemic problem. The attempt to resolve these dilemmas exclusively from within the political system can at best result in proposals and decisions of a new technocratic–rationalizing power which conceals itself behind its capacity for innovation.

However, a careful consideration of the connection between the political dilemmas of contemporary western societies and their multi-faceted systemic logic, together with a recognition of the specificity and autonomy of political relationships, are necessary if the problem of democracy is to be faced in its entirety. To believe that the essence of democracy still consists in securing the competition of interests and the rules that make their representation possible is to fail to appreciate the scope of the socio-political transformations that are taking place within the complex systems. The early modern conception of democracy corresponded to a capitalist system founded on the separation of the state from civil society, a system in which the state simply translated the 'private' interests formed in civil society into the terms of 'public' institutions.

Today, this distinction between the state and civil society, upon which the political experience of capitalism was based, has become unclear. As a unitary agent of intervention and action, the state has dissolved. It has been replaced, from above, by a tightly interdependent system of transnational relationships, as well as subdivided, from below, into a multiplicity of partial governments, which are defined both by their own systems of representation and decision-making, and by an ensemble of interwoven organizations which combine inextricably the public and private. Even 'civil society', at least as it was defined by the early modern tradition, appears to have lost its substance. The

171

'private' interests once belonging to it no longer have the permanence and visibility of stable social groups sharing a definite position in the hierarchy of power and influence. The former unity (and homogeneity) of social interests has exploded. Drawing upon a spatial image, and seen from above, it could be said that they assume the form of general cultural and symbolic orientations which cannot be attributed to specific social groups; seen from below, these interests are subdivided into a multiplicity of primary needs, including those which were once considered to be natural.

The simple distinction between state and civil society is replaced by a more complex situation. Processes of differentiation and 'secularization' of mass parties have transformed them increasingly into catch-all parties which are institutionally incorporated into the structures of government. At the same time, the parliamentary system tends to accentuate both its selective processing of demands and its merely formal decision-making functions. On another plane, there is an evident multiplication and increasing autonomy of systems of representation and decision-making. This process results in the pluralization of decision-making centres, but also carries with it the undoubted advantages associated with their diffusion. Finally, on a further plane, there is an evident growth of collective demands and conflicts which assume the form of social movements aiming at the reappropriation of the motivation and sense of action in everyday life.

Under these conditions, it would be illusory to think that democracy consists merely in the competition for access to governmental resources. Democracy in complex societies requires conditions which enable individuals and social groups to affirm themselves and to be recognized for what they are or wish to be. That is, it requires conditions for enhancing the recognition and autonomy of individual and collective signifying processes. The formation, maintenance and alteration through time of a self-reflexive identity requires social spaces free from control or repression.

These spaces are formed by means of processes (of organization, leadership, ideology) that consolidate collective actors, ensure the continuity of their demands, and permit their confrontation and negotiation with the outside world. Freedom

172

to belong to an identity and to contribute to its definition thus supposes the freedom to be represented. But belonging is not identical with being represented – it is in a certain sense its opposite. Belonging is direct, representation is indirect; belonging means the immediate enjoyment of the benefits of an identity, whereas representation means deferred enjoyment; and so on.

Under pressure from this contradiction between belonging and representation, democracy must entail the possibility of refusing or modifying the given conditions of representation, as well as the possibility of abandoning constituted signifying processes in order to produce new ones. A non-authoritarian democracy in complex societies presupposes the capacity of foreseeing and supporting this double possibility: the right to make one's voice heard by means of representation or by modifying the conditions of listening, as well as the right to belong or to withdraw from belonging in order to produce new meanings. These freedoms would facilitate the generation, for the first time, of certain 'rights of everyday life', such as those relating to space, time, birth and death, individuals' biological and affective dimensions, and the survival of the planet and the human species.

A necessary condition of democracy in this sense are public spaces independent of the institutions of government, the party system and state structures.[2] These spaces assume the form of an articulated system of decision-making, negotiation and representation, in which the signifying practices developed in everyday life can be expressed and heard independently from formal political institutions. Public spaces of this kind should include some guarantees that individual and collective identities are able to exist; 'soft' institutionalized systems favouring the appropriation of knowledge and the production of symbolic resources; and open systems in which information can be circulated and controlled. Public spaces are characterized by a great fluidity, and their size may increase or diminish according to the independence they are accorded. They are by definition a mobile system of instances kept open only by creative confrontation between collective action and institutions. Inasmuch as public spaces are situated between the levels of political power and decision-making and the networks of everyday life, they are structurally ambivalent: they express the double meaning of the terms representation and participation. Representation means the possibility of presenting interests and demands; but it also means remaining different and never being heard entirely. Participation also has a double meaning. It means both taking part, that is, acting so as to promote the interests and the needs of an actor, as well as belonging to a system, identifying with the 'general interests' of the community.

The public spaces which are beginning to develop in complex societies are points of connection between political institutions and collective demands, between the functions of government and the representation of conflicts. Contemporary social movements can act within these public spaces without losing their specificity. The main function of public spaces is that of rendering visible and collective the questions raised by the movements. They enable the movements to avoid being institutionalized and, conversely, to ensure that society as a whole is able to assume responsibility for (i.e., institutionally process) the issues, demands and conflicts concerning the goals an meaning of social action raised by the movements. In this sense, the consolidation of independent public spaces is a vital condition of maintaining – without seeking to falsely resolve – the dilemmas of 'post-industrial' democracy. For when society assumes responsibility for its own issues, demands and conflicts, it subjects them openly to negotiation and to decisions, and transforms them into possibilities of change. It thereby makes possible a 'democracy of everyday life', without annulling the specificity and the independence of the movements ot concealing the use of power behind allegedly neutral decision-making procedures.

Invisible dilemmas

If complex systems are characterized by uncertainty, change and differentiation, decision-making is a crucial part of their government. In the decision-making process a plurality of interests confronts each other within an accepted framework of rules. Selection and risk-taking allow choice between alternatives, and permit the reduction of uncertainty.

Selection is therefore central to decision-making: it is the price to be paid for reducing uncertainty. But it is also the least transparent part of the decision-making process, the area in which both power relations and the unavoidable dilemmas and risks involved in decision-making are submerged. The government bodies of complex systems – political units and large corporate organizations alike – devote a large part of their activity to preparing, generating and executing decisions. It is an area in which power tends to concentrate; as such it is invariably characterized by secrecy and unaccountability.

Contemporary forms of collective action act as 'revealers' by exposing that which is hidden or excluded by the decision-making process. Collective protest and mobilization bring to light those elements of silence, obscurity or arbitrariness buried within complex systems.

Decisions within these systems, it is often claimed, are based on consensus and guaranteed by procedural rules. In this way, power tends to be masked by procedures: the greater and more constant the need for decisions, and the more they depend upon a growing mass of technical data, the less visible power becomes. It seems to disappear behind a neutral mask of 'rational' measures to achieve a given goal, of 'technical' evidence based upon the available facts. Against this tendency, collective mobilization forces power into the open and exposes the interests behind its apparently neutral reasoning.

Decisions are also presented as based upon a series of means, of operations and techniques whose effectiveness must be maximized. As the range of options broadens and the value of problem-solving techniques grows, the decision-making process tends to avoid the question of ends altogether, concentrating instead on the choice and optimization of means alone. Against this, collective mobilization and protest reopen public discussion about ends by revealing non-negotiable needs and creating an area of debate in which the alleged neutrality of means is thrown into question.

As I have explained, decisions are essential in governing any large or complex systems. But to draw this conclusion is to neglect a number of important dilemmas, which should be considered more carefully.

When information becomes a key resource, the basis for social production and exchange, individuals must act as competent and reliable terminals in a complex network of communications. In other words, they must be capable of both receiving and transmitting information and using the right languages. This is only possible if they have access to resources that enable them to solve problems and to learn. However, individual abilities must be integrated into an ordered and coherent flow, which in turn requires greater conformity and more predictable behaviour. This produces the dilemma between *autonomy* and *control*, between placing a greater value on individual capacity and choice, and the formation of all-encompassing systems of manipulation that today go so far as to impinge on the individual's cerebral processes and genetic structures.

Contemporary societies are self-generating, extending their range of intervention into the internal and external nature of the human species. Nuclear science and genetic engineering are, in different ways, witnesses to this infinite capacity of human society to transform itself, even to the point of self-destruction. The survival and evolution of the species is no longer left to uncontrollable forces of nature, but becomes subject to deliberate choices. Thus there appears a new dilemma between *responsibility* and *omnipotence*, between the urge to extend society's capacity to operate on itself, and the need for responsibility, for recognizing the constraints of survival that bind society to its eco-system.

A further dilemma arises from the extension of human power over both the human species and its environment. This process depends on the irreversible swelling of available scientific knowledge: the advances in physics, chemistry and biology that have made possible nuclear energy and genetic manipulation comprise a body of fact that can never be obliterated (at least, not without some catastrophic regression that would nullify our present stage of evolution). Meanwhile, how we use this knowledge depends on choices – policies on energy, science, defence and other decisions taken by governing bodies – that are indeed reversible. Today we can see that this dilemma between the *irreversibility of information* and the *reversibility of decisions* opens up hitherto unexplored areas of thought and action bearing upon our immediate future.

The all-encompassing character of the present world system admits of no 'outsiders'; nations and cultures have come to represent mere facets of a single planetary system. This development opens up a further dilemma between *inclusion* and *exclusion*. Inclusion presses for a levelling of differences, turning peripheral cultures into insignificant 'folk cultures' which are appendices of the few 'centres' responsible for producing and diffusing cultural codes through the great media market. Resistance to such homologization leads almost inevitably to exclusion, which in effect means silence and cultural death.

These deep dilemmas linger, usually silently, in the shadows of the decisions made by the governing institutions of complex systems. The apparent neutrality of these decision-making procedures masks from sight, and therefore from discussion and control by society at large, many of the fundamental questions to do with the lives of individuals, the future of the species and the nature of its possible evolution. Collective action has brought to light some of these dilemmas and has already begun to subject once shadowy areas of power to scrutiny and direct control by society as a whole. But the growing visibility of these fundamental contemporary dilemmas has an even more fundamental implication. It forces us to redefine the notion of freedom inherited from the modern era.

Transforming freedom

Behind the major mobilizations of the modern era were demands for economic rights and rights of citizenship. This era is certainly not over. What we are presently seeing, however, is the growth of new claims for, and, definitions of, freedom. Rights to do with everyday life and people's relationship with the eco-system are opening up new frontiers for democracy.

In post-material society, in which the primary needs of the population are to a large extent satisfied, freedom *from* needs is being replaced by freedom *of* needs. Awareness grows that needs are subject to choices and are not mere necessities imposed by want. The cultural dimension of needs supercedes their material determination and opens up new unexplored territory: human needs are viewed as cultural creations, while recognition is given to desires which are not imposed by 'nature' and, hence, can be experienced as freely chosen and mutually accepted.

The freedom to *have* which characterized *homo economicus* in industrial society is replaced by the freedom to *be*. The right to property has been, and remains, the basis of both industrial capitalism and its competitor model, 'real socialism'. In post-material society there emerges a further type of right, the right to existence or, rather, to a more meaningful existence. This is prompted by the fact that in crucial areas of human life – in such matters as birth, death and sickness – new needs, demands and powers are emerging. Birth and death cease to be matters of biological fate and become objects of individual and social choice – even though in matters such as health and sickness, individuals' claim to determine the quality of their own lives is frustrated by the intervention of impersonal apparatuses that impose from above criteria of normality and pathology.

The right to *equality*, under whose banner all modern revolutions have been fought (and the battle for which is still far from won), is being replaced by the right to *difference*. The recognition of diversity and the respect for individual difference opens the way for a new definition of solidarity and coexistence centred on mutual respect and an awareness that the species as a whole is bound to the future of the eco-system and perhaps even to the universe.

New rights also develop within the *temporal* and *spatial* dimensions of life. In matters of time, a need emerges to escape from external constraint and to achieve a level of self-determination of both the complete life cycle and of daily life. The need to establish a new rapport between inner time and social time creates a demand for reversible time, for autonomously chosen and regulated units of duration unburdened from the rhythms of clocks and calendars.

The right to space similarly assumes the form of a demand for autonomy. The safeguarding of space in daily life against administrative regulation conflicts with the pressures of a hyper-socialized world in which all space is governed by the requirements of instrumental efficiency. The right to space extends to the protection of other living creatures and the natural environment, which together with the human species constitutes both a single physical and biological universe and the context for a meaningful human life. Individual space and eco-systemic space are linked by a fine thread that is none the less real: they represent the ultimate terrain, the limit placed on human beings' destructive activity. This terrain deserves a measure of silence and respect precisely because it exists. Its boundaries, which are never established once and for all, have been recognized in different ways by every previous society. Present-day complex societies, with their power to create or destroy themselves, must redefine these boundaries in novel ways; in other words, they must decide the point at which speech and action must cease so as to allow beings the right simply to exist.

These various rights of everyday life define areas of conflict that go far beyond the problems of pollution. They indicate the need for a future which gives recognition to both our membership in the species and our relationship with the eco-system. The growing wave of support for Green mobilizations is only a forewarning of the debates, opportunities and risks that lie before us. The recognition of these opportunities and risks constitutes a challenge for every one of us. Life on this planet is no longer assured by a divine order. It now lies in the shaky and uncertain grasp of human hands.

Notes and reference

1 For a review of this literature, see especially Offe (1984) and Schmitter and Lehmbruch (1980).

2 The contemporary revival of the debate on civil society is moving towards this conclusion. See Cohen (1982, 1984); Cohen and Arato (1984); Keane (1984, 1988a, 1988b).

9

New perspectives on social movements: an interview with Alberto Melucci*

Q: Most of your sociological research during the past two decades has focused upon the growth and significance of social movements in contemporary modern societies. Much of this work is still unavailable to English-speaking readers. Could you therefore tell us what experiences – personal, intellectual and political – have most attracted your interest in these movements?

Several personal and intellectual experiences have shaped my understanding of social movements. I was born into a working-class family and raised in a left-leaning Catholic culture. I studied at the Catholic University in Milano, where I completed a master's degree in philosophy. By 1968 I had become a university assistant – and a disenchanted young intellectual. I was dissatisfied with my involvement in the Catholic youth movement – with the contradiction between the spiritual side of my religious experience, which I did not reject, and the highly traditional social and political practices of the Italian Catholic Church.

This mood was strengthened by the growth of the student movement in 1968. As a young university assistant, I was sympathetic towards the movement. Yet I quickly realized that the student mobilizations were afflicted with the same kind of intolerance and yearning for integralism that I had already

*An interview conducted by John Keane and Paul Mier in Milano, Italy, on 26 and 27 February 1988.

encountered – and rejected – in my previous commitment to Catholic youth activism. Precisely because I had been involved deeply in a communal experience, I was sensitive to its reappearance in the student movement and 'vaccinated' against its charm. What troubled me about integralism is its rejection of a pluralist and 'disenchanted' attitude to life. Under the influence of integralism, people become intolerant. They search for the master key which unlocks every door of reality, and consequently they become incapable of distinguishing among the different levels of reality. They long for unity. They turn their backs on complexity. They become incapable of recognizing differences, and in personal and political terms they become bigoted and judgmental. My original encounter with totalizing attitudes of this kind has stimulated a long-lasting interest in the conditions under which integralism flourishes. And to this day I remain sensitive to its intellectual and political dangers, which my work on collective action attempts to highlight and to counteract.

My early contacts with the PCI and the 'real socialist' world reinforced my allergy to integralism. I never joined the Communist Party, although some of my friends and colleagues had done so. I participated in certain political campaigns – against the Vietnam War, for instance – and I became aware of the extent to which the Communist experience in Italy closely resembled Catholic fundamentalism. My distance from both was deepened by several research visits to Poland. In 1968 I received a fellowship to enable me to work with Leszek Kolakowski at the Polish Academy of Sciences. I arrived in Warsaw one week after he had been fired for political reasons. Since he was a *persona non grata*, I had this very strange and unnerving Kafkaesque experience of being somebody with whom nobody wanted to talk. Each day I had official meetings with people who might have been police, intellectuals or university administrators – it was impossible to tell – and yet the ritual was always the same 'Well, now that you are here, Mr Melucci, what are your plans?' I usually explained that I had a grant to work with Kolakowski. The typical reply was 'Well, of course, we'll see what we can arrange.' I never met Kolakowski, but in this way I experienced at first hand the reality of life under totalitarianism. My doubts about socialism, classes and Marxism –

which in the Italian context meant the PCI – were reinforced, and I realized more clearly the fundamental difference between everyday life in 'real socialism' and democratic countries.

My personal experiences were not the only sources of my later interest in social movements. I was also dissatisfied intellectually with the dominant sociological paradigms, Marxism and functionalism, which had influenced me most strongly during the 1960s. As a young graduate student in the early years of that decade, my philosophical and sociological interests had focused upon the relationship between Marxism and religion. In Italy, there was at that time considerable debate about this subject among intellectuals. I explored some of its aspects in my master's dissertation, which attempted – it now seems very remote – a case study of the Polish system and proposed some answers to two key questions. Which kind of class divisions exist in a socialist country? And how does Polish culture coexist with socialism? My questioning of both religion and Marxism deepened my interest in sociology. I went on to complete a two year postgraduate programme in sociology at the State University of Milano. I studied with the best Italian sociologists, including Gallino, Pagani and Pizzorno. They deepened my knowledge of the sociological tradition, Parsonian functionalism and empirical research methods. At that time, sociology in Italy was influenced deeply by American sociology. In opposition to the influence of philosophical idealism, which was still dominant in Italian culture, including even Marxism, Italian sociology attempted to legitimate new concepts and methods. Yet I felt trapped between the functionalist theoretical framework, which structured my empirical interest in contemporary social reality, and the Marxist approach, which seemed to me incapable of looking empirically at conflict and other social phenomena.

This discomfort with the two irreconcilable sources of my intellectual formation persisted until I encountered the writings of the Frankfurt School, especially Habermas, and until I went to Paris in 1970 to do my doctorate with Alain Touraine at the Ecole Pratique des Hautes Etudes (as the Ecole des Hautes Etudes en Sciences Sociales was called at that time). Meeting Touraine was intellectually very important for me. I realized that Touraine's approach escaped the shortcomings of both the economism of the Marxist tradition and the ideology of functionalism. It emphasized the importance and autonomy of social action, and this has had a lasting impact upon my work. Intellectually speaking, the theme of social movements developed by Touraine helped me come to terms with all my previous sociological work on conflict and classes.

A final source of my concern with social movements is my interest in psychology and clinical practice. While I've always had an interest in the psychological dimensions of individuals, I found myself at first mainly attracted to social problems. I never considered becoming a professional psychologist. But partly by chance I became one. For personal reasons I entered psychotherapy, and I developed a deep commitment to the field. I also discovered that I had certain personal qualities and skills, such as intuition and the ability to communicate with others and to make contact with their deep inner realities. For these reasons, during the 1970s I continued my training in clinical practice and I completed a second doctorate, this time in psychology at UER Sciences Humaines Cliniques at the University of Paris. All of this is highly relevant to my interest in social movements because it has sensitized me to the ways in which collective action effects not only social change but also transformations of individual experience.

My training in psychology also sharpened my understanding of some of the important methodological and epistemological issues in the study of personal and social life. I went through psychoanalysis. I also carefully studied psychoanalysis. However, I was unsatisfied with its theoretical foundations – with its causal and sometimes mechanistic explanations of psychic life. In the clinical situation, psychoanalysis often searches for the past causes of an individual's present problems. I found myself more attracted to the phenomenological and existentialist approaches, including the humanistic psychologies – such as Gestalt therapy and body therapies – which were developing at that time. I came to see the importance of the phenomenological attitude, which is not centred on causal explanations, but which is more concerned with how people act and how they can change their lives if they so wish. It is a process-oriented approach which, in contrast to psychoanalysis, is therefore less fixated on the contents of experience, particularly those from the past. My preference for the phenomenological approach is evident in my empirical research methods and indeed in my whole attitude towards social movements.

Q: During the past two decades, there has been considerable debate among social scientists about the changing nature of western societies. Older terms such as organized capitalism, industrial society and monopoly or advanced capitalism have been replaced by new terms such as post-industrial society, technocratic society or, as you have suggested, complex society. Much of your analysis of social movements rests upon assumptions about the novelty of contemporary societies. It seems important to explicate them, if only because an essential ingredient of your definition of a social movement is that it is a type of collective action which breaks the limits of the social system in which it operates. What do you mean when you say that contemporary western societies are complex? What kind of system are we living in?

This question is important and unavoidable in research on social movements. But the fact is that nowadays nobody has a convincing answer. There is a general reliance upon metaphors, adjectives and prefixes to describe the nature of the system in which we are living. And – as the use of such terms as neo-capitalism and post-industrial society suggests – the two leading models of modernity, the Marxian theory of capitalist society and the Weberian theory of industrial society, are undergoing modification. Most people feel that our systems have changed, but very few admit that we lack a language to describe the way in which they have changed. I prefer to acknowledge this impasse, to declare it openly in order to make possible its resolution through different questions and answers. This is why all the terms you mention are used rather indiscriminately in my more recent writings.

Q: Are you saying that you intentionally deploy these various concepts in an undisciplined way, in the hope that this will produce dissatisfaction with them and encourage the formulation of new concepts?

Yes. I'm convinced that we are entering an era qualitatively different from both the capitalist model of modernity and socialism as we've known it historically. At least three main processes are taking place, the acknowledgement of which can help broaden the discussion about the nature of our society – and its limits. First, within this system information has become the core resource. Our access to reality is facilitated and shaped by the conscious production and control of information. 'Forms' or images produced through perception and cognition increasingly organize our relationship to the material and communicative environment in which we live. The transformation of natural resources into commodities has come to depend on the production and control of these cognitive and communicative 'forms'. Power based upon material production is therefore no longer central. Second, this system has become planetary, a completely interdependent World system in which nothing or nobody is external to its boundaries. In this respect it differs from the capitalist system, which only laid the foundations for planetarization. A third development is individualization, the fact that the main actors within the system are no longer groups defined by class consciousness, religious affiliation or ethnicity, but – potentially at least – individuals who strive to individuate themselves by participating in, and giving meaning to, various forms of social action. I really don't know what kind of system we are entering. But I would say that if these three processes are indeed significant then, correspondingly, the questions we ask about the present system must also change. So also must our understanding of the disequilibria and social conflicts within the system, which I do not assume to be monolithic and totally administered.

Q: Many of your views on complex societies are at odds with a Marxist approach, which attempts to establish the causal links between the macro-structures of capitalist society and its conflicts. Some of the key themes of recent Marxist analyses of the present system – such as the fiscal crisis of the state, the restructuring of the global capitalist economy and corporatism – are virtually absent in your analysis of 'complex society'. Why? Is it because you think that this type of macro-analysis is inappropriate in

complex societies? That it belongs to a past era – that of industrial capitalism? Or that it is fundamentally unhelpful in analysing the formation of social movements?

Macro-structural analyses of the Marxian type are unavoidable, as I've tried to explain in my criticisms of recent American analyses of social movements. These market-based analyses, such as resource mobilization theory, dispense with conceptions of structural boundaries and macro-power relations and reduce everything – illegitimately – to calculation, bargaining and exchange. I therefore accept as a strong working hypothesis the Marxian point that we live within a system which has a definite logic and definite limits – even if these limits are presently obscure and difficult to specify. This is why recent Marxian analyses of the system in terms of fiscal crisis, corporatism and economic restructuring are interesting and stimulating. They help to explain certain important mechanisms of the system. But my objection to these analyses is that they present their *particular* account of contemporary society as a *general* theory. They appear to be explaining the universe, when in fact they are presenting 'regional' explanations of only certain key mechanisms of present-day society. No doubt, these theories can provide us with a sense of intellectual and emotional security, they help to close our circle of uncertainty by incorporating new phenomena into pre-existing intellectual frameworks. But in my view they constitute a form of intellectual reductionism. They deny the need to creatively declare the impasse I've spoken of already. Instead of openly admitting the limits of our present understanding of the system and our inability to explain the complex problems confronting us, they resort to totalizing concepts which are simplistic and incapable of embracing reality as such.

Q: There is a strong ambivalence in your earlier work about the use of class analysis. A central feature of the Marxian project for analysing collective action is its focus upon class struggle. While you argue that such analysis is inadequate for examining collective action, your earlier writings nevertheless refer to the 'class relationships' which lie at the root of the new social conflicts. Why this ambivalence? What is wrong with Marxian class analysis?

My earlier work certainly displays an ambivalence about class analysis. As I've mentioned already, my original research considered the subject of class divisions and conflicts in terms influenced by the Marxist tradition. It became evident to me during this research that the Marxian discourse of class in fact specifies two different sets of phenomena which are often confused. The term class refers both to the patterns of social differentiation and stratification within a society and to the conflictual relationships defined by the production and distribution of the basic resources of a society. The Marxian analysis of social stratification considers *classes* as real social groups, but it also utilizes the concept of *class relationships* to analyse the dynamics of social production. I further realized that the latter sense of the term – the thesis that there are conflicts generated by the relationships through which social actors produce and appropriate their basic resources – is crucial for the analysis of collective action. I still retain the originally Marxian idea that the production of a society's basic resources is riddled with conflicts. But I am not convinced that we need the term class to describe and analyse all of these conflict-ridden relationships. Class relationships are only one very specific historical form of production relationship; they are unique to modern capitalist society, in which they assume the form of struggles between the bourgeoisie and the proletariat, that is, between social groups defined by their position in the economic system.

The Marxian model of class analysis is inadequate for a second reason. Since the classical era of industrial capitalism of the nineteenth century, patterns of social differentiation and social conflict have altered. No doubt, in sociological terms class divisions in certain fields of contemporary society continue to be evident; they have not disappeared completely, and therefore the concept of class should not be dismissed from sociological analysis. But since the phase of industrial capitalism, the social structure has become ever more flexible and subject to change. The relationship between social position and collective action has also become more contingent, while social conflicts concerning basic resources can no longer be adequately understood in class terms.

Q: A more serious, if less obvious objection to the

Marxian class analysis is that it relies upon a particular view of history, in which a subject is privileged and destined to transform society through revolution. As Marx and Engels say in *The Holy Family*: 'It is not a question of what this or that proletarian, or even the whole proletariat, at the moment *regards* as its aim. It is a question of *what the proletariat is*, and what, in accordance with this *being*, it will historically be compelled to do'. Didn't this view rest upon metaphysical assumptions peculiar to the age of revolution? Isn't the very idea of a social movement – which Marx certainly embraces – an invention of this period? Doesn't its employment condemn its users to fictional images of technical mastery, struggle, revolution and progress which are now obsolete?

My doctoral dissertation in sociology examined the ideology and practice of nineteenth-century French entrepreneurs. France underwent industrialization later than England, with the result that French entrepreneurs openly debated fundamental questions concerning the nature of progress and industrialization. Their discourse was saturated with the images of a world in motion – of progress, industrial revolution, railways, machines, global conquest and the domination of nature by human beings. What struck me about this dominant entrepreneurial discourse was its similarity to that of its socialist opponents. The work ethic is common to each discourse. So too are metaphysical assumptions about the teleological course of history and the belief that a particular actor is capable of recognizing and fulfilling the truth of this historical process. The concept of a social movement belongs to this shared constellation of metaphysical images. It expresses the idea that there is a central actor whose every action is caught up in a linear process of motion towards a final destination. The concept of a social movement is difficult to disentangle from the concepts of Progress and Freedom, and I therefore find myself uncomfortable with its use in the present period.

Q: You remark in *Nomads of the Present* that contemporary movements are no longer guided by the sense that they are completing a universal plan. You claim that they don't even have long-term goals, that their mobilization is limited to specific times and places, and that they resemble nomads who dwell entirely in the present. Is this why you consider the concept of a social movement no longer plausible?

Yes. But my discomfort with the concept is further reinforced by its association with grandiose political programmes which have in practice resulted in violence and totalitarianism. This tragic scenario presently appears to be repeating itself in the Third World. The vision of a new system of transparent power replacing the old and unjust system has claimed too many victims in our century. At the very least, respect for these victims obliges us not to feed such grandiose and dangerous illusions any longer.

Q: The view of history as destiny, upon which Marxism rests, is arguably problematic for another reason. It turns a blind eye to other, often important types of collective action which coexisted, not always peacefully, with the working-class movement. For example, Craig Calhoun has pointed out in *The Question of Class Struggle* that the conventional view, defended by E. P. Thompson *et al.*, of the early British workers movement is quite misleading. According to Calhoun, the movements of the 1810s were not primitive or backward-looking nor should they be treated as part of the linear development of the working-class movement. Rather, this decade saw the formation of populist movements which acquired distinct and different forms of protest and collective action. The social basis for this movement, according to Calhoun, lies in their communal foundations. In other words, the radicalization of this movement was inspired by the uprooting of traditional communal life, and not by the new factory system of class exploitation. Not only was this early social conflict not a class movement in Calhoun's view; it was more radical by virtue of not being a class movement. Calhoun's thesis has wide and important implications. It suggests that the classical Marxian view of collective action was highly one-dimensional. It also raises the question of whether other non-class forms of action – such as the early movements of women, citizens and struggles against slavery – were significant features of the age of 'industrial capitalism'. In the light of Calhoun's claims, doesn't a contemporary theory of collective action need to fundamentally rethink their roles and importance – against the narrowness of the original Marxian approach? Aren't you too faithful to classical Marxism?

I am unsure whether there were forms of action more radical than the working-class movement. But I agree that even during the period of industrial capitalism collective action had a multidimensional quality. The tendency to unify the heterogeneity of collective action by means of either a key concept – such as class struggle or the objective historical role of the proletariat – or through empirical generalizations is rooted deeply in the whole tradtion of research on social movements. This tendency is misleading because collective action always has a composite and plural quality. It contains a multiplicity of levels, meanings and forms of action – even when in particular contexts certain types of action are most efficacious and eye-catching – and for this reason collective mobilizations cannot be summarized in simple formulae, such as progress or reaction. Charles Tilly's writings vividly illustrate this point. The historical research presented in his *The Rebellious Century* and *From Mobilizations to Revolution* is very informative and provides much empirical evidence of the heterogeneity of collective action. But in theoretical terms he still works within a basic Marxian framework. His claim that interests motivate people into action is founded upon the Marxian idea of class interests. His framework of analysis is further burdened by its heavy emphasis upon the political dimensions of collective action. This bias – which again obscures the multidimensional character of social movements – is evident in Tilly's preoccupation with the effects of collective action upon the political system, as well as in his reliance upon public data sources, which probably are biased towards types of action which impinge directly on the political authorities. While this type of political analysis of social movements is important, it obscures their complexity.

Q: Your attempt to develop a sociological theory of social movements is not only critical of the Marxist tradition. It is also at variance with the received mainstream sociological theories of collective action. Among the most influential of these mainstream theories during the post-world war period is the view – associated with the work of Kornhauser, Smelser *et al.* – that collective action is pathological reaction to the strains produced by modern society. Emphasis is given to the non-rational, even irrational components of collective behaviour. Collective behaviour is seen to result from structural changes, which trigger a breakdown of the organs of social control and legitimation. The resulting strains, discontent and aggression drives anomic, frustrated and maladjusted individuals into collective behaviour, which itself feeds upon volatile goals and rumours, propaganda and other crude forms of communication. What are your objections to this view?

The belief that social movements are a pathological reaction to the stresses and strains of modern society was influenced understandably by the experience of Stalinism and Nazism, which prompted intellectuals' fear of insurgent masses and their manipulation and control by totalitarian parties and leaders. Considered from our quite different historical situation, it nevertheless becomes clear that the analytical foundations of this view are very weak. To begin with, this view makes the questionable assumption that social order is a normal state of affairs. Collective action is therefore seen as a form of social pathology which is produced by the disequilibrium within a social order. This view also ignores the constructive or creative dimensions of collective action. Even in less structured forms of collective behaviour, people do not act in a void. They are always enmeshed in relations with other actors, and through this interaction they produce meanings, express their needs and activate their relationships. Collective action is never a purely irrational phenomenon. It is always to a degree socially constructed and meaningful to its participants, even when it appears to be anomic or marginal behaviour. This point is actually implied in Smelser's important contributions to a theory

191

of collective behaviour, which diverge in this respect from Kornhauser's and others' view that collective action is pathological.

Q: Since the early 1970s, resource mobilization theory has dominated research on social movements. In contrast to traditional theories of collective action, this approach claims that grievances and deprivations are not a sufficient (or very important) condition in explaining the rise of social movements. Resource mobilization theory accepts your criticism of the traditional view that a low-level of organization is a feature of social movements. It points instead to the crucial importance of pre-existing organizations in the rise and growth of social movements. Resource mobilization theory emphasizes the fundamental importance of factors such as the availability of resources – recruitment networks, the costs and benefits of participation, organizations, funding, and the availability of professionals – in analysing the recent growth of social movements. This approach seems plausible and helpful in analysing, for example, the successes of the American civil rights movement. According to some writers, resource mobilization theory nevertheless de-emphasizes the grievances and injustices that _normally_ motivate protest movements. Isn't your critique of resource mobilization theory subject to the same objection?

My own research has drawn upon resource mobilization theory and extended it in ways not intended by its proponents; in a sense, I have tried to push this approach beyond itself. Resource mobilization theory attracted me initially because – as you say – it calls into question the naive premise, evident in the whole Marxist tradition, that 'interests' are the motivating force of collective action. It also rejects the comon-sense assumption that suffering and social inequality leads necessarily to collective action. Resource mobilization theory adopts a sceptical attitude towards these views. It suggests that pre-existing injustices and grievances are not sufficient conditions of explaining action, and thereby it opens up an important theoretical space in which questions can be asked about how movements produce themselves. It suggests the need to analyse the complex and dynamic relationship among three dimensions: a pre-existing social problem; the development of a shared sense of common interests among actors; and collective action itself. I have tried to incorporate these insights into my own understanding of the formation of social movements, for I am convinced that people do not decide to act together simply on the basis of injustice or commonly shared or ascribed interests.

Q: Shouldn't this point be extended? Perceived grievances and injustices are not simply a point of departure for collective action, as you imply. Their recognition by actors as grievances and injustices is always in part an *outcome* of interaction itself. During the past ten years, for example, the west European peace movements did not merely react to a pre-existing nuclear threat. They also helped construct and heighten the public sense of a nuclear threat. Isn't this typical of all recent movements?

That's certainly true. Actors' definition of a grievance as such presupposes that they have cognitive and interactive skills which enable them to recognize that an objective problem is problematic *for them*. Objective problems don't exist in themselves. They come to exist as problems because people are capable of perceiving and defining them as such within processes of interaction.

Q: It is a striking fact that resource mobilization theory has enjoyed considerable popularity, particularly in American social science. One could almost say that resource mobilization theory is an American phenomenon. Why is this? Is it to do with specifically American intellectual traditions? The different nature of American social movements? Or perhaps the predominance of 'business thinking' (Perrow) or the emphasis on 'entrepreneurial' models (McCarthy and Zald)?

Resource mobilization theory is indeed an American phenomenon, and in three ways. First, its focus upon the availability of social resources as a key factor in the life of social movements expresses an important difference between American and west European collective action. American social movements have always been interwoven more closely with civil life and, hence, founded upon pressure groups and voluntary associations. By contrast, European social movements have always been tied more closely to class actors and political parties and much more concerned to transform class interests into political goals. This important difference probably reflects the contrasting social structures and patterns of state intervention in Europe and the United States. The relative openness of American society and the absence of centralized state structures has permitted more dispersed and non-political forms of mobilization, whereas in Europe centralized state structures have operated as something of a magnet for collective action. In countries such as Italy and France, every articulated social grievance is confronted by the omnipresence of state power. The temptation has therefore been strong to rely upon parties and other political organizations which can interact with or oppose state power. An extreme historical example of this general trend was the Bolshevik strategy of confronting the bureaucratic and centralized Czarist regime with a professional revolutionary organization.

Resource mobilization theory is also a product of the specific patterns of intellectual life within the United States. In that country, there has been an unprecedented development of organization theory in the analysis of business and administration. Resource mobilization theory is in this sense an American phenomenon because it has managed, in intelligent and fruitful ways, to translate concepts and insights from the paradigm of organization theory into the field of social movements research. But the resource mobilization approach is a specifically American intellectual phenomenon in another sense. In the United States, Marxist and radical thought has not strongly influenced the sociological tradition. In the field of social movements research, resource mobilization theory has therefore played the role of an *ersatz* radicalism. It *appears* to be a form of radical opposition to the conservative orientations of American sociology. But its critique of the older theories of collective behaviour we've discussed is rather restrained. Resource mobilization theory has in fact become a new orthodoxy. It is a form of institutionalized radicalism: it is, for instance, the dominant paradigm in the new section on social movements in the American Sociological Association. In terms of intellectual legitimation, resource mobilization theory has been a big success. It has even begun to conquer the world academic market in the field of social movements research.

Q: In Western Europe so called structural theories continue to be more influential in the analysis of social movements. Structural theories focus upon the socio-economic and political levels of the present system in order to explain collective action as a response to crises or adjustments in the macro-levels of the system. For example, Habermas has claimed that the new social movements are best understood as a by-product of the colonization of the life world by economic and political mechanisms that operate in abstract and reified ways and 'invade' and consequently destroy spheres of social life in which individual and collective identities are constituted and defended. Movements – with the exception of the women's movement, which is seen as genuinely universalistic – are interpreted by Habermas as a defensive reaction against the bureaucratization of everyday life. Arising in areas of cultural reproduction – at the interface between the life-world and the political economy – the new movements are engaged primarily in resistance and retreat, in the search for personal and collective identity. Why do you have reservations about this type of analysis of the origins of new social movements?

The colonization of the life world is certainly an observable trend in complex societies. But I have theoretical and empirical reservations about Habermas's thesis. Theoretically speaking, its analysis of contemporary movements is not differentiated enough. It treats these movements as unified entities. It thereby conceals the different realities – the variety of actors and orientations – within contemporary movements. This theoretical objection to Habermas's thesis is reinforced by some empirical doubts. The evidence suggests that forward-looking and pro-active forms of resistance are at least as evident within these movements as backward-looking and reactive forms of action.

People within movements invest a great deal of time and energy in the creation of groups, centres and communities. Such action is not simply defensive, for it is also the means through which they experience personal growth and develop a sense of security – against the (threatened) manipulation of large-scale organizations. Paradoxically, such action is facilitated by the phenomenon of colonization itself.

Q: Are you saying that Habermas understates the way in which the colonization process turns unwittingly against itself?

I'm sure of that. Colonization is a deeply ambiguous process. It entails the (attempted) domination of the life world as well as the injection of resources which can be used by people to transform the conditions of everyday life. The health policies of the welfare state are a typical example. Health information and sickness prevention policies – as the campaign against AIDS illustrates – invade everyday life more than any other policy field. Health care services manipulate and control people in the most intimate sense. And yet at the same time people acquire through these same channels new information about the conditions of health and a new awareness of their health needs and rights. This enables people to organize themselves in new and more meaningful relationships. Of course, this process of inventing new forms of action is always frustrated by inequalities of power and resources, and this is why conflicts and movements are a fundamental aspect of the colonization process. Nevertheless, the colonization of everyday life by large-scale organizations is not a one-dimensional process. It extends forms of administrative control *and* encourages new meanings and forms of sociability.

Q: All that you've said so far indicates your dissatisfaction with the whole nineteenth-century and twentieth-century theoretical tradition of analysing social movements. You've clarified your disagreements with previous approaches – such as Marxian class analysis, resource mobilization theory, and Habermas's structural theory. We'd therefore

like to explore your own positive contributions to the understanding of the main features of new social movements. One intriguing argument in *Nomads of the Present* is that all previous approaches have relied upon dualistic thinking, and have therefore neglected the complex processes through which collective action is *produced*. Could you explain this point?

Dualistic thinking emphasizes either the objective or subjective dimensions of social life. It stresses either the powerful forces inscribed in the structures of society – such as its laws of motion in the sphere of economic production and exchange – or the importance of actors' beliefs, intentions, representations and cultural productions. Such thinking is evident in the whole of modern social science and especially in the philosophies of history which have so far guided the analysis of social movements. These philosophies typically assign social movements a revolutionary role; or they assume that the capture of state power is the principal goal of collective action; or they embrace the conservative myth that collective action is subversive of social order. My broad objection to dualistic thinking is that it fails to understand the ways in which social action is constructed and 'activated' by actors who draw upon the (limited) resources offered by the environment within which they interact. Structural theories have something to contribute to the explanation of the environmental limits of action. But social action is never a given fact. It is always socially produced. Within the boundaries of certain structures, people participate in cognitive, affective and interactive relationships and creatively transform their own social action and to a certain extent their social environment as well. I am aware that this is at best a preliminary formulation – something like a first step in transcending dualistic analyses of collective action. But I think it is an important step to take in both a theoretical and empirical sense.

Q: Your empirical research on various movements in the Milano area is one of the distinctive – but least well known aspects of your work. What methods have you used to study collective action? What are the aims of this empirical research?

The Milano research project extended over a four-year period. It was conducted by a team of ten researchers and it involved spending a considerable amount of time with groups of movement activists in four different areas: among women, urban youth groups (such as punks and social centres [centro sociale]), ecologists and neo-religious groups which operate outside the official churches and have a strong spiritualist orientation. The overall aim of the project was not merely to enhance our general knowledge of contemporary social movements, but also to examine how the process of constructing collective action actually takes place.

Q: This is arguably one of the most central – but least explored – issues in the field of social movements research. It touches upon the simple but fundamental question of why individuals become involved in social movements.

Precisely. And it raises some difficult methodological problems, which remain unresolved in the two dominant types of empirical research into collective action. One approach tries to show the empirical links between the location of actors in the social structure and their patterns of belief and action. Through surveys and interviews and other means, it collects data on the social origins and attitudes and activities of groups such as workers, students or movement militants. This approach tries to explain the relationship between the structural and behavioural variables of collective action. Another approach concentrates instead on the ideologies of social movements, that is, on what social actors say about themselves and their social reality in their documents and speeches.

Both approaches are very useful, in my view. But neither tells us anything about how people come together and construct something called a movement. My empirical research has concentrated on this problem and attempted to develop an appropriate methodology for examining it. Basically, the research methodology involved three phases. Initially, we conducted a survey of the wide spectrum of groups involved in collective action in the Milano area. This first phase rested on the empirical assumption that these groups belonged to a social movement by virtue of their self-definition as active members of one or other movement. During a second phase, we conducted in-depth interviews with all these groups. Here the immediate aim was not merely to gather information about the group, but to establish a working relationship between us as researchers and the group itself. This phase, which involved much hard work and intensive training by the research group, was methodologically very important, precisely because it enabled us to pass to the third and final phase of research. In this final 'experimental' phase the prior relationship established during the in-depth interviews was deepened and extended. From each movement, we selected one group for observation. In this experimental phase, the members of the group acted for themselves as well as for us in video-recorded sessions. This provided us with information about their action. It also provided the members of the group with an opportunity to activate their relationships, to reflect on what they were doing, and in this way simulate the processes through which they create new meanings and produce a collective identity, that is, come to define themselves as participants in a movement.

Q: The empirical research method you've sketched here is clearly at odds with Touraine's method of sociological intervention. Touraine sees the role of the sociologist as truth-teller of social movements: the researcher views social movements as a potential unity, whose highest meaning is open to causal explanation. The research programme consists in intervening by 'incitement' or 'hypothesis' in the actors' self-analysis of their struggle. The researchers' ultimate aim is to achieve successful conversion – to formulate hypotheses which enlighten movement participants about the 'highest possible meaning' of their action – and, hence, to help the young social movement find its true identity. What's wrong with this methodology?

Touraine's methodological contributions to the analysis of the self-production of action – of action in action – have been very important. Certainly, some of the methodological problems involved in observing action were posed long ago by Kurt

Lewin. Awareness of these problems is also evident in the disciplines of psychology and social psychology, but in both cases – as my training in psychology has made clear – the methodological techniques are only applicable to individuals or small groups. To my knowledge, Touraine was the first to point out the need for a specific method for analysing the field of action of social movements. This is no small achievement: awareness of this methodological lack is already the first step in overcoming it. In this respect, my own techniques of empirical research have been influenced by Touraine's method of *intervention sociologique*. But I'm critical of two aspects of his research methods.

One objection concerns Touraine's supposition that there is a 'highest possible meaning' of social movements. The idea of a 'highest possible meaning' rests upon the value-laden assumption that there is one central social movement in any given historical period. It follows from this assumption that all other forms of collective action are 'lower'. My research method avoids this normative assumption. It does not suppose that it knows the truth of collective action, nor does it presume to know what is good for actors. It does not set out to save anyone's soul. My research method instead acknowledges and accepts the different levels and meanings of collective action. It tries to understand these differences without supposing that they are hierarchically ordered. This is the point of the experimental phase of investigation described above. It encourages all these different meanings of collective action to surface. In the experimental phase, my only assumption is that actors know the meaning of their action, even if never completely so. As individuals, we always partly know what we are doing. Of course, when we become confused or involved emotionally in what we are doing we don't see certain things – until we become aware of our actions by analysing their different meanings. Something similar occurs within collective action. Since collective actors participate in a system of knowledges, exchanges and relationships which they control only in part, they tend to act ideologically. But since collective actors also know something of the meaning of their action, they are therefore capable of recognizing the need to know more about their action. And this is why there can be a contractual relationship between researchers and actors. The researcher needs information in order to complete his or her scientific research. The researcher possesses certain kinds of skills and resources – of knowledge, for instance – which the actors can recognize as valuable for clarifying their own action. The researcher never has a monopoly on these resources, but he or she can offer analyses to actors who cannot be actors and analysts of themselves at the same time. In this way, the researcher can pursue his or her own scientific goals as well as facilitate actors to heighten their awareness of the interactive nature of their action. The researcher can facilitate actors to locate themselves in their patterns of action, and hence enable them to take greater responsibility for their choices and actions. But this possible outcome is not inspired by the missionary role of the researcher. It is rather a by-product of the contractual relationship between researcher and actor, each of whom pursues his or her particular goals.

Q: This is very different from Touraine's techniques of 'conversion', which both imply the need for an hierarchical relationship between researchers and actors, and concentrate on altering the content rather than the form of collective action.

Yes, although I don't think that this hierarchical relationship is necessarily implied by Touraine's methodology.

Q: What is your other methodological objection to Touraine?

It is a technical point to do with the logic of his procedures for achieving 'conversion'. Let's for a moment ignore the previous criticism and suppose that a researcher wants to know – and transmit to a movement – the 'highest possible meaning' of its actions. The problem is that the researcher can never be sure whether or not the observed action is the product of his or her interventions. Touraine's research procedure is unable to control its own effects. It cannot know whether or to what extent the conversion process is simply the product of its own interaction with the group it is observing. Our research in Milano tried to overcome this difficulty by concentrating, during the experimental phase, on the *formal*, phenomenological level of action. In other words, we tried carefully not to introduce any interpretative contents into our exchange with the groups under observation. We attempted only to feed back to the groups information about the *how* and not the *why* of their action. In this way, we were able to control to an acceptable degree the effects of our presence upon the actors being observed. We were thus able reasonably to assume that what the group actually revealed to us was the product of the group itself and its conscious interaction with us. In the final stage of research, we were then able – separately from the actual interaction with the groups – to interpret our observations through explanatory hypotheses.

Q: There seems to be another important disagreement with Touraine. He claims that in any society there is only one central social movement, and he therefore continually poses the question: which new social movement will tomorrow assume the central role that the workers' movement held in industrial society? You seem uncomfortable with this line of questioning. Is this because of your objections to holism?

Yes. Touraine's idea of *the* central movement still clings to the assumption that movements are a *personnage* – unified actors playing out a role on the stage of history. This idea simply doesn't correspond to present-day conditions in complex societies. As I've explained already, it is wise not to turn our backs on the task of analysing the dominant structures and limits of the system – and, hence, the way in which its key resources are produced, appropriated and struggled over. But this type of analysis neither implies that the system is monolithic nor that collective action within this system is expressed as a unified movement. Within complex societies, as Touraine himself recognizes, collective action is highly differentiated. It shifts from one location to another, depending on the resources and issues at stake. It thus becomes difficult to explain why it is that certain conflicts become core conflicts, but only for a limited period and in relation to certain issues.

Q: In *La Voix et le regard* and *Le Mouvement ouvrier*,

Touraine argues that the workers' movement has lost its role as the central social movement, and that it has become institutionalized politically. Do you accept this view?

Although I agree basically with Touraine that the working-class movement in western Europe and North America has been drawn more and more into the institutionalized political arena, there are still examples of working-class conflict in the traditional capitalistic sense. And new types of collective action specific to post-industrial forms of production – actions by women, youth, immigrants and other groups defined by their social existence outside the workplace – appear to be emerging and merging with more traditional industrial conflicts.

Q: In *La Prophétie anti-nucléaire* Touraine claims that anti-nuclear struggles are crystallizing into the central social movement of our times. According to him, other struggles remain within the paradigm of modern indus-trialism, whereas the ecological movement is a revolutionary force. It questions the dominant images of modernity, fundamentally challenges the dominant economic and political structures and forces public debate about how we want in future to work and to live. Do you also have reservations about this view of the ecological movement?

Term 'movement' – which at best is only a conversational tool – risks exaggerating the degree of (possible) unity of this form of collective action. As Touraine himself points out, the ecological movement in Europe contains different levels of action, ranging from political conflicts to defensive reactions and challenges to the codes of everyday life. The movement also contains a variety of meanings. Consider the example of a mobilization against the proposed siting of a nuclear power plant near a rural community: for the peasants of this community, the plant may represent a threat to the traditional ways of life. But for a group of young people who studied in the capital city and who have returned to their rural community, the proposed plant may symbolize something quite different, for instance a threat to their attempts to live autonomously. This intricate collage of different meanings and forms of action within ecological mobilizations is further complicated by evidence that they are keeping ever greater distance from institutional politics. Initially, the ecological movement was engaged mainly in political action, whereas today it gives greater emphasis to an 'everyday ecology' and to the transformation of individual identity.

Q: Any analysis of contemporary social movements is only complete if it addresses the vital question: 'What do they achieve?' Your writings argue that to answer this question in terms of 'success' or 'failure' (as is traditionally done) is fundamentally inappropriate. You say that movements operate primarily in the field of culture. Your argument is concerned mainly with the shift of emphasis in complex societies from the management of economic resources to the production of social relations, including symbols, identities and needs. Corresponding to this shift, you claim, are changes in the nature of contemporary conflicts – away from production-based conflicts. Are you saying that 'new social movements' are concerned essentially with 'post-material questions', that is, with redefining cultural codes? And is this what is 'new' about new social movements?

I was among the first writers to introduce the term 'new social movements' into English, and so I must also be implicated in the misunderstandings it has created! I am not opposed to the continued use of the term, but – as *Nomads of the Present* tries to explain – I have become dissatisfied with its reification and convinced of the need to clarify and specify its meaning. The term is often used loosely in a chronological sense to refer to the growth, since the early 1960s, of forms of action which diverged from the then dominant types of collective action. But this sense of the term wrongly assumes that the 'new' movements are unified entities. My main theoretical objection to the literature on 'new social movements' is that it fails to recognize their *composite* character. It therefore neglects a vital question: given the differentiated nature of contemporary social movements – the fact that they contain a plurality of levels, including very traditional forms of action – do they nevertheless display novel types of action which cannot be explained by the traditional analyses of class conflict or political struggle?

Q: An answer to this question presumably requires not only empirical research along the lines of your Milano project. In analytic terms, it also forces a clarification of the various dimensions of present-day social movements as well as requires a definition of the meaning of 'novelty'.

Yes. In my view there are new dimensions of action and meaning within contemporary movements. But I am convinced that this novelty can be explained only by introducing fresh hypotheses – terms different than those used to analyse the workers' movement. A key hypothesis is that there are four novel structural characteristics of today's movements. The first is the central role played by information resources within some sectors of these movements. Today's movements operate primarily as 'signs'. They are not preoccupied with the production and distribution of material goods and resources. They are instead concerned mainly with information – in both the narrow sense of demands for 'factual information' about, say, the siting of a nuclear power plant, and in the broader sense of struggles over symbolic resources, as in the challenge of the women's movement to sexist advertising. Second, parts of the movements invest much time and energy in constructing forms of organization which are not considered instrumental for the achievement of social and political goals, but are viewed primarily as a way of experiencing collective action itself. Networking within the European peace movement and consciousness-raising groups within the women's movement are model examples of this new trend. Participants within contemporary movements act in the present tense. They are not driven by grandiose visions of the future; their organizations are not vehicles for the implementation of such visions. Rather, those who participate within the organizations of a movement view their participation as an end in itself. Their 'journey' is considered at least as important as their intended destination. A third novel feature of contemporary movements is their integration of the latent and visible dimensions of collective action. In the tradition of socialist and working-class politics, particularly among militants, there tended to be a split between private life and public life. The emotional investments, cognitive frameworks and patterns of life within each sphere were different. This is not the case in contemporary movements. There is instead a complementarity between private life, in which new meanings are directly produced and experienced, and publicly expressed commitments. Living differently and changing society are seen as complementary. Within the new movements there is a more balanced sense of the proper relationship between the latent and visible dimensions of action. Involvement in public–political action is perceived as only a temporary necessity. One does not live to be a militant. Instead, one lives, and that is why from time to time one can be a public militant. Finally, contemporary movements display the seeds of a new awareness of the global dimensions of complex societies. This 'planetary' consciousness is broader than the more limited 'internationalism' of the working-class movement. It involves an awareness of living as a member of the human species in a fully interdependent human and natural world system. I was reminded of its fundamental significance several years ago when white middle-class American students mobilized against apartheid in South Africa – despite the fact that they had no direct political connections with apartheid. This new sense of totality is also strongly evident in the peace and ecological movements, which emphasize the connections between humanity and the wider global universe.

Q: An unusual feature of your view of contemporary social movements is the claim that their form is itself a message – an idea that seems to closely parallel McLuhan's thesis on the 'medium is the message'. Are you saying that the form of a movement is not only a vehicle for achieving certain goals, but that it is also a goal in itself, an alternative experience (or naming) of reality as such?

Yes. My claim that movements operate as a 'message' or a 'sign' – a claim which certainly draws upon McLuhan – is designed to highlight the way in which they express something more and other than the particular substantive issues for which they are usually known. From their particular context, movements send signals which illuminate hidden controversies about the appropriate *form* of fundamental social relations within complex societies. An important example is the way in which the movements help ensure that difference – the possibility for particular individuals or groups to affirm their specificity – is a controversial issue in complex societies. In this way, movements increase the already high learning capacity or 'reflexivity' of complex systems. They initiate and publicize new fields in which society acts upon itself. But this in turn generates an evident tension within the movements between the particularism of their participants' claims and fields of operation and the general formal problems which they raise. This tension is inescapable, because actors are always prisoners of the particular language, actions, contexts and resources upon which they draw. The women's movement, for example, addresses issues specific to women as well as prompts consideration of the importance of difference in a complex society. Women speak of themselves by drawing upon the particularity of their condition as women in a gendered society; and they struggle for the difference which is denied or repressed by the dominant culture. But women do more than this. They also speak of the difficulty of dealing with difference in a society which is becoming ever more integrated and differentiated at the same time. They show that in complex societies the need for communication – for solidarity, love and compassion – increases along with the need for recognizing and affirming differences.

Q: You've observed that an important characteristic of recent social movements is their 'invisibility' – their operation through subterranean networks of mainly part-time membership. You imply that this invisibility is one of the movements' strengths. This view is surprising, if only because others have seen this characteristic of new social movements as a sign of their decline, loss of momentum and impotence. Far from 'breaking the limits of the system', these observers claim, social movements are (compared with a decade ago) presently in decline – in the process of slowly burning themselves out. How do you respond to this pessimistic view?

Mobilizations and whole movements can and certainly do disappear. But the pessimistic view fails to understand that a great deal of important activity takes place during the invisibility phase. The submerged networks of social movements are laboratories of experience. New problems and questions are posed. New answers are invented and tested, and reality is perceived and named in different ways. All these experiences are displayed publicly only within particular conjunctures and only by means of the organizing activities described by resource mobilization theory. But none of this public activity would be possible without the laboratory experiences of the submerged networks. The pessimistic view which you described misses this essential point because it concentrates narrowly on the political effectiveness of movements. In the extreme, it ends up embracing the Leninist view that only intellectuals and political organizers prepare the new experiences which are later displayed in public form.

Q: Your emphasis on submerged networks also seems to rest upon a conception of power which is quite at odds with that underlying the view you are criticizing. Isn't it true that this pessimistic view fails to recognize that large-scale organizations, such as state bureaucracies and capitalist corporations, rest upon complex, molecular networks of everyday power relations? Doesn't it therefore underestimate the ways in which the transformation of these molecular powers by social movements necessarily induces effects upon large-scale organizations?

You're right. In complex societies, power relations become subject to 'microchipization'. In other words, actors become aware that changes in everyday life have institutional effects, and that is why the small subterranean networks of the movements resemble laboratories in which experiments are conducted on the existing relations of power. My understanding of power differs in this respect from that of Foucault, Deleuze and Guattari and others. They share a one-dimensional view of power – as the construction and administration of subjects – whereas reality as we experience it in complex societies is in my opinion the resultant of powerful organizations which attempt to

208

define the meaning of reality *and* actors and networks of actors who use the resources of these same organizations to define reality in novel ways.

Q: A serious objection to your thesis that the new movements issue important challenges to the dominant cultural codes is that they sometimes become infused with narcissistic impulses that are essentially apolitical. This point has been emphasized, for instance, in interpretations of the decline of the American Movement of the 1960s. The impulse of self-fulfilment, the desire 'to move personally' (Keniston) was strongly evident in that movement. Arguably, it put excessive emphasis on personal gratification, on achieving intimacy, expression and freedom. This trend was evident in the decline of political commitment and the advance of 'political tribalism' (Castells): drug culture, sexual experimentation, the cult of Eastern religions, rock music, 'drop outs' and 'hippies'. Woodstock and Altamont gradually replaced Port Huron and the Siege of Chicago as the Movement's defining moments. But this search for challenging the codes of everyday life – a search for what Norman O. Brown called the Dionysian ego – led to the fading political commitment of thousands of young people, thereby undermining the Movement. Doesn't this example illustrate the danger of narcissistic withdrawal in all of the new movements?

The dangers of narcissistic withdrawal which you illustrate are real, and they can produce tragic results. But I think that the argument conflates two different aspects of the phenomenon of narcissism. One aspect is the desire for individualization. Each individual has the potential to become a unique and self-determining being. Within contemporary movements, and in the society at large, this desire for self-realization is very strong, and it is encouraged by the production and distribution at the systemic level of such resources as education, technical skills and universalistic codes.

Narcissism has another aspect: the yearning for communal identity, or 'political tribalism' as you called it. Paradoxically, this yearning for solidarity is encouraged by the possibility of individualization. The more we are exposed to the risks associated with personal responsibility for our actions, the more we require security. We actively search for supports against insecurity. This is why the desire for self-realization can easily turn into the regressive utopia of a safe and transparent environment which enables individuals to be themselves by becoming identical with others. This utopia was certainly evident in the movements of the 1960s in the United States and elsewhere. It tended to get the upper hand over the more creative need for individualization, which was frustrated by restrictive youth policies, weak educational reforms and other inadequate responses of the system. This overpowering of self-realization by communal solidarity could be prevented, and a new relationship between personal needs and a commitment to shared human responsibilities could be ensured by creating or strengthening a civil society which enabled individuals to satisfy their needs for self-determination.

Q: What about the oft-heard claim that contemporary movements cannot achieve this goal of self-determination because they do not question the existing property system? According to this view, movements may raise important cultural questions, but they leave untouched the fundamental questions – to do with property and its private appropriation – addressed by the workers' movement. This reaction has been summarized by Ralph Miliband: 'the "primacy" of organized labour in struggle arises from the fact that no other group, movement or force in capitalist society is remotely capable of mounting as effective and formidable a challenge to the existing structures of power and privilege as it is in the power of organized labour to mount. In no way is this to say that movements of women, blacks, peace activists, ecologists, gays, and others are not important, or cannot have effect, or that they ought to surrender their separate identity. Not at all. It is only to say that the principal (not the only) "gravedigger" of capitalism remains the organized working class.' How do you respond to this plea for the continuing strategic importance of struggles centred on property?

210

The fundamental issue to be clear about is what we mean by property. In the era of industrial capitalism, property took the form of natural resources, material goods and capital. The form of property was externalized, and its ownership conferred upon human beings the power to control external nature. Property in this sense has not disappeared from complex societies. It probably remains one of the problems confronting us today. But Miliband's reaction overlooks the fact that there is another kind of property – property in our biological and psychological existence – which is becoming more and more important. The form of property is becoming 'internalized'. What is at stake is not who owns what, but who owns whom and whether that ownership is legitimate. This trend is evident in the legal and political controversies aroused by genetic engineering, reproductive technologies, medical research and other direct interventions in our internal nature. It is also evident in the debate generated by the ecological movement, which has broadened the old concern about controlling material property into new questions concerning attempts to control both outer nature and the inner nature of human beings.

I therefore agree with Miliband that struggles centred on property remain important. But I understand property to include much more than property in material goods and capital. It would be interesting to explore this difference by comparing the contemporary conflicts about property in my expanded sense with the controversies about property in goods during the era of capitalist development. Such comparison might show up the inadequacy of traditional definitions of property as well as deepen our understanding of contemporary forms of property. It could enrich and extend the debate, which has developed since the 1930s, about ownership versus control of property, the growth of collective consumption and the changing nature of capitalism. It would probably show, for instance, that the power of multinational corporations is problematic not only because they privately appropriate common goods, but because they interfere deeply with both our natural environment and the biological and psychological existence of individuals – with their sense of genetic destiny, sexual choices, and patterns of consumption.

Q: There is a long sociological tradition – which has its political supporters – which stresses the importance of cultural tradition in weaving together the members of a complex differentiated society. Lacking tradition, said Edmund Burke, individuals are naked, isolated and miserable creatures, who are as frail as flies at the end of summer. This old warning about the dangers of anomie has been repeated more recently by Daniel Bell, who defends the need for cultural conservatism in the face of atomizing, hedonistic challenges to everyday life. How would you respond to the claim of cultural conservatives that movements are enemies of tradition, that they foster cultural breakdown and anomie?

It is curious that the conservative claim is sometimes countered with exactly the inverse point: that the movements are too tradition-bound and backward-looking, and not progressive and modernizing enough. I prefer to think differently about the relationship between tradition and contemporary forms of collective action. In my view, systemic trends in complex societies are slowly destroying traditions. The processes of increasing differentiation and complexity characteristic of these systems is gradually eliminating the barriers of tradition that hindered the growth of capitalist systems. Yet what is interesting is the simultaneous growth of a sensed need for roots. This need, as I've explained already, is stimulated by the uncertainty and insecurity which accompanies the increased opportunities for individualization fostered by complex systems.

The attempt to fend off insecurity and to preserve and develop memories is most evident in regionalist or ethno-nationalist movements. In our study of nations without a state, *Nazioni senza stato*, Diani and I tried to show how these movements contain elements of traditional resistance to state-building and modernization processes as well as attempts to draw upon the particular linguistic and cultural traditions of a region and its people in order to symbolically express new and different things. We found that these movements are not simply orientated to the past. Rather, they orient themselves to the present system in order to preserve and develop their particular cultural traditions against the generalized pressure towards

212

conformity and homogenized cultural patterns. They indicate how traditions, far from being static, can be developed in novel ways. And they indicate why the nineteenth-century distinctions between 'progressive' and 'conservative', and Left and Right are inadequate for understanding this innovative development of traditions by contemporary movements.

Q: There is an additional sense in which contemporary movements re-tie the threads of historical memory. They also feed upon the themes and patterns of organization of previous movements. They keep alive and cultivate traditions of collective action. This is one of the paradoxical features of present-day movements: while they diverge in many ways from older social struggles (such as the workers' movements), at the same time they rekindle a whole series of past experiences of struggle. They bring these experiences back to life and give them a new shape.

There are certainly pre-modern experiences which contemporary movements retrieve and develop. Gerlach and Hine's work on the organizational form of the new movements makes this point by drawing on Marshall Sahlin's writings on hunting and gathering tribes. They argue that the reticular and segmented structure of contemporary movements can be understood as a functional response to conditions of uncertainty and complexity, and that in this limited sense they have a pre-industrial form reminiscent of so-called primitive tribes, which duplicated and multiplied their group functions in order to deal with the uncertain environment in which they moved.

Q: But there are also continuities between contemporary movements and early modern forms of collective action. Many examples come to mind: the infusion of 'red' and 'black' themes within the Green movement; the deliberate efforts of social movements to rescue and develop endangered democratic traditions in the central-eastern half of Europe; and the ongoing references within the women's movement to earlier mobilizations of women.

213

Don't these examples refute the conservative claim that today's movements raze tradition?

Yes.

Q: But then your earlier claim that there are some things which are 'new' in contemporary social movements is jeopardized. In the workers' movements of the nineteenth century, for example, all four of the features which you consider to be novel were already evident. The workers' movements were certainly concerned with information resources – as is evident in their agitation against the ideology of classical political economy. These movements also experimented with new forms of organization, such as the co-operative, mutual aid society and trade union. They also operated through invisible networks, especially in countries in which these movements were illegal and under constant harassment by the political authorities. And the early threads of a planetary awareness are evident in workers' attempts to organize underneath and across the boundaries of nation-states. Doesn't all this suggest that contemporary movements have revived and extended forms of action already evident in early modern movements? That they are active 'agents' of a *modern tradition* of collective action?

I agree that the 'new' social movements preserve these traditions of collective action. But they do not simply preserve them as if they were on display in a museum. They use these traditions to confront new problems, to ask new questions and to offer new answers. Historical continuities are always observable within present-day social movements. The crucial question is how and to what extent contemporary actors render these elements of tradition meaningful by synthesizing them with completely new elements.

Q: Not everybody within movements experiences challenges to cultural codes as a discovery and a liberating, joyful struggle. Arguably, most people feel it as a dis-orientating and sometimes painful crisis. They feel nostalgic

214

for the certainties of times past. They worry about the loss of friends and acquaintances; feel inadequate in political discussions; feel guilt at what they are doing; and they feel compelled to conform to new norms which they neither comprehend fully nor accept. Has your research uncovered this kind of reaction? If so, how do actors in movements cope with this? Is it a potential source of fragmentation and decline in movements, the stony ground upon which actors' appeals can and do fall?

Involvement in collective action always entails the experience of disruption and disorientation you describe. In the contemporary movements it is especially acute. These movements are filled with many different processes and tensions and conflicts, all of which makes individuals' commitment to them risky and uncertain. As I have explained, the image of movements as a character or *personnage* is misleading, precisely because in sociological terms the experience of being involved in a movement is both temporary and highly fragile. The quality and length of individuals' commitment depends very much on the resources available to them. In the Milano research project, for instance, I observed among groups within the youth movement wide discrepancies in the availability of resources. Some groups were marginalized by their inability to translate their emphasis upon internal solidarity and expressive drives – guitar playing and smoking joints – into public action. They suffered implosion because their limited personal skills and resources prevented them from translating their guitar playing and opposition to the system into a viable activity in the outside world. Other groups fared better. Young people working with video, for example, developed certain technical skills within their group. This linked them with the outside world of information production, and in turn enabled them to have a public presence, or even to become professionals and to abandon the movement altogether.

Q: Given these internal tensions and wide discrepancies of resources within the movements, why do people join them in the first place? Why do they submit themselves to

215

forms of collective action which are multi-layered, fragmented and highly precarious?

This is a very important – but enormous – question. Let me try simply to summarize the three different levels of explanation which must be acknowledged if a plausible answer is to be given. First, individuals participate in collective action because they belong to a specific social sector which is exposed to the contradictory requirements of complex systems. This structural explanation is not sufficient, however, because not all individuals who belong to a self-contradictory social sector actually participate in collective action. A second type of explanation – emphasized by resource mobilization theorists – is therefore also required. This concerns the availability of specific resources to individuals who engage in calculations about the costs and benefits of involvement. Resources such as prior membership in networks are of course never 'neutral'. They are always conditioned by the specific social sector to which an individual belongs. For example, while all women are exposed to contradictory pressures and obligations, their participation as women in collective action depends upon such resources as their level of education, their access to employment and their previous membership in leftist political groups.

A third level of explanation – to do with the psychology of individual commitment – is often underestimated and sometimes forgotten. Yet it is fundamental, because individuals ultimately participate for highly personal reasons, and not only because they are 'students' or 'women' or 'young' or 'black' or 'urban dwellers'. I tried to show the importance of individual variables in *Corpi estranei* (*Extraneous Bodies*). Based on my clinical work, this book analyses the deep psychological reasons why individuals withdraw from movements and seek therapeutic advice. It illustrates how individuals sometimes confuse the three different levels of explanation of why they get involved in collective action. It shows that the analytical separation of these interdependent levels can help individuals to recognize that their commitment to collective action is based in part on deeply personal reasons. And it suggests, on that basis, that those individuals can resume their social activities, and even their involvement in collective action.

Q: One of the formal criteria you use to define a new social movement is its emphasis upon internal solidarity. Doesn't this neglect the chronic internal divisions within movements? Such divisions can sometimes be productive. In the United States, for example, the rebirth of the women's movement (as Sarah Evans and others have pointed out) derived largely from the civil rights movement and the New Left. But divisions can also be paralysing. For example, within the Green movements of western Europe there are serious paralysing divisions about the very meaning of 'green politics'. Doesn't such heterogeneity and conflict contradict your definition of social movements as based upon solidarity? Isn't it more accurate to say that they are at best only ever defined by a dynamic and *contested solidarity*? Don't you yourself recognize this when you emphasize, against those who speak of movements as characters, that movements are invertebrate phenomenon – heterogeneous, fragile, complex?

Along with the terms conflict and breaking the limits of the system, the concept of solidarity was used in my early writings to define a social movement as a specific form of collective action. At the time, it seemed to me important to overcome the theoretical confusion which plagued discussions about collective action. I was troubled particularly by the tendency of researchers to conflate different forms of collective action – to define everything as similar to everything else. But I soon realized that solidarity is not a given state of affairs, and that a social movement is a multifaceted reality. I therefore became convinced of the need to clarify how collective actors come to define themselves as a unity. So when I now use the term solidarity I use it as an ideal-type. It refers to a dynamic and unstable reality, to the *product* of intense interaction, negotiation, conflict and compromise among a variety of different actors.

Q: It seems to us that the phrase contested solidarity is still more appropriate for expressing, in an ideal-typical manner, the permanently contested sense of collective identity within social movements. And it also ser healthy reminder that it is usually the leaders of pa

217

movement organizations who emphasize, against their opponents, the appearance of unity within the movement.

This is what I also wish to emphasize. We know, and my research confirms, that it is normally the spokespeople, the ideologists who speak on behalf of other participants, who place most emphasis on unity. But careful observation reveals the chronic tensions and differences within the fabric of the movements. Collective actors invest an enormous quantity of resources in the on-going game of solidarity. They spend a great deal of time and energy discussing who they are, what they should become and which people have the right to decide that. This on-going process of construction of a sense of 'we' can succeed for various reasons: for instance, because of effective leadership, workable organizational forms or strong reserves of expressive action. But it can also fail, in which case collective action disintegrates. The task of sociological analysis is to understand how and why the game of solidarity succeeds or fails.

Q: Your work plays down the importance of analysing the social background – e.g. the social class – of those who participate in new social movements. Isn't it nevertheless an important dimension to understand? For instance, sociological analysis indicates that support for the Greens is strongest among young people, women, metropolitan dwellers, groups with higher levels of formal education and workers in key sectors of the information economy. Doesn't this type of analysis tell us about the degree to which the new movements are (capable of) drawing upon sectors crucial for the functioning – and therefore the transformation – of the present system? And doesn't it therefore help us estimate the mobilization potential of the movements?

This kind of research is very important in generating knowledge of how social movements function. Even though I don't do this research myself, I find its results very useful for understanding certain features of contemporary movements. But it is limited by its supposition that collective action derives spontaneously from social conditions. We've already discussed the serious weaknesses of this view.

Q: One of the characteristics of the new social movements, you claim, is their refusal of a certain type of revolutionary politics – the Leninist model of capturing and transforming state power – as well as more conventional Left political strategies. Could you explain this point? Are you saying that the conventional distinction between Left and Right is obsolete in thinking about the cultural and political potential of the new social movements?

The dream of many nineteenth-century utopias was to harness social actors to the project of transforming the state. At one and the same time, social actors were viewed as the motor of civil society and the creators of a new form of political power. Today, in my opinion, this view is obsolete, because there is a growing divergence between the patterns of social action within civil society and political action within state institutions. Political action involves making and implementing decisions through processes of selection and, hence, by means of pressure, competition, calculation and representation. By contrast, social action is a reticular and multifaceted experience, which is more and more concerned with the meaning of individual, interpersonal and collective life. The problem with Leninism is that it reduces everything which is social to political matters; social actors, social judgements and knowledge of social phenomena are compressed into political terms. This is an extreme form of reductionism, but it has been highly influential. Still today we usually judge collective action in terms of its impact on the political system. This short-circuiting of the relationship between social movements and political power and conflict is best avoided. It weakens our understanding of the independent processes at work within social movements as well as their impact upon the political system.

My dissatisfaction with reductionism of the Leninist kind indicates why I am doubtful about applying the traditional distinction between Left and Right to social movements. This distinction probably remains valuable in the political arena. To be on the Left in political terms is to oppose the backward-looking conservatism of the Right. It stands for the expansion of human rights, legal guarantees for citizens, greater equality and democracy, and the toleration of political differences. The difficulty is that these criteria cannot be applied to social movements. The heterogeneity of contemporary forms of collective action cannot be contained in these simplifying categories. Moreover, as I've tried to explain to you, many features of the new social movements are simply not describable as progressive or conservative, forward-looking or backward-looking. These old terms are obsolete in a sociological sense.

Q: But there are a number of contemporary movements which articulate some key themes of the political Right. Religious fundamentalism, racialist and nationalist movements (e.g., Le Pen's Front Nationale), and the 'right to life' movement also have all of the formal qualities of new social movements as you understand them. Why then doesn't your analysis deal with these 'right-wing' movements? Doesn't your research implicitly *assume* that the new movements are (potentially) democratic? Don't you thereby understate the fundamentalist or anti-democratic 'dark side' of movements?

It is true that my research has not concentrated on these movements, although in the Milano project I experienced at first hand the neo-religious movement. In the Italian context, this movement comprises an eclectic network of groups attempting to develop a new spiritual experience. These groups are situated mainly on the fringes of the established churches, and some of them are guided by orientalist themes. I personally found this neo-religious movement highly troubling. It raised many conceptual problems and political doubts. In particular, it forced me to reflect upon the deeply ambiguous role played by 'spiritualism' in several of the new movements. For some collective actors, spiritualism is highly attractive because it provides an alternative to the allegedly flat one-dimensionalism of present-day reality. It is a means of denouncing and transcending the given reality – of developing a radically different vision from a standpoint 'beyond' that reality. But the embrace of spiritualism does more than create a sense of difference for its believers. It also defines itself in opposition to a reality which pretends to be without limits. In the realm of sexual experience, for example, complex societies emphasize the right to pleasure as if it were an Eleventh Commandment. This produces new obligations and controls: we are supposed to get our pleasure by following the rules of the sex manual. Spiritualism feeds upon and reacts against this reduction of sexual experience to techniques and gymnastic exercises. It offers a transcendent perspective of the kind found in certain forms of radical feminism and eco-feminism. Spiritualism provides the important reminder that we cannot live without ethics, even in a disenchanted world. But it supposes – incorrectly, in my view – that the dilemmas of life in complex societies can be overcome by taking refuge in higher 'ethical' principles such as love and harmony.

Q: Spiritualism certainly originates as a reaction against the perceived homogenization of life in complex systems. But there are other forms of fundamentalism – evident in Le Pen's Front Nationale – which are prompted by the inverse experience of fragmentation. For example, the Front Nationale in France draws some of its support from manual working-class voters, some of them ex-Communists, who feel threatened by de-industrialization, unemployment and 'foreigners'. These nationalists embrace a transcendent ideology not because they feel that they are living in a flat, homogenized reality. They rather feel the earth to be shaking under their feet. They yearn for certainty in the face of uncertainty, and that is why they are intolerant of difference and fascinated by unifying symbols such as 'France'.

Yes. This is the other face of fundamentalism in its reactionary or fascist form. It embraces the myth of a de-differentiated society in order better to impose it upon others.

Q: You have mentioned several times that you are troubled personally by the spiritualist tendencies within the new social movements. Is this because spiritualism is intolerant of diversity – a lapse into the very same

integralism which you found originally in both Catholicism and Marxism?

More than this is at stake. I think that transcendent perspectives – spiritualism is not exactly the right word since it is often associated with formal religions – are as necessary as they are dangerous. The issues and problems with which we are confronted today cannot be addressed simply on the basis of an appeal to the private interests of people. Consider the issues raised by the ecological movements. Certainly, people become concerned when a nuclear power plant is built near their homes or when the seaside where they live becomes polluted. But what interest do they have in the fate of forests in the Amazon Basin or aboriginals in Australia? Why should people be concerned about the fate of the planet? They can only become interested in such matters on the basis of an overriding set of ethics which motivate them into action. Hence my discomfort: movements cannot survive on rational calculation alone, and yet their necessary resort to supra-ethical standards easily risks turning them into a church preaching a new gospel.

Q: This brings us to your claim that the new social movements keep their distance from politics, that they have a deeply anti-political quality. Why is it that these movements are suspicious of parties, governments and state institutions?

Rather than speak of the anti-political quality of contemporary movements, I would prefer to discuss their pre-political and metapolitical qualities. Movements operate in the pre-political dimensions of everyday life. Within its informal networks, collective actors collaborate in the laboratory work of inventing new meanings and testing them out. But movements also contain a metapolitical dimension. They publicize the existence of some basic dilemmas of complex societies which cannot be resolved by means of political decisions. They reveal that we are confronted by general problems for which there are at best only partial and temporary solutions.

Q: Would you give some examples of these metapolitical issues raised by social movements?

We know for instance that the elimination of currently available knowledge of nuclear energy is impossible – except of course by means of a final and ultimate global disaster. Given the manifest dangers of nuclear power and weaponry – which the peace and ecological movements have well publicized – it follows that neither the elimination nor the free use of nuclear knowledge is feasible. This is an example of a dilemma which will remain no matter what decisions are taken by the political authorities. Another example is the crucial dilemma resulting from the growing technological power we as human beings exercise over ourselves and our environment. This power is becoming virtually infinite even though at the same time we remain rooted inescapably within the boundaries of human biology and our natural eco-system. We cannot choose either human omnipotence or a regression to a fully 'natural' existence. We are caught necessarily between these two extremes, which political decisions can never resolve fully. The contemporary movements have helped us become aware of these kinds of dilemmas. They remind us that politics has its limits, that not everything is reducible to negotiation, decision-making and administrative control, and that *non-political* forms of action must therefore be kept alive as a reminder of this fact.

Q: To what extent do your views on the pre-political and metapolitical character of movements reflect the high degree of 'closure' within the Italian political system?

My early thinking about the relationship between movements and parties was certainly influenced by the pecularities of the Italian political system. An especially important fact is the inherited pervasiveness of the state in nationalized industry, the media, the arts and many other spheres of Italian daily life. Nearly every single problem is dealt with or refracted through the political system. Social action is hyperpoliticized. The scope for autonomous civil initiatives is comparatively limited. The political system therefore tends to be viewed as illegitimate and blocked. This feeling that the state is omnipresent yet unresponsive is reinforced by its malfunctions: the system of justice works clumsily, the universities are overcrowded and the health service is highly inefficient.

During the 1970s in particular, the hyperpoliticization and under-representation of social action in Italy resulted in the suffocation of the demands of the new social movements. The Radical Party was the political party most sensitive to these issues raised by civil society, and this resulted in two important social reforms, which swept away laws against divorce and abortion. Other questions raised by the new mobilizations were ignored by political actors. This resulted in clashes with the governmental authorities, who often responded with authoritarian and repressive measures. Every attempt was made to contain the new social demands within the established political equilibrium. The PCI which aspired to the ranks of government, did not play the role of a left opposition in a democratic two-party system. It failed to represent the new radical demands; until the late 1970s, its policies and public statements concerning students, women, and ecology poorly acknowledged the legitimacy of their demands. Under these conditions, it is not surprising that the New Left groupings embracing the tradition of revolutionary Marxism were temporarily successful. The student movement in particular fed small political organizations and parties, such as Lotta Continua, Il Manifesto and Avanguardia Operaia. Although they were sensitive to the new themes and demands of the social movements, they tried to translate them into Leninist political terms, thus failing to recognize their novelty as *social* phenomena. This is the background against which the non-political forms of action of the 1980s emerged.

Q: One of the most troubling developments of the past two decades has been the growth of terrorist organizations in complex societies. You locate the development of terrorism in Italy in the processes of distorted modernization and the institutionalization of the Left. You say that the expectations of the new movements were thwarted by the newly modernized institutional arrangements; and, as the example of Autonomia demonstrates, the movements thus became disillusioned and felt betrayed. Your view is that terrorism is the result of the decomposition of social movements. Could you explain this point, perhaps with reference to the Italian developments you have just sketched?

When I began writing on social movements in the mid 1970s, there were two prevailing interpretations of the growth of violence and terrorism in the Italian political system. Either these phenomena were seen as an effect of the irrationality and madness of the individual terrorists, or they were viewed as the necessary outcome of social and political phenomena which contained seeds of violence from the outset. In opposition to these interpretations, I tried to show, in the Italian case, that there was a link between the wave of modernization which effected civil society from the end of the 1960s, the growth of social movements and the malfunctioning of the political system. I tried to show that terrorism was the resultant of these three processes.

Q: Would you describe for us these processes in more detail?

The details are complex and difficult to summarize accurately. From the mid-1950s onwards, the Italian economy was transformed in ways comparable to other neo-capitalist economies. New forms of industrial organization, expanding markets, and the growth of middle-class consumption patterns were not matched, however, by corresponding changes in the cultural and institutional life of civil society. At the end of the 1960s, this contradiction erupted in demands for the reform and democratization of industrial relations, the education system, the judiciary, and the health system. I use the term modernization to refer to all these dramatic changes which effected economic and cultural life in Italy during this period. A second factor in my analysis of the origins of terrorism was the emergence of new demands from within the new social movements, which we've already discussed. The third important factor was the blocked political system, which was controlled by the Christian Democrats, the dominant party in the governing coalition. The political system tried to contain the new social demands. It left behind much unfinished business and dissatisfaction. The fate of student demands well illustrates this trend. The most vocal demand of the students was for a different university system. The universities became marginally more democratic as a result. But other student demands – to do with war, the role of science, the international system, the need for a lessening of authoritarianism in interpersonal relations and other issues common to student movements around the world – were ignored completely. This resulted in widespread disillusionment and a radicalization of the student movement in a Leftist political direction. The factory unrest produced by economic modernization had facilitated changes in the industrial relations system, but it also produced disillusioned, fundamentalist fringe groups. The New Left organizations, whose ideological and political framework was Leninist, but who in practice acted as a 'wildcat' democratic opposition, were unable to satisfy both the fundamentalists and those people searching for personal and cultural change. Some militants therefore concluded that political violence was the only solution. In this way, the terrorism of the 1970s synthesized the disillusionment produced by the half successful institutionalization of social demands and the repression and neglect of the claims of new groups of urban youth.

Q: You have explained, at least for the Italian case, how the systematic use of violence grows out of social movements. But isn't it also important to explain why violence is so rare within contemporary movements? Compared with the early years of this century, when parts of the workers' movement were driven by fantasies of violent confrontation with employers and the state, contemporary movements rely almost exclusively on civil disobedience and other non-violent forms of action. Why is this?

There are several reasons. First, the over-use or crude use of violence by political authorities in the past normally provoked counter-violence by their opponents. To some extent, this old rule has been learned by present-day pluralist political systems. Political power has become shrewder. A related factor, second, is the democratization of political systems by the struggles and violence of the past. Open and violent confrontations between movements and western states are today less common because there are alternative means available for negotiating their differences. Finally, the inner culture of today's movements is decidedly against the use of violence. The contrast with traditional socialist and working-class culture is clear. That culture considered violent confrontation with employers and the state legitimate. Its theories sometimes even supposed violence to be necessary and inevitable. Contemporary movements distance themselves from these old assumptions. They have an aversion to grandiose plans and political ideologies – they dwell within the present tense – and they therefore emphasize pacifism, personal experience and the need to avoid frequent open confrontations with the state. Having said this, I doubt whether we are seeing the withering away of violence. Violence will probably continue to be the shadowy underside of movements. Paradoxically, the weakening links between violence and social movements might make terrorist campaigns by disillusioned and impatient individuals and isolated 'grouplets' even more likely.

Q: Your writings emphasize that the demands of new social movements are not negotiable, even though they require political mediation. A similar point has been made by Manuel Castells. In his study of urban social movements, *The City and the Grassroots*, Castells suggests that there is a contradictory relationship between dominant urban life and the alternatives offered by social movements. Yet he argues that urban social movements, in their quest for an alternative city, cannot provide a political alternative because the image they project cannot be linked with an alternative mode of development, nor to a democratic state. He concludes that urban social movements are directed at transforming the meaning of the city without being able to transform society. They are a reaction not an alternative. You also recognize this problem. What the movements require, you suggest, is the formation of new intermediate public spheres within civil society. Would you elaborate this point?

I am convinced that the expansion and official recognition of public spaces is essential for protecting contemporary movements – and for enriching democracy as we know it at present. A new process of 'post-industrial' democratization based on the widening and consolidation of public spaces would build on the principles of rights, citizenship and equality of the early modern era. It would also enable the movements to live more fully their double existence within the invisible networks of civil society and in the temporary mobilizations through which they become publicly visible. The consolidation of independent public spaces would help the movements to articulate and publicize to the rest of society the themes and dilemmas which they consider to be important. And it would enable political actors to receive the messages of the movements more clearly.

Q: Would you give some examples of the new institutions of representation which you have in mind?

These public spaces already exist to some extent. But their further development would be especially important in three areas of complex societies. Among the most important would be knowledge-producing institutions, such as universities, cultural foundations and research institutes. Knowledge is a key resource of complex societies. It is produced by professionals and appropriated by corporate and state power as well as by the general public. These actors could negotiate more openly with each other through bodies set aside for their purpose within the knowledge-producing institutions themselves. Public spaces could also be strengthened within the field of collective consumption – in the areas of transportation, housing, health and other public services where the everyday needs and demands of civil society could interface more freely with the established policy-making bodies. Finally, public spaces could also be strengthened within the field of communications media. I am aware of the enormous difficulties here, and I don't have any ready-made solutions. But attempts to create spaces of confrontation and negotiation among various actors within the media would help to ensure their greater accessibility and responsiveness. The public spaces I have in mind for each of these three policy areas would not necessarily function as arenas of conflict. They would neither be dominated by political parties nor would electoral success be their guiding criterion. Since they would not be burdened by the pressures of reaching final decisions, they might resemble neutral territory, in which different interests could interact without necessarily clashing head on. They would require legal protection. And they

228

certainly would include task forces, committees, and other temporary forms of representation – 'bio-degradable organizations' as the Italian Greens call them – which matched the sporadic mobilizations of the new social movements.

Q: Wouldn't the development of these public spaces suppose a radical break with conventional views about the primacy of political parties in relation to social movements?

It certainly implies a dramatic change of attitude among traditional political actors, including political parties, who could not expect immediate electoral or political gains from these spaces.

Q: Even when that point is granted, your proposal still seems to understate the reasons why movements are compelled – even if only to survive – to directly enter the party-political arena. The point is that competitive, democratically organized political parties can perform several functions which the public spaces you have in mind cannot. For example, parties can help crystallize disparate opinions into stable coalitions of interests; they can develop, under pressures of time and circumstances, policy programmes; and they can help citizens to defend their social interests while keeping an eye on state power. These functions of democratic political parties have often been ignored within the new movements. But there are signs, awareness of the necessary dependence of movements upon parties. Daniel Cohn-Bendit is a case in point. In 1968 Cohn-Bendit remarked: 'To bring politics into everyday life is to get rid of the politicians.' He now accepts the need for movements to get involved in party politics: 'The problem with the social movements is that they are not obliged to institutionalize and protect themselves. They have spread rapidly, sure, but we have learned . . . that you can spread very fast and then get beaten back very fast. That is what happened to us in '68. What we are now concerned to do is to give a presence to what has been achieved, and that is very, very difficult now. . . . I want to be able to say that we can try to achieve this with a political party, but a political party is by definition a bureaucratic organization. The thing is that the Greens are pushed by the social movements which force them to bargain with their political power. With a party like the Greens we can begin to change the institutions of the country. I now accept that this is as important as anything else.' How do you react to Cohn-Bendit's change of heart?

I would emphasize that the functions performed by political parties are also performed by other organizations. Trade unions, pressure groups and voluntary associations can also stabilize opinions, represent social demands and formulate long-term policy programmes. I would also stress that the functions performed by social movements are not reducible to those of political parties. This point should be clear from our discussion. Political parties and other political bodies mostly exercise power at the macro-levels of complex societies. The role of public spaces is different. They permit movements to articulate the demands of civil society and to render the power relations of complex systems more visible. Given that power in these systems tends to conceal itself behind a veil of allegedly neutral or technical decision-making procedures, this critical function of public spaces is indispensable and probably of primary importance in the present period.

Q: Sympathetic observers and supporters of the new social movements often express alarm about their fragility and vulnerability to political and social repression. For example, this fear is presently evident within the gay and lesbian movements. Everywhere these movements are being subjected to a wave of cultural, legal and political harassment. Your writings don't address this problem of the forcible elimination of movements. In fact, you say in *Nomads of the Present* that the new movements have a permanent and non-conjunctural nature – that they are a stable and irreversible component of complex societies. What is the basis of this conviction? Isn't it overly optimistic?

Some might consider my view hopelessly Italian – as somehow

based on voluntarist and optimistic assumptions. This judgement would be unfair, since I am aware that considerations of the future of social movements should not be reduced to questions of optimism or pessimism, personal taste or political preference. Moreover, our conversations during the past two days have emphasized the fragile and ephemeral character of contemporary social movements. Their existence evidently depends on conjunctural factors, such as the degree of political democracy in a country, and their normal destiny is either to become institutionalized – to produce new elites and to introduce cultural changes in everyday life – or to disappear into the streams of daily existence.

I grant these points. Nevertheless, I maintain that social movements are permanent and irreversible features of complex societies. This is partly because these societies produce – as well as require – the forms of individual participation and collective mobilization generated by these movements. In functionalist terms – which I normally don't use – a sub-system of movements is a permanent feature of complex systems. What I mean is that these systems, which are both highly centralized and complex, encourage the development of spaces in which collective action becomes possible. These systems resemble an organization equipped with several mainframe computers, which are linked together and accessed by a network of terminals. The central computers require the periphery of terminals as a condition of their own operation. Without the information resources provided by the terminals, the computers simply couldn't operate. The same is true of complex societies. They require for their functioning constant inputs of individual and collective motivation. This requirement is the soil in which social movements grow. They exploit the fact that there is a deeply ambivalent relationship between the 'centres' and 'peripheries' of complex systems, and that the centres of these systems cannot impose their power, but must exercise it in co-operation with the peripheries. This structural tension lies at the heart of complex systems, and that is why social movements are likely to continue to play a role in questioning their cultural codes and power relations.

There is another reason why social movements are unlikely to disappear. This has to do with the fact that life cannot be reduced permanently to the level of simple reproduction. Human beings want more than to eat, sleep, procreate and to stay alive. They are also motivated to transcend their given forms of existence. Awareness of this fact is growing in our times because metasocial principles, such as the Will of God or the Laws of History, are losing their grip on society. For the first time ever, society itself senses that it is contingent and in need of continuous reconstruction. Social movements feed upon this sense of contingency as well as reinforce it. They have heightened our awareness of our own ability to create and to destroy ourselves as a species. We live in an unprecedented situation. No previous form of society has exercised such power over itself. Our future now depends almost entirely on our own choices and decisions. Social life has never been so risky. That is why social movements are unlikely to disappear. They are a sign of this awesome power we have over ourselves – and of our enormous obligation to exercise this power responsibly.

IV

APPENDIX

10

Collective action as a research problem

Research and intervention

Empirical research on social movements has been marked traditionally by the legacy of dualistic thinking. In general a set of instruments and techniques has been established, to be applied to two distinct areas of analysis: to the structural variables which determine behaviour, and to the orientations, representations and ideologies of actors themselves. In addition, there have been attempts to correlate both levels of analysis. What is lacking, however, is an approach concerned with *action systems*. The lack of a methodological tradition in this area is due primarily to the difficulty of capturing these action systems 'in action'.

In anthropology and experimental and social psychology, research techniques have been developed which are capable of 'capturing' action systems in action. In sociology, with the exception of participant observation, research has only begun recently to develop qualitative methods for the observation of action systems. Recent sociological contributions emphasize a more direct intervention by the researcher in the observed field. The role of the researchers is to develop qualitative techniques capable of detecting behaviour in its formation, or stimulating the behaviour in order to observe it under experimental conditions.

As part of the methodological discussion I will refer to the research conducted under my direction between 1980 and 1984 in metropolitan Milano. The research, utilizing an experimental qualitative method, was designed to investigate the processes of forming a collective actor. This type of investigation presented a number of specific risks: 1) that the actors might refuse prolonged interaction with the researchers; 2) that the latter might become too intimately involved, both through an effective identification, and by tending to become 'demiurges' of the collective action; and 3) that investigation might turn into an instrument of social engineering, even if more illusory than affective These risks prompted the researchers to tackle new questions, such as the problem of the contractual relationship between researchers and groups; the multiple levels of analysis involved; and the possible factors influencing the relationship of researchers and actors.

Following the experimental practice of other social sciences, contemporary sociological research seems to have opened itself up towards an analysis of the qualitative and affective dimensions of individual experience.[1] In terms of the sociology of knowledge, this development corresponds to changes in the objects observed, the emergence in society of a shift towards qualitative values (such as the quality of life and the environment), individuals' need for self-realization, and the attention to the emotional dimensions of experience. In this context it is not surprising that the kind of research study on contemporary movements conducted by myself was potentially more sensitive than other studies to these new orientations.

However, the trend towards qualitative sociological research has no direct link with the analysis of social movements. Touraine is the only author who has proposed a method of research intervention in the field of social movements, but even he does not seem particularly sensitive or interested in these sweeping changes in qualitative methodology. Despite this, in the field of movements research, reference to Touraine is obligatory. His work represents an appropriate starting point for any discussion of the contributions that have shaped the development of my own techniques of empirical research.

Touraine's method of *intervention sociologique* tries to reconstruct a movement's field of conflict (Touraine 1978a, 1980b, 1982a and 1982b). Several stages are involved. First, the researchers assemble a group composed of militants from the various sectors of the movement. Second, the group is observed in a series of confrontations with its adversaries and with other social actors. The researchers' objective is to identify the issues at stake in the conflict and to communicate to the group an interpretation of its action that reflects its 'highest' possible meaning. This initiates a process of self-analysis by the group: the researcher's task is then to guide the group towards a 'conversion', that is, to the recognition (or not) of its true meaning as a social movement. The results of the self-analysis are then announced and compared within the movements at the so-called 'permanent sociology' stage.

Intervention sociologique explicitly tackled the problem of creating a research method designed specifically for examining social movements. Moreover it stressed the need to concentrate attention on the *system of relations* between the actors, drawing from this the meaning of the action. Finally, it pointed out the importance of establishing a researcher–actor relationship which is not based on mutual identification between the parties. These methodological contributions have enormous value and are not vulnerable to the method's numerous critics.[2]

The real problems, in my view, concern the method's underlying conceptual framework. The basic assumption is that there exists a 'high' meaning of the movement's action. It is the task of the sociologist, through his or her interpretation, to reveal to the movement the meaning of its action. The group in turn recognizes itself (or not) to the degree to which it becomes a movement. (One is tempted to use a capital M!) The question this method intends to answer is whether or not the phenomenon observed is *the* central movement of post-industrial society. The central problem of the method – apart from the obvious disproportion between the weight of the question and the empirical field under observation, and a certain missionary spirit on the part of the sociologist – is that it lacks the tools necessary to identify the meanings it sets out to reveal.

In a small group many levels of action operate simultaneously, ranging from affective dynamics to the possible identification of itself as a movement. Even if the group's action has a 'highest' possible meaning (and this is already problematic) what guarantees its emergence unless the 'lower' meanings have been identified or kept under control? Touraine's method pays no attention to the problems of affective dynamics. Furthermore, no instruments are provided to isolate those aspects of action which are guided by the logic of calculation or exchange. Finally, observation is centred on the group's verbal output, thereby completely ignoring the grammar of communication, the forms of interaction, and non-verbal communications.

In such circumstances there is no guarantee that the outcome of the 'conversion' is not the result of other factors that have little relation to the procedures, but are instead a function of 'weaknesses' in the conceptual apparatus. Thus one might imagine a permanent threat from the 'surfacing' of those variables not under control (especially the affective dynamic, in an *ad hoc* group set up solely for research purposes). Another serious weakness is the lack of control over the group–researcher relationship which is taken as a quasi-natural fact. In fact the relationship is founded upon the researcher's promise to reveal to the group the meaning of its action. The problem here is not, as some critics have suggested, that the researcher may manipulate the group. The real dilemma in establishing such a relationship is that it provides no group autonomy or scope for reflection on the relationship itself. Here again there is no guarantee that what is produced is what the researchers expect (e.g., the 'meaning' of the action) and not, on the contrary, the way in which the group gratifies or disappoints the researchers, wins their attention or defends itself against them.

Touraine's methodology shares the same limitations of the action research approach. In the 1950s, American action research aimed to resolve social conflicts (in particular the integration of ethnic minorities) by field-testing ways of 'improving the social climate'. By contrast, its current counterpart presents itself as a learning process involving both researcher and actor equally. The only common link between the new and old forms is a few technical aspects (inspired by Kurt Lewin's type of social psychological theory) and the direct intervention of the researcher in the field. Recent action research, with its emphasis on learning situations, was developed by the post-1968 generation of researchers trained in the atmosphere of German Critical Theory.[3] Action research aims to trigger processes of change in society and transform the field during the research process. The concept of 'emancipation' is as central as the relationship between researcher and object.

The limitations common to these approaches, including Touraine's, concern essentially two points:

1 The missionary–teacher role assigned to the researcher (evident in the concepts of 'emancipation' or 'conversion') is a respectable ethical option, but as such it is not a valid procedure or a guarantee for methodological rigour. If anything it increases the risk of confusing research with political agitation. As such, it can become a convenient outlet for the frustrations felt by intellectuals who feel 'cut off' from reality. In terms of the sociology of knowledge, it is no accident that interest in these methods is cyclical – greater during periods of social turbulence or rapid change.

2 The problem of the researcher–actor relationship is left unsolved. In the case of action research there is a simple identification, while Touraine, though insisting on the separation of roles, provides no instrument to make the relationship a conscious field of analysis. On the contrary, the problem is not even taken into consideration.

The provisional alliance

These limitations can be overcome only by making the relationship between researchers and actors itself an object of analysis,[4] and by defining the researcher's specific role.[5] The solution to these shortcomings depends upon the recognition of a number of arguments, which in turn can guide the development of a method for analysing the formation of collective action.

1 We cannot study social action as a mere 'thing'. Action is a process whose meanings are constructed through interaction. Hence the point is not that the actors themselves *are* the object of analysis; rather, they *produce* the object of analysis and supply its meanings. The researcher who comes into contact with the field activates a process in which the actors play as significant a role as he or she does. In other words, the researcher–actor relationship is not a problem external to the research.

2 The process of self-reflection is distinct from action. There is

a distance between action and its meaning. The size of the gap depends on the permanent tension between actor and system. The system is something more than the sum of its parts, but it is constituted by their interaction. Actors are therefore always part of a system of relations that gives meaning to their action, but actors also contribute to this definition. Knowledge of the relations of the system is therefore a necessary resource for social actors maximizing the effectiveness of their actions.

3 At this point the relationship between researcher and actor can take the form of a *contractual relationship*. Both parties control specific resources. The researcher possesses 'know-how', consisting of a research hypothesis and techniques which cannot be verified or utilized without the participation of the actors. Meanwhile actors exercise control over action and its meanings, but they also require reflective knowledge to increase their potential for action: here they may value the researcher's analysis of their action. The relationship is thus one of interdependence, but not of coinciding or overlapping roles. Indeed, this difference in roles – declared and understood mutually – is the only element that justifies the provisional alliance between the two parties. It is the only factor that gives meaning to the *contract*.

The contract is therefore founded on a temporary convergence of two demands: the scientific objectives of the researcher; and the actors' need to respond to problems arising from their social practice. The researcher offers information resulting from the application of concepts and techniques; the actors offer information about their own action. On this basis an exchange is possible which is neither authoritarian nor instrumental.

4 The contract serves to safeguard the distance that exists between the parties – their non-identification. Each pursues a different goal: the researcher pursues the scientific (or personal, or professional, or political) interests that motivates his or her work; the actors want to learn something about their activities to help them increase their potential for action. The distance is never fixed, but it must be reassessed continually by treating the researcher–actor relationship as a constant object of analysis. Each side thereby maintains control over, and responsibility for, its investment in the relationship. Only in this way can one

guarantee sufficient transparency to a relationship that is temporary and open permanently to revision. When it ends both parties can make use of the results for their own respective purposes.

Two further problems concerning the distance between researcher and actor still have to be considered because they have methodological implications for any research practice based on a direct interaction between actors and researchers. These include, first, the role of interactive and communicative processes in which face to face contact with small groups is involved; and, second, the 'experimental' character of a research situation that separates the actors from the 'natural' conditions of their action. In terms of the first problem, communications are an important level of analysis which cannot be ignored by the research procedures. This is because communications determine the *quality* of the information gathered: we know, for example, how similar verbal content in a situation of interaction can assume quite different meanings depending on the emotional, interactive and gestures through which it is expressed.[6]

The second problem concerns the inherent artificiality of the research context: in Touraine's or in action research methods the framework is intended to recreate 'natural' conditions. These methods require the group to act as if it were in the real world; but this is clearly in sharp contrast to the contrived nature of the experimental situation.

It seems impossible to avoid this problem without making an *explicit break* with the 'natural' situation, one that allows the group to assume the experimental framework as its field of interaction, without, however, annulling the logic of its action. In other words we need to shift our observation from the *contents* (which can only partly reflect the group's actual behaviour) on to the *process* of action which lies beneath the content.[7]

A research process

The provisional alliance between researcher and social actors underlies the procedures employed during the research conducted in the Milano area. Before discussing the problems associated with a contractual relationship between researcher and actors, I shall summarize the various stages of the Milano project.

1 The first stage of the project involved conducting a survey to identify and locate four movement networks: the youth, women's, ecological and neo-religious movements. In-depth interviews were then carried out with all groups who had shown empirical evidence of their membership in the network. The interviews, conducted with one or more core members of the group (or sometimes with the entire group), aimed to gather information on the group's history, composition, structure and forms of action. They also served to select one 'natural' group from each network for the experimental part of the research. This meant determining the characteristics of the various groups, their position in relation to the network as a whole and their eventual willingness and/or conditions of participation in the research proposal. This information also served to single out those groups which, by their character or willingness to co-operate, could be used for the network debates (or constructed groups, see below).

2 On the basis of this information, the second stage involved choosing one group from each network. With this group we proceeded to the 'laboratory' stage. The tendency was to choose a group occupying a central position in the movement as a whole. If a movement area had polarized or dispersed, then the polar positions were chosen.

It was decided to target research at the grass roots level rather than on the more complex structures of the movement. This focus brought out more clearly the points of tension and plurality of meanings within the movement. These dimensions tended to be obscured by the unifying ideology of the organizations, where the need for integration is paramount. Meanwhile these basic groups were compared easily with other more structured forms and with other definitions of the movement by, for instance, spokespersons, 'politicians' and observers.

Working with 'natural' groups seemed to temper the artificiality of the laboratory situation, enabling actors to refer to a more or less consolidated collective identity. A particular group always has a separate existence beyond the objectives of the research allowing it to retain, within the experimental situation, a certain autonomy (and at times opaqueness) in its normal functioning.

This procedure is not without its risks. While a particular group may not reflect accurately the network as a whole, it also can resist the experimental situation (i.e., remain opaque) through recourse to well-practiced rituals, complicity over internal codes and hidden rules. But these limitations can be overcome by comparing information gathered in the natural group with that on the rest of the movement and by special group-leading and observation techniques. In any case, the risks are minor compared to those involved with purpose-built research groups. Touraine's experimental groups, for example, are formed with militants from different organizations within the movement, and are artificially submitted to prolonged interaction. This prolonged interaction tends to encourage a group identity founded on affective relations generated by the experimental situation. In Touraine's method the group exists solely as a basis for research and, regardless of the origins of the individuals, this produces internal dynamics that distort significantly the quality of the interaction.

The idea of comparing differences and tensions within the movement nevertheless seemed interesting. Thus we decided to set up, alongside the natural group, a series of network debates, assembling groups composed of activists from different areas of the movement. Interaction was, however, kept brief (one session) and discussion focused on one specific theme. Several debates were held and the composition of the group changed on each occasion. In this way we hoped to practically eliminate the influence of affective dynamics on group interaction, by concentrating discussion each time on a problem crucial for the identity of the network.

3 Drafting a contract with the basic research groups was a particularly delicate stage. As outlined above, the researcher's objective was to gather – through observation and recording – a mass of information on group behaviour for subsequent analysis. For the actors, meanwhile, interest in the experience (aside from the motives specific to each group) lay in its offering an opportunity for self-reflection. Where a group's collective

identity was either forming (as in the ecological and neo-religious groups) or undergoing restructuring (as in the youth and women's movement), there was a breathing space for discussion which was not immediately linked to action, and which represented a valuable and desirable resource for both groups and individuals.

It was important, however, that the research be presented as an open space, in which the objectives of researchers and actors could meet without coinciding. It also required the possibility for both parties to retain responsibility for their respective investments in the experience. The objectives of the researchers and actors were negotiated at the outset and remained negotiable throughout the experience. The process of self-reflection was not the object of the research. It was in part a methodological tool for gathering information on the object under investigation, i.e., the process of forming and maintaining a collective identity. And in part the process of self-reflection formed the means of exchange for a contractual agreement with the group.

The researchers have no message for the movements. The results of their investigations are placed at the disposal of the participant groups in two ways: first, by direct feedback during the course of the research and, second, through scientific and cultural communications, available to any reader of ordinary scientific output or to the general public.

4 The experimental stage (to be discussed in detail below) entailed a series of videotaped encounters. The usual sequence was to expose the group to certain stimuli, to select the most significant passages and then to play these back to the group as new input. In a final 'feedback' session the researchers presented an edited montage of what the group had produced.

5 The last stage of the research consisted in analysing and comparing the videotaped material with the other information gathered (interviews and documents concerning the movements, plus data on each movement's activity in Italy and abroad). The interpretation of the video material took into account the various levels of meaning at issue. Precisely because the group simultaneously had different functions – as part of a larger movement; as a market for a range of interests in which

processes of exchange and decision operate; as a role system; as a network of affective relations; and as a sum of individual motivations – it was necessary to adopt different levels of observation. This included observing non-verbal communication; affective interaction; alliances and conflicts; the use of language; and the motivational aspects of individual behaviour. The alternation between micro- and macroanalysis was adopted according to the researchers' theoretical hypothesis.

In terms of the procedures adopted in the experimental stage, the groups were invited to participate in a series of sessions in a specially prepared environment. This was an ordinary assembly room with seats arranged in a semi-circle around a researcher who conducted the session. An operator of a mobile VTR recorded the sitting on videotape. Two other researchers, visible but out of shot, acted as observers, taking notes on both the verbal and non-verbal interactions. The videotape followed the speaker, occasinally providing a panoramic view of the group.

Two types of stimulus situations were introduced: first, the *who we are* situation – the group was asked to define itself. The techniques used attempted to draw out the various faces of group identity of the movement to which they belong; second, the *who you are* situation – the group was presented with definitions from outside itself.

At each stage a feedback session was conducted in which the group was shown an edited version of the recorded material selected according to the observation levels mentioned above. The playback served as a stimulus for further discussion and the feedback session was itself videotaped. There was a final feedback session recapitulating the entire experience and allowing the participants to take stock.

Let us look now at the various stages in more detail.

1 The *who we are* phase is divided into three parts: memory, self-representation and how:

a) In terms of *memory* we are not so much interested in factual content (which can be acquired by other means) as in locating the multiplicity of interacting and contradictory elements – representations, actors, interests and roles – constituting the reality of collective identity. The group abandons the harmony and cohesion of its customary representations and begins to manifest itself as an action system. The stimuli in this phase are designed to multiply the voices and points of view through which the history of the group (the persons, events and places) can be told.

b) For the *self-representation* stage imaginary situations are proposed and the group is encouraged to simulate and play games with its identity. Again the object of this stage is to draw out the various components – the systems of exchange and opposition – that make up the collective identity. The game-playing situation and the reference to a medium which projects the group identity breaks down the more explicitly ideological self-image of the group and once again creates a puzzle around its meaning. To begin with, the context for simulation moves from highly exaggerated to more realistic situations. In the imaginary situations, the group is asked to confront situations of adversity and to make choices. The games also allow the group to test their decision-making procedures, exposing the mechanisms through which leadership and other roles are established. As the imaginary situations become more realistic so also do the external constraints on group action. This 'conical' progression is of the utmost importance because the group is in a position to experience the development of its own self-definition as a group when faced with uncertainty under different circumstances.

c) The *how* phase consists in feeding back to the group the terms it has used to define itself. Significant or recurring terms describing the group or its action are extracted from the taped recordings. From this list of terms actors are asked to indicate those terms which best represent the positive and negative qualities of group action. Each participant is then invited to use his or her chosen words to talk about the group. The degree of convergence or divergence of choices serves to stimulate discussion within the group. The researcher meanwhile reintroduces the remaining terms, which invariably mask submerged difficulties, and asks the group to make use of them.

The three sessions were followed by the first playback, which the group was asked to discuss.

2 In the *who you are* stage the group compares itself with the

video pre-recorded definitions proposed by three types of outsiders: 'spokespersons', i.e., people who speak on behalf of the movement; 'observers', i.e., people such as journalists who are close to the movement but not involved directly; and by 'adversaries'.

This is followed by a second playback of material from the *who you are* phase. Finally, the group is shown a montage of material covering all the previous sessions, including discussions of the intermediate playbacks. The entire experience involves eight sessions, each lasting three hours.

Some final clarifying remarks about the research process.

1 The decision to use videotape arose out of a need to record group behaviour as efficiently as possible with the minimum loss of information. In addition, video is an ideal means for providing feedback. However the use of video inevitably implies selectivity in framing and content, and therefore also in the information gathered. One method of ensuring a more or less consistent bias was to use the same professional video operator throughout, with instructions to film the speaker as far as possible. The other corrective measure was the presence of two observers. One attempts to keep the most faithful and complete record possible of the verbal exchanges, noting also the direction of communication and the issues around which discussion is concentrated. The other observes and records several elements of non-verbal communication of the participants (such as their spatial distribution, dress, flow of speech and patterns of silence, positions, facial expressions, glances and gestures).

2 Apart from indirect references by the participants, their observable leadership models, and certain ways in which the interaction is structured, the organizational characteristics of the natural group cannot emerge satisfactorily in an experimental situation. The experimental context must therefore be supplemented with participant observation of the group in its natural environment. The research is thus completed by attendance, before and after the laboratory work, at various group meetings. Movements as a whole are observed at demonstrations and other public mobilizations.

3 Network debates using constructed groups are a valuable

source of additional information. For example, they provide information on the structure of the movement and offer an overview of its ideological spectrum. However these purpose-built groups can only function as 'movement groups' as long as their interpersonal dynamics do not predominate. This explains the decision noted above to limit them to single sessions focusing only on one topic. Work with the natural groups reveals the range of problems each movement confronts when constructing its collective identity. Thus for each network we devised a stimulus, which served as a topic of debate and an hypothesis for testing the structure of the movement. The groups were assembled by taking the one or two militants from each group who made themselves available during the preliminary survey (hence always core group members). For each area three groups were prepared with three respective topics: one based on a central problem revealed during the *who we are* stage with the natural group; and two from the *who you are* phase (one from a 'spokesperson' or 'observer' and one from an 'adversary'). The participants changed with each session, which lasted around three hours.

Actors and analysts

We can now discuss the methodological problems emanating from a research process based on a direct contractual relationship between actors and analysts.

In this type of a research project there are no preliminary or '*instrumental*' stages, i.e., phases which instrumentalize the actors for the purposes of data-gathering. From the outset, contacts during the pre-experimental phase serve a dual purpose: first, to collate data on the groups belonging to the movement; and second, to present the research project to potential participants and to acquire the information needed to select the natural group and the individuals for the constructed groups. This double objective results in a particularly delicate situation: to keep contact within the limits of the first objective without compromising the second. The problem is to obtain the necessary data without falsifying the nature of the relationship.

At the same time there is the need to control the field of assessment which remains the professional responsibility of the research team.

This means that the information must be obtained 'honestly', without extortion or false pretences, and with the research objectives declared openly. Similarly, the information concerning the research must be congruent with the level of interaction. Thus the very first contacts already contain elements of the second objective and are therefore crucial to the success of any future relationship. In this sense the problem is to assess the extent of the group's need for self-reflection and to furnish enough information to transform this need into an attitude of co-operation. Much of the information transmitted consists in the behaviour of the researchers themselves; this behaviour reveals the logic that guides the relationship throughout.

The approach adopted therefore involved channelling back, from the outset, analysis to the contact group in exchange for the information it provides. In this way the relationship may be seen to terminate on each occasion with a balanced exchange that leaves nothing hanging in the air, but which at the same time allows room for contact to be resumed at a later stage. Thus the first contacts already anticipate the kind of research relationship and offer a concrete example of it. However, they do not strain the group's willingness to co-operate at any given stage, but remain respectful of the existing quality of interaction. The openness of the exchange removes all trace of instrumental 'exploitation' from the data-gathering process. It also offers the opportunity from the beginning for a contract that may be successively renegotiated into its final form (through participation in the research) or, alternatively, terminated at an earlier stage without leaving loose ends.

Consistent with this orientation, contacts with the networks follow a set sequence of steps leading to the experimental stage: informal contact, in-depth interviews, and then the researcher's decision to effect or abandon the relationship on the basis of what has emerged so far. The invitation to participate at the experimental stage depends on the assessment of both the information already obtained and the nature of the conditions specified by the participants. Out of this comes the choice of the natural group and the selection of participants for the constructed groups. This is followed by the contract stage, which involves a detailed presentation of the contents of the research proposal, and decisions about both the environment in which it is to take place and the organizational forms to be adopted. In reality none of these phases is truly 'preliminary' because each one constitutes an integral part of the research and its overall logic.

Another problem linked with a research method based on a contractual relationship between actors and analysts concerns the role of feedback. Feedback remains a constant feature of the entire experimental process. It is manifested most explicitly during the video playback phases, but the exchange of information is a permanent feature of the relationship between the researcher and the group. At the end of every session, both with the natural groups and the network debates (and occassionally during the sessions themselves), the research leader communicates the results of his or her observations of the session. What these feedbacks have in common is the attention given to the *how and not to the why*: the information delivered verbally plays virtually the same role as the video playbacks. That is to say, it concerns the phenomenological elements of behaviour, which are not subject to causal explanation. Thus every feedback serves as a stimulus for self-examination which makes visible each time the contract between the two parties. During the final feedback the group gives its impressions and assessments of its experience.

The contract between the two parties allows the research procedures to distinguish between two distinct levels of analysis: first, the *phenomenological* level during the course of the experience; and second, the *interpretative* level which comes after the experiment.

During the experimental phase both verbal feedback and visual playbacks are designed to nourish self-reflection, leaving the group complete freedom to use these stimuli as it pleases. Obviously, the choice of observations and images to be fed back cannot be entirely neutral; out of necessity it involves some subjective criteria. But this does not mean employing a series of *causal hypotheses* about the group's action – that is, an emphasis on *why* the group acts in certain ways. Rather, it relies upon a *phenomenological hypothesis* about the role played by particular types of behaviour in structuring the *Gestalt* – that is, in giving coherence to group and/or individual action. Here the question is *how* the group acts. In other words, the concern is with how the behaviour is structured and what gives the group its collective character. Here we might profitably use the term *systems of relevance* (Schutz, 1975). Attention shifts from the causes of behaviour to its regularity, pauses and rhythms. What is observed and fed back is conduct which is concentrated or diffused around certain nodes, the breaks and silences in the flow of communication, the capacity for definition, and the position of individual action and the single events in the system of action.[8]

This non-causal, non-interpretative orientation frees the researcher from any function as 'midwife' of the movement's meaning. At the strictly methodological level, this orientation also allows the researcher to escape the circularity inherent in research-intervention methods. In these methods researchers continue to speak of *research* and not of political agitation or militancy, since it is assumed that the goal of intervention is knowledge of the movement's meaning. Indeed it is presumed that any change in the actors must derive directly from the introduction of this knowledge. However, a vicious circle is always produced: if the observer modifies the field under observation, without the tools necessary to control such changes, then his or her knowledge will be worthless. Nothing can assure the researcher that what is observed is attributable to the group and not instead to his or her *input*, or to chance. Knowledge generates action and the action generates knowledge.

This dilemma is evident in Touraine's method of *intervention sociologique*. He attempts, through observation of the group in an experimental context, to discover the 'highest possible meaning' of the movement. One of the fundamental points in this experience is the 'conversion', that is, the response of the group to the interpretative hypothesis proposed by the researcher. The result of this conversion – the acceptance or rejection of the proposed interpretation – is itself employed to establish the 'meaning' of the movement, i.e., to establish the basis for the research findings. But nothing can guarantee that the outcome of the conversion corresponds to the 'meaning' of the group's action and not instead to the content introduced by the researcher.

Unlike some moralistic critics (see note 2), I am not accusing Touraine of manipulation. This type of criticism implies that the groups in question are unable to defend themselves against the pressures exerted by the researchers. The problem is of a totally different character, and resides on the epistemological plane. What the researcher discovers about the 'meaning' of the movement depends upon what he or she contributes. In this 'constructed' situation, where the purpose of the study is to elicit the 'meaning' of the movement, the researcher adopts a stimulus which has the same character as the thing to be discovered. The stimulus is therefore indistinguishable from its effects. The terms of the experiment are turned on their heads – the stimulus becomes simultaneously both cause and effect. The observed behaviour and the interpretation of the meanings of the movement cannot be interpreted properly as products of group action. At best they may be seen as the result of the interaction with the researcher's interpretative hypothesis. The fact that the group recognizes itself (or not) in the hypothesis tells us nothing about the 'meaning' of its action, but only about how close, in cultural or affective terms, the group stands in relation to the researcher.

The non-interpretative approach (here I am referring only to the experimental phase) would seem to offer an escape route from the vicious circle inherent in any experimental situation where the observed field is modified by the observer and by uncontrolled stimuli. By introducing phenomenological stimuli (the *how* feedback), self-examination modifies the field of resources and constraints in which the group acts, or better, it modifies the perception of this field. The group redefines the opportunities and limits of its action and makes its decisions not on the basis of *contents* – specific orientations proposed by the researchers – but on the basis of a redefinition of the field prompted by the feedback process.

This redefinition process remains under the control of the group. It evolves in the experimental situation without receiving any value-laden 'hints' or suggestions about the direction it is taking or should take. Of course, the observed field also changes here, as with any situation entailing a direct interaction between researcher and actor. But in this case we can, to a reasonable extent, control the effects of the stimulus and distinguish between what the group produces and what the researchers introduce. Ideally, the *how* feedback resembles an open forum, allowing the group the freedom to redefine its field of action as it proceeds by incorporating the contents produced throughout the experience by the group itself. In other words, this type of experimental framework permits us to observe the formation and definition of group action as it develops. The results of the experiment, i.e., the videotaped material, may thus be interpreted as a series of reports on the ways in which the group – by redefining autonomously its field of action through self-reflection – constructs, sustains or modifies its collective identity.

At this juncture the role of *interpretative analysis* – performed on the recorded material at the end of the experimental stage – becomes clearer. Interaction with the group, and thus the basis of the experiment's validity, are no longer at stake. Causal hypotheses can now be applied to the records obtained to explain the various levels of behaviour by relating them to actor/movement variables or to a wider context.

The failure of current research to distinguish between the content and the process of the observed action generates a third methodological problem concerning research in an artificial situation. To isolate a group from its natural 'habitat' for the purpose of research implies necessarily creating an artificial situation. We cannot begin with a naïve assumption about the 'naturalness' of observed group behaviour. Rather, we must develop and improve upon the artificial situation to make it capable of supplying the required information. This occurs only if both researchers and actors accept the experimental framework as the field in which their exchanges take place. For the actors this means accepting the contrived context as a condition of the process of self-reflection, i.e., as a means of acquiring the information resources they seek. For the researchers it certainly does not imply producing a situation which resembles reality; on the contrary, it means giving explicit emphasis to its artificial character. This entails creating a context capable of activating and revealing the logic of the action hidden behind the specific content, and at the same time distributing among the actors the information that motivates their investment.

The artificiality of the research experience affects the group in several ways. First, the stimuli employed and the use made of the video recordings (e.g., playbacks):

a) changes the object of the group's attention and facilitates different perspectives of the field;

b) heightens thereby the perception of the resources and limits of action as well as exposes contradictions and crises;

c) stimulates internal interaction, and the circulation and exchange of information (on more than one occasion actors were heard to say: 'This is the first time we've talked about these issues.');

d) accelerates the group's normal rhythms: one of the most delicate problems in the laboratory experience is that the acceleration may be too fast for the group's rate of development. The only guarantee against this possibility is the contract, that is, the opportunity for the group to measure its involvement and set the pace of its own evolution; and

e) feeds the aspect of ritual and play, more than occurs under 'natural' conditions.

Second, the self-reflective character of the procedures encourages the group to stand back from and to examine its ordinary action. The practice of self-reflection has a cumulative effect, building gradually upon itself as new elements are acquired and absorbed. The group changes and redefines itself throughout the entire experience. Several common characteristics apply to all the groups that participated in the experimental phase: a) they acquire information which was unavailable previously or was not in circulation among the members; b) the group's field of action alters between the first and the last sessions; c) they become conscious of the difference between group action in an experimental situation and action in the real world; and d) they recognize the effects of the experience (this was viewed positively by all participants).

Third, the research experience is marked by the absence of the 'outside world' which the groups confront in everyday life. In the experimental situation the group is isolated from the external conditions against which it normally measures its action. To reconstruct the external conditions in the laboratory is to attempt the impossible, but there remains the problem of re-creating the system of relations in which the actor is involved. Touraine's solution of physically producing interlocutors for the group to interact with is open to two main objections.

The first is methodological. It consists in the fact that in face to face interaction personal qualities and affective dynamics tend to prevail over the 'role' the interlocutor is supposed to fulfil for the group. What one observes therefore is largely the group's interaction with person X and not its relations with, for example, an adversary in the social field.

The second objection, of a theoretical nature, is that the adversaries of social conflicts in highly differentiated systems never meet face to face. In complex societies social relations are mediated by the opaqueness and complexity of institutional apparatuses.

In our research project the 'outside' was represented by the researchers and the pre-recorded interviews which were presented to the group during the *who you are* stage. Since the researchers belong to a scientific institution often identified with the establishment, the researcher–group relationship may be read as an indicator of relations with the outside world. The group has direct relations with its immediate environment and only 'systemic' relations with the wider world. Thus the individuals selected for the interviews – here there was a degree of abitrariness which depended upon the researcher's opportunities and decisions – represented the group's symbolic field of reference.

The artificiality of the experimental context poses two problems: first, how to encourage the participants to take part in and accept the conditions and rules of the experiment; and second, how to measure the distance or the 'distortion' of the artificial situation from the 'natural' situation.

The first problem is one of motivation. In our research model the contract between researchers and actors is the only instrument for motivating the participants. In other words, there is no assurance that the experimental stage will produce the expected results. Indeed if the contract is open constantly to review, the outcome will depend entirely on the investment of the 'partners'. The information received by the researchers does not follow automatically from the stimuli employed, but from the investment of the actors and their willingness to play the game. By contrast, the feedback received by the actors is not dependent upon the a priori knowledge of the researchers, but on what the group itself is capable of producing within the experimental context.

A group that is reticent or unwilling to have its action questioned soon reaches an impasse: the conditions of the research are such that the proceedings can be terminated at any given moment. This situation never arose with any of the groups, but the degree of involvement varied from one area to another. The natural group from the youth movement was an example: for reasons related to the poverty of internal resources (such as educational level and professional skills) and the anti-institutional culture of the movement, this group showed the most difficulty in adjusting to the artificial research context as a field of action.

This exemplifies another point concerning the researcher–group relationship. In this relationship there is no imbalance of power, but only a diversity of resources. If the researchers have control over certain aspects of the experimental situation, then the group in effect possesses very extensive powers of veto. The researcher's task (or power) consists of proposing stimuli and of selecting the video footage to be played back to the group. But the discussions at the end of the sessions and the initial presentations of the simulations (which, however, do not reveal the key to the game) reduce continually the researcher's control. Meanwhile the group is free, merely by absenting itself, to cancel at any moment the entire investment of time and materials made by the researchers. Similarly, the group is always in a position to consciously falsify the information.

A final problem concerns the 'distortion' of the results by the artificial context. Stating the problem in this way is obviously misguided. The research situation is *intentionally* artificial – there is no question of comparing it with a 'natural' situation. The experimental context is designed to provide a field in which the group can produce and redefine its action through self-examination. The real dilemma therefore consists in eliminating (as far as possible) any interference capable of altering the object of observation, i.e., the logic of collective action within a movement. Stimuli are used to focus the group's attention on its sociological self-definition: the only real threat to the accuracy of the results is that the encounter may turn into an affective relationship or assume a therapeutic dimension.

A fundamental factor preventing this possibility was the control exercised over the actor–researcher relationship. During the research much of the researchers' energies were directed at this task. To this end, a series of instruments was adopted:

1 training of the research team, which involved the team using itself as an object of self-analysis. Without turning it into a therapeutic situation, and under the direction of a qualified external supervisor, the researchers experimented on themselves with some of the instruments later used with the groups. Each stage of the research – initial contact with the groups, negotiation of the contract, observation of the sessions, selection of video footage, etc. – required the specific skills of the researchers. Steps were therefore taken to measure the researchers' different capacities, and to heighten awareness of these differences within the research team itself. In this way a training procedure was tailored to the study of interaction, thus minimizing the effects of the various researchers' individual perceptions or affective qualities;

2 to ensure uniformity in the style and manner of proposing stimuli or presenting feedback, one person – with clinical qualifications, training and experience – was chosen to lead the sessions;

3 analysis of the researcher–group relationship. This level of observation was fundamental for maintaining the exchanges within the boundaries of the established sociological context. At the initial contact stage the researchers had to analyse the group's demands, while at the same time remaining conscious of their own involvement. For instance, it was discovered that many difficulties arise from the researchers' own fears and assumptions, rather than from real resistance on the part of the groups, who in fact proved willing and interested in proceeding

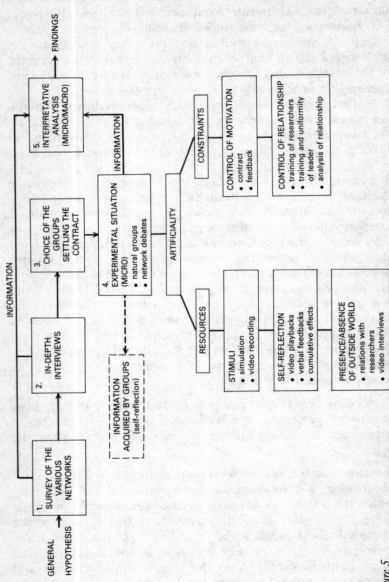

Figure 5

with the relationship. At the experimental stage a designated period of time was devoted regularly to analysing how the sessions had been conducted as well as the affective dimensions of the relationship.

Figure 5 presents an overall model of the research procedure and the problems I have discussed. In conclusion, it can be claimed that the experimental situation was kept within the limits of the contract and concentrated on the strictly sociological level of group action – as required by the original objectives of the research. By exerting a reasonable level of control over the effects of the stimuli introduced, and by reducing – if not eliminating completely – the influence of other variables, the research model was capable of reconstructing the intermediate level of action between the system and the actors, between the conditions and the actions, in which the formation of a collective actor takes place.

Notes and references

1 On the comparison between qualitative and quantitative methods and on the search for new research models in the social sciences see Bulmer (1981); Morgan (1983); Zeller and Carmines (1980) and Mehan (1982). For a general discussion of qualitative orientations and research methods see Bogdan, Taylor (1975) and Schwartz, Jacobs (1980). On the 'creative' aspect of this type of research see Morris (1977); Eriksson (1978); and Van Maanen (1982).

Many experimental approaches explore new ways of solving new problems: from 'clinical sociology' which applies clinical methods to observation and the handling of groups (Glassner and Freedman 1979), to 'behavioural sociology', which applies the premises of behaviourism to analysis and intervention on groups (with the intention of social engineering, but sometimes with interesting experimental solutions); see Burgess and Bushell (1969); Kunkel (1975); Hamblin and Kunkel (1977); and Michaels and Green (1978).

Apart from essential contributions by Goffman (1967, 1969, 1971, 1974) and ethnomethodology, renewed interest in the individual, intimate, dimension of behaviour is suggested by the new role of biographical research in sociology. Among the numerous contributors in this area see Chevalier (1979); Williams (1978); and Cavallaro (1981). For an overview of this development see Ferrarotti (1981) and Bertaux (1981). In the area of the re-evaluation of the emotional aspects of individual behaviour are approaches such as 'existential sociology' (Douglas and Johnson, 1977) and the 'sociology of emotions' (Kemper, 1978; Schott, 1979). For a critique of these approaches see Bogart (1977).

2 See Touraine (1978, 1980, 1982a). For a critical discussion of Touraine's method see Amiot (1980); and Minguet (1980). See also the contributions of Melucci and others in Touraine (1982b).

3 See in particular Moser (1977); and Lukesch and Zecha (1978). For a discussion of action research see Oquist (1978); Exner (1981); and Lerbet (1980). See also the 'militant' research techniques applied to the movements evident, for example, in the 'laboratories of the future' (Jungk, 1978), a kind of collective brainstorming through which a social group projects in utopian form the solution to a problem. Following the same direction are certain applications in France of *socioanalyse*, which is linked with post-1968 *gauchiste* culture (see note 4).

4 The concern with the relationship between researchers and actors is broached by institutional analysis or socio-analysis. This is a current of analysis and intervention in institutions developed primarily in France by Lapassade (1970, 1971) and Lourau (1969, 1973), with connections to psychosocial intervention and institutional psychotherapy. The fields of application are above all complex organizations, educational and welfare structures, and voluntary associations. For a summary see Hess (1975, 1981). Institutional analysis still maintains a missionary–teacher orientation: the institutions tend to disguise the institutional act that founded them and the task of analysis is therefore to reveal the 'hidden energy' that is opposed to the crystallization of the institutions. The more interesting aspects instead lie with the criteria of intervention: a) analysis of the demand; b) self-management of the applicant; c) the rule of complete freedom of expression; d) the analysis of the role and implications of the analyst/researcher; and e) the identification or construction of analysts, who provoke contradictions in the organizations so as to reveal their deeper logic.

5 The work of Crozier (Crozier and Friedberg, 1977) provides some useful insights. His studies on actors' behaviour in organizational situations are based on strategic analysis. However irrational and contradictory it might appear, actors' behaviour in fact corresponds to an intrinsic rationality, to strategies that the actors set in motion within the system of relations to which they belong. The researcher alternates between two poles: the critical position of external observer and the 'viewpoint' of the actors within the field.

6 Symbolic interactionism and ethnomethodology on the one hand, and on the other hand the Palo Alto school which draws upon Bateson's work, signalled an irreversible step forward that renders obsolete any qualitative research method which ignores communicative processes. For the initial studies on the development of ethnomethodology see Garfinkel (1967); Garfinkel and Sachs (1970); and Cicourel (1964, 1974). For a discussion of

the debates within the field of ethnomethodology see Pfohl (1975); Mehan and Wood (1975) and Cicourel (1981). A discussion of the contributions made by ethnomethodology to the field of research is found in Zimmermann (1979); O'Keefe (1979) and Giglioli and Dal Lago (1983). On the Palo Alto school see Watzlawick *et al.* (1967) and Watzlawick *et al.* (1970).

7 Simulations and games can provide stimuli that activate real relationships, which are at the same time bound by the limits of the experimental framework and the play fiction. For a theoretical discussion of simulation and games in sociology see Dal Lago (1978); Coleman (1969); Stein Greenblat (1971); Hamburger (1979) and Inbar and Stoll (1972). Problems related to the construction and assessment of games are discussed in Megarry (1977) and Dukes and Waller (1976). On specific applications, presentations and the analysis of games see Gamson (1971); Geiger (1975); Laver (1979); Stadsklev (1975); Muir (1979); and Stein-Greenblat and Duke (1982).

8 Besides phenomenology, the reference is obvious here to Gestalt theory of perception (Köhler, 1947) and to its application to the study of communication and relationships during the last twenty years. Though divergent in many respects, both the Palo Alto school (Watzlawick *et al.* 1967) and Fritz Perls (1976) share a Gestaltic, phenomenological approach, more concerned with process than with causes.

Bibliography

Agamben, G.
   1978 *Infanzia e storia*, Torino, Einaudi.

Alberoni, F.
   1977 *Movimento e Istituzione*, Bologna: Il Mulino.
   1981a *Movimento e Istituzione*, Bologna, Il Mulino. (new edition)
   1981b *Le ragioni del bene e del male*, Milano, Garzanti.
   1982 *L'albero della vita*, Milano, Garzanti.

Amiot, M., Touraine, A.
   1980 'L'intervention sociologique, la science et la prophetie', *Sociologie du travail*, XX no 4.

Arditti, R., Duelli Klein, R., Minden, S.
   1984 *Test-Tube Women: What Future for Motherhood*, London, Routledge and Kegan Paul.

Attali, J.
   1977 *L'ordre cannibale. Vie et mort de la medecine*, Paris, B. Grasset.

Baffoy, T.
   1978 'Les sectes totalitaires', *Esprit*, no. 1.

Baudrillard, J.
   1979 *Lo scambio simbolico e la morte*, Milano, Feltrinelli.

Baumgartner, E.
   1983 'L'identita nel cambiamento', Quaderni del Dipartimento di Politca Sociale, University of Trento.

Bejin, A., Pollak, M.
   1977 'La rationalisation de la sexualité', *Cahiers Internationaux de Sociologie*, 62, no. 1.

Bendix, Reinhard
   1964 *Nation-Building and Citizenship*, New York: Wiley.
   1978 *Kings or People*, Berkeley, University of California Press.

BIBLIOGRAPHY

Berger, P.L., Berger, B., Kellner, H.
1979 *The Homeless Mind*, Harmondsworth, Penguin Books.

Bertaux, D. (ed.)
1981 *Biography and Society. The Life History Approach in the Social Sciences*, Beverly Hills, Sage.

Beywl, W., Nelles, W.
1983 'New Self-Organizations', Paper presented at the 6th EGOS Colloquium, Florence, November.

Bianchi, M., Mormino, M.
1984 'Militanti di sé stesse', in A. Melucci (Ed.), *Altri Codici*, Bologna, Il Mulino.

Biorcio, R., Lodi, G.
1983 *La sfida verde*, Padova, Liviana.

Bogart, R.W.
1977 'A Critique of Existential Sociology', *Social Research*, no. 2.

Bogdan, R., Taylor, S.J.
1975 *Introduction to Qualitative Research Methods*, New York, Wiley.

Bourdieu, P.
1979 *La distinction*, Ed. de Minuit, Paris.
1982 *Ce que parler veut dire*, Paris, Fayard.

Brand, K.W. (ed.)
1985 *Neue soziale Bewegungen in Westeuropa and den USA*, Frankfurt, Campus Verlag.

Breines, W.
1982 *Community and Organization in the New Left 1962–1968: The Great Refusal*, New York, Praeger.

Brown, M. H., Hosking, D. M.
1984 'Distributed leadership and skilled performance as successful organization in social movements.' Paper presented at the 'Egos Working Group on New Social Movements.' Aarhus, August 27–29.

Bruckner, P., Finkielkraut, A.
1977 *Le nouveau desordre amoureux*, Paris, Seuil.

Bulmer, M.
1981 *Social Research Ethics*, New York, MacMillan.

Burgess, R.L., Bushell, D. (Ed.)
1969 *Behavioral Sociology*, New York, Columbia University Press.

Calabrò, A.R., Grasso, L.
1985 *Dal movimento femminista al femminismo diffuso*, Milano, Angeli.

263

Capra, F.
  1982 *The Turning Point. Science, Society and the Rising Culture*, New York, Simon and Schuster.

Carlstein, T., Parkes, D., Thrift, N. (Eds.)
  1978 *Human Activity and Time Geography*, New York, J. Wiley.

Castel, F., Castel, R., Lovell, A.
  1979 *La société psychiatrique avancée*, Paris, Grasset.

Castel, R.
  1976 *L'ordre psychiatrique*, Paris, Ed. de Minuit.
  1981 *La question des risques*, Paris, Ed. de Minuit.

Castells, M.
  1983 *The City and the Grassroots*, Berkeley, University of California Press.

Cavallaro, R.
  1981 'L'individuo e il gruppo. Riflessioni sul metodo biografico', *Sociologia*, 15, no. 1.

Cavalli, A. (Ed.)
  1985 *Il tempo dei giovani*, Bologna, Il Mulino.

Chambers, I.
  1985 *Urban Rhythms. Pop Music and Popular Culture*, London, MacMillan.

Cherfas, J.
  1982 *Man Made Life*, Oxford, Blackwell.

Cherniss, C.
  1980 *Staff Burnout. Job Stress in the Human Service*, Beverly Hills, Sage.

Chevalier, Y.
  1979 'La biographie et son usage en sociologie', *Revue Française de Science Politique*, no. 1.

Chombart de Lauwe, P.H.
  1975 'Les sociétés en proie au désir', *Cahiers Internationaux de Sociologie*, 22, no. 58.

Cicourel, A.V.
  1964 *Method and Measurement in Sociology*, New York, Free Press.
  1974 *Cognitive Sociology*, New York, Free Press.
  1981 'The Role of Cognitive-Linguistic Concepts in Understanding Everyday Social Interactions', *Annual Review of Sociology*, no. 7.

Cipolla, C.M.
  1981 *Le macchine del tempo*, Bologna, Il Mulino.

Clastres, P.
  1974 *La Société contre l'Etat*, Paris, Ed. de Minuit.

BIBLIOGRAPHY

Cohen, J.L.
  1982a 'Crisis Management and Social Movements', *Telos*, no. 52, Summer.
  1982b *Class and Civil Society*, Amherst, University of Massachusetts Press.
  1984 'Rethinking Social Movements', *Berkeley Journal of Sociology*, 28, Fall.
  1985 'Strategy or Identity: New Theoretical Paradigms and Contemporary
  Social Movements', *Social Research*, 52, no. 4.

Cohen, J.L., Arato, A.
  1984 'Social Movements, Civil Society and the Problem of Sovereignty',
  Praxis International, 4, October.

Coleman, J.S.
  1969 'Games as Vehicles for Social Theory', *American Behavioral Scientist*,
  no. 6.

Conrad, P.
  1979 'Types of Medical Social Control', *Sociology of Health and Illness*, no. 1.

Crespi, F.
  1982 *Mediazione simbolica e società*, Milano, Angeli.

Crouch, C., Pizzorno, A. (Eds.)
  1978 *The Resurgence of Class Conflict in Western Europe since 1968*, London,
  MacMillan.

Crozier, M., Friedberg, E.
  1977 *L'acteur et le système*. Paris, Seuil.

Dal Lago, A.
  1978 'Simulazione, lotta e strategia: sulla natura e sulla funzione del gioco
  in sociologia', *Rassegna Italiana di Sociologia*, XIX, no. 3.

Davies, J.C.
  1962 'Toward a Theory of Revolution', *American Sociological Review*, 27, no.
  1.

Davies, P.C.
  1977 *Space and Time in Modern Universe*, Cambridge (Mass.), Harvard
  University Press.

De Leonardis, O.
  1980 'Devianza: Crisi critica', *Quaderni Piacentini*, 74, April.

De Leonardis, O.
  1982 *Dopo il manicomio. L'esperienza psichiatrica di Arezzo*, Roma, Pensiero
  Scientifico.

De Leonardis, O., Mauri, D.
  1980 'Note sull'istituzione psichiatrica', *Rassegua Italiana di Sociologia*, 21,
  no. 3.

De Santillana G., Von Dechend, H.
1977 *Hamlet's Mill. An Essay on the Myth and Frame of Time*, Boston, Godine.

Della Porta, D.
1985 'Left-wing Terrorism in Italy during the Seventies: The Formation of Terrorist Organizations', Paper presented at the XIII IPSA Conference, Paris.
1987 Organizzazioni politiche clandestine, Doctoral Dissertation, Istituto Universitario Europeo, Florence.

Della, Porta, D., Tarrow, S.
1986 'Unwanted Children: Political Violence and the Cycle of Protest in Italy, 1966–1973', *European Journal of Political Research*, no. 1.

Devereux, C.
1976 'Normal et anormal', in *Essais d'Ethnopsychiatric Génér zale*, Paris, Gallimard, 3rd ed.

Diani, M.
1987 Le mobilitazioni ecologiste tra lobby e movimento sociale, Doctoral Dissertation, University of Turin.

Diani, M., Lodi, G.
1986 'On participation in the ecological movement.' Paper presented at the International Workshop 'Transforming structure into action.' Amsterdam, June 12–15.

Dizard, W.
1983 *The Coming of the Information Age*, London, New York, Longman.

Donati, R.
1984 'Organization between movement and institution.' *Social Science Information*, 23, no. 4–5.

Donzelot, J.
1988 *L'invention du social*, Paris, Fayard.

Dörner, K.
1975 *Il borghese e il folle*, Bari, Laterza.

Douglas, J.D., Johnson, J.M. (Eds.)
1977*Existential Sociology*, New York, Cambridge University Press.

Dukes, R.L., Waller, S.J.
1975 'Toward a general evaluation model for simulation games: GEM', *Simulation and Games*, VII, no. 1.

Eckert, R., Williams, H.
1984 'Youth Conflicts and Public Policy Challenges in Western Europe', Paper presented to the XXth International CFR Seminar, Melbourne, August.

BIBLIOGRAPHY

Eder, K.
  1985 'The "New Social Movements": Moral Crusades Political Pressure Groups, or Social Movements?', *Social Research*, 52, no. 4.

Eiser, J.R.
  1980 *Cognitive Social Psychology*, London, McGraw Hill.

Ennis, J.G., Schreuer, R.
  1987 'Mobilizing Weak Support For Social Movements: The Role of Grievance, Efficacy and Cost', *Social Forces*, 66, no. 2.

Ergas, Y.
  1986 *Nelle maglie della politica*, Milano, Angeli.

Eriksson, I.
  1978 'Soft-Data Sociology', *Acta Sociologica*, 21, no. 2.

Exner, H.J.
  1981 'Ist die Aktionsforschung gescheitert?', *Zeitschrift für Arbeitswissenschaft und Arbeit und Leistung*, 35, no. 2.

Fachinelli, E.
  1979 *La Freccia ferma*, Milano, Erba Voglio
  1983 *Claustrofilia*, Milano, Adelphi.

Ferguson, M.
  1980 *The Aquarian Conspiracy*, Los Angeles, Tarcher.

Ferrarotti, F.
  1981 *Storia e storie di vita*, Bari, Laterza.

Ferree, M.M., Miller, F.D.
  1985 'Mobilization and Meaning: Toward an Integration of Social Psychological and Resource Perspectives on Social Movements', *Sociological Inquiry*, 55: 38–61.

Fireman, B., Zald, M.N., Gamson, W.A., McCarthy, J.D. (eds.)
  1979 'Utilitarian logic in the resource mobilization perspective,' in *The Dynamics of Social Movements*, Cambridge, (Mass.), Winthrop.

Forester, T. (ed.)
  1982 *The Microelectronics Revolution*, Oxford, Blackwell.

Fornari, F.
  1975 *Genitalita' e cultura*, Milano, Feltrinelli.

Foucault, M.
  1961 *Histoire de la folie à l'âge classique*, Paris, Plon.
  1975a *Surveiller et punir*, Paris, Gallimard.
  1975b 'Pouvoir et corps', *Quel Corps*, no. 2.
  1976 *Histoire de la sexualité. I. La volonté de savoir*, Paris, Gallimard.
  1977 *Microfisica del potere*. Torino, Einaudi.

Frank, J.D.
1979 'The present status of outcome studies', *Journal of Consulting and Clinical Psychology*, 47.

Fraser, J.T., Lawerence, N., Park, E. (eds.)
1978 *The Study of Time*, New York, J. Wiley. Vol. III.

Freeman, J. (ed.)
1983 *Social Movements of the Sixties and Seventies*, London, New York, Longman.

Fraser, J.T.
1978 *Time as Conflict*, Basel, Birkhauser Verlag.

Friedrichs, G. (ed.)
1982 *Microelectronics and society: for better or for worse. A report to the Club of Rome*, New York, Pergamon Press.

Gamson, W.A.
1971 'Simsoc. Establishing Social Order in a Simulated Society', *Simulation and Games*, no. 3.
1975 *The strategy of social protest*. Homerwood (Ill.), Dorsey Press.

Gamson, W.A., Fireman, B., Rytina, S.
1982 *Encounters with Unjust Authority*, Homewood (Ill.), Dorsey Press.

Garfinkel, H.
1967 *Studies in Ethnomethodology*, Englewood Cliffs, (N.J.), Prentice Hall.

Garfinkel, H., Sacks, H.
1970 'On the Formal Structure of Practical Actions', in McKinney, Tiryakian (Eds.), *Theoretical Sociology*, New York, Appleton.

Garner, R., Zald, M.N.
1981 'Social movement sectors and systemic constraint'. Ann Arbor, University of Michigan, CRSO Working paper no. 238.

Geiger, M.
1975 'Simulation de jeu pour la solution de conflits relatifs à la politique de planification', *Revue Internationale de Sciences Sociales*, 27, no. 3.

Gherardi, S.
1985 *Sociologia delle decisioni organizzative*, Bologna, Il Mulino.

Giglioli, P.P., Dal. Lago, A.
1983 *Etnometodologia*, Bologna, Il Mulino.

Giovannelli G., Mucciarelli, G.
1978 *Lo studio psicologico del tempo*, Bologna, Cappelli.

Glassner, B., Freedman, J.A.
1979 *Clinical Sociology*, London, Longman.

Goffman, E.
1967 *Interaction Rituals*, New York, Doubleday.
1969 *Strategic Interaction*, Philadelphia, University of Pennsylvania Press.
1971 *Relations in Public*, New York, Basic Books.
1974 *Frame Analysis*, Cambridge, (Mass.), Harvard University Press.
1979 *Gender Advertisments*, New York, Mac Millan.

Gorz, A.
1977 'Nature, valeurs vitales et valeur du corps', *Temps Modernes*, 32, no. 367.
1983 'The Reconquest of Time', *Telos*, no. 55, Spring.

Gosselin, G.
1983 'Movements sociaux et volontarisme chez A. Touraine', *Cahiers Internationaux de Sociologie*, no. 72.

Grazioli, M., Lodi, G.
1984 'La mobilitazione collettiva negli anni Ottanta: tra condizione e convinzione', in A. Melucci (Ed.). *Altri codici.*, Bologna, Il Mulino,

Gundelach, P.
1984 'Social Transformation and New Forms of Voluntary Associations', *Social Science Information*, no. 6.

Gurney, J.W., Tierney, K.J.
1982 'Relative Deprivation and Social Movements. A Critical Look at Twenty Years of Theory and Research', *The Sociological Quarterly*, 23, Winter: 33–47.

Habermas, J.
1976 *Zur Rekonstruktion des Historischen Materialismus*. Frankfurt, Suhrkamp.
1981 'New Social Movements', *Telos*, no. 49, Fall.
1984 *The Theory of Communicative Action*, Boston, Beacon Press, Vol. 1.
1987 *The Theory of Communicative Action*, Boston, Beacon Press, Vol. 2.

Hall, J.R.
1978 *The Ways Out: Utopian Communal Groups in an Age of Babylon*, London, Routledge and Kegan Paul.

Hamblin, R.L., Kunkel, J.H. (Eds.)
1977 *Behavioral Theory in Sociology*, New Brunswick, Transaction Books.

Hamburger, H.
1979 *Games as Models of Social Phenomena*, New York, Freeman.

Hegedus, S.
1983 'Pacifisme, neutralisme ou un nouveau mouvement transnational pour la paix?,' Paper presented at Feltrinelli Foundation Conference, Milan, June.

Hess, R.
1975 *La socioanalyse*, Paris, Ed. Universitaires.
1981 *La sociologie d'intervention*, Paris, PUF.

Hirschman, A.O.
1970 *Exit, Voice and Loyalty*, Cambridge (Mass.), Harvard University Press.

Hosking, D.M.
1983 'Leadership Skills and Organizational Forms: The Management of Uncertainty', Paper presented at the 6th EGOS Colloquium, Florence, November.

Illich, I.
1975 *Medical Nemesis*, Calder and Boyars, London.

Inbar, M., Stoll, C.
1972 *Simulation and Social Science*, New York, Free Press.

Inglehart, R.
1977 *The Silent Revolution*, Princeton, Princeton University Press.

Jenkins, J.C.
1983 'Resource mobilization theory and the study of social movements', *Annual Review of Sociology*, no. 9.

Jervis, G.
1975 *Manuale critico di psichiatria*, Milano, Feltrinelli.

Jungk, R.
1978 'Staff auf der grossen tag zu warten uber pläneschmieden von unten', *Kursbuch*, no. 53.

Keane, J.
1984 *Public Life and Late Capitalism*, Verso, New York and Cambridge.
1988a *Democracy and Civil Society*, Verso, New York and London.
1988b (Ed.), *Civil Society and the State. New European Perspectives*, Verso, New York and London.

Kemper, T.D.
1978 'Toward a Sociology of Emotions', *American Sociologist*, 13, no. 1.

Kerbo, H.R.
1982 'Movements of Crisis and Movements of Affluence. A Critique of Deprivation and Resource Mobilization Theories', *Journal of Conflict Resolution*, 26, no. 4.

Kitschelt, H.
1985 'New Social Movements in West Germany and the United States', *Political Power and Social Theory*, vol. 5: 273–324.

Kitsuse, J.I.
1975 'The New Conception of Deviance and Its Critics', in Gove, W.R. (Ed.), *The Labeling of Deviance*, New York, Halsted Press.

Klandermans, B.
1984 'Mobilization and Participation: A Social Psychological Expansion of Resource Mobilization Theory', *American Sociological Review*, 49, October.
1986 'New Social Movements and Resource Mobilization: The European and American Approach', *Journal of Mass Emergencies and Disasters*, no. 1.

Klandermans, B., Oegema, D.
1987 'Potentials, Networks, Motivations and Barriers: Steps Towards Participation in Social Movements', *American Sociological Review*, 51, August.

Klandermans, B., Kriesi, H., Tarrow, S. (eds.)
1988 *From Structure to Action, Comparing Social Movements Participation*, New York, JAI Press.

Klapp, O.E.
1977 *Opening and Closing: Strategies of Information Adaptation in Society*, Cambridge, Cambridge University Press.

Köhler, W.
1947 *Gestalt Psychology*, New York, Liveright.

Kornhauser, A.
1959 *The Politics of Mass Society*, Glencoe, (Ill.), Free Press.

Krause, E.A.
1977 *Power and Illness*, New York, Elsevier.

Kriesberg, K. (ed.)
1981 *Research in social movements, conflict and change*, vol. 4, Greenwich, Jai Press.
1982 *Research in social movements, conflict and change*, vol. 5, Greenwich, Jai Press.

Kriesi, H.
1985 'Structural determinants of latent political potentials: cycles of protest and cycles of protest generations', Paper presented to the CES Research Planning Group Workshop, Ithaca, August.

Kriesi, H.
1986 'Local mobilization for the people's petition of the Dutch peace movement.' Paper presented at the International Workshop 'Transforming structure into action,' Amsterdam, June 12–15.

Kunkel, J.H.
1975 *Behavior, Social Problems and Change*, Englewood Cliffs (N.J.), Prentice-Hall.

Landes, D.
  1984 *Revolution in Time: Clocks and the Making of the Modern World*, Cambridge (Mass.), Harvard University Press.

Lapassade, G.
  1970 *Groupes, organisations, institutions*, Paris, Gauthiers-Villars, 2nd ed.
  1971 *L'analyse et l'analyste*, Paris, Gauthiers-Villars.

Lasch, C.
  1978 *The Culture of Narcissism*, New York, Norton.

Laver, N.
  1979 *Playing Politics*, Harmondsworth, Penguin Books.

Lemert, E.M.
  1974 'Beyond Mead: The Societal Reaction to Deviance' *Social Problems*, 21, no. 3.

Lerbet, G.
  1980 'Essai sur un complexe d'Athéna. De la recherche-action comme revelateur des blocages heuristiques', *Archives de Sciences Sociales de la Coopération et du Développement*, no. 51.

Lijphart, A.
  1977 'Political Theories and the Explanation of Ethnic Conflict in the Western World', in M. J. Esman (Ed.), *Ethnic Conflict in the Western World*, Ithaca, Cornell University Press.

Lourau, R.
  1969 *L'instituant contre l'institué*, Paris, Anthropos.
  1973 'Pour une theorie des analyseurs', *Connexions*, no. 6.

Lukesch, H., Zecha, G.
  1978 'Neue handlungforschung?', *Soziale Welt*, no. 1.

Maisonneuve, J.
  1976 'Le corps et le corporeisme aujourd'hui', *Revue Française de Sociologie*, 17, no. 4.

Manacorda, A., Montella, V.
  1977, *La nuova psichiatria in Italia*, Milano, Feltrinelli.

Marsh, A.
  1977 *Protest and Political Consciousness*, London, Sage.

Marx, J.H., Holzner, B.
  1975 'Ideological Primary Groups in Contemporary Cultural Movements', *Sociological Focus*, 8, no. 4.

Marx, J.H., Seldin, J.
  1973a 'Crossroads of Crisis: Therapeutic Sources and Quasi-Therapeutic Function of Post-Industrial Communes', *Journal of Health and Social Behavior*, 14, no. 1.

1973b 'Crossroads of Crisis: Organizational and Ideological Models for Contemporary Quasi-Therapeutic Communes', *Journal of Health and Social Behavior*, 14, no. 2.

Matte Blanco, I.
1975 *The Unconscious as Infinite Sets. An Essay in Bi-Logic*, London, Duckworth and Co.

Mauri, D. (Ed.)
1983 *La libertà é terapeutica? L'esperienza psichiatrica di Trieste*, Milano, Feltrinelli.

McAdam, Doug
1982 *Political Process and the Develoment of Black Insurgency*, Chicago, Chicago university Press.
1986 'Micro-mobilization contexts and recruitment to activism.' Paper presented at the International Workshop 'Transforming structure into action.' Amsterdam, June 12–15.

McCarthy, J.D., Zald, M.N.
1973 *The Trend of Social Movements in America: Professionalization and Resource Mobilization*, Morristown, (N.J.), General Learning Press.
1977 'Resource Mobilization and Social Movements: A Partial Theory', *American Journal of Sociology*, 86, no. 6.

Mehan, H., Wood, H.
1975 'On the Morality of Ethnomethodology', *Theory and Society*, 2, no. 1.

Mehan, H.
1982 'Le constructivisme social en psychologie et en sociologie' *Sociologie et Sociétés*, 14, no. 2.

Megarry, J.
1977 *Aspects of Simulation and Gaming*, London, Kogan Page.

Melucci, A.
1974a *Lotte sociali e mutamento*, Milano, Celuc.
1974b *Classe dominante e industrializzazione*, Milano, Angeli.
1976 (ed.) *Movimenti di rivolta*, Milano, Etas Libri.
1977 *Sistema politico, partiti e movimenti sociali*, Milano, Feltrinelli.
1980 'The new social movements: a theoretical approach', *Social Science Information*, 19, no. 2.
1981a 'Ten Hypotheses for the Analysis of New Movements' in D. Pinto (Ed.), *Contemporary Italian Sociology*, Cambridge, Cambridge University Press.
1981b 'New Movements, Terrorism and the Political System', *Socialist Review*, no. 56.
1982 *L'invenzione del presente. Movimenti, identità, bisogni individuali*, Bologna, Il Mulino.

1984a (ed.) *Altri codici. Aree di movimento nella metropoli*, Bologna, Il Mulino.
1984b 'An End to Social Movements?', *Social Science Information*, 24, no. 4/ 5.
1984c *Corpi estranei. Tempo interno e tempo sociale in psicoterapia*, Milano, Ghedini.
1985a 'The Symbolic Challenge of Contemporary Movements', *Social Research*, 52, no. 4.
1985b 'Multipolar action systems: systemic environment and individual involvement in contemporary movements', Paper presented to the CES Research Planning Group Workshop, Ithaca, August.
1986 'Getting involved. Identity and mobilization in social movement', Paper presented at the International Workshop 'Transforming structure into action', Amsterdam, June, 12–15.
1987 *Liberta' che cambia. Una ecologia del quotidiano*, Milano, Unicopli.

Melucci, A., Diani, M.
1983 *Nazioni senza stato. I movimenti etnico-nazionali nelle società occidentali contemporanee*, Torino, Loescher.

Michaels, J.W., Green, D.S.
1979 'Behavioral Sociology', *American Sociologist*, 13, no. 1.

Micheli, G.
1982 *I nuovi catari. Centralità della conoscenza nell 'esperienza psichiatrica di Perugia*, Bologna, Il Mulino.

Minguet, G.
1980 'Les mouvements sociaux, la sociologie de l'action et l'intervention sociologique. A propos de deux ouvrages d'Alain Touraine', *Revue Française de Sociologie*, 21, no. 1.

Morgan, G.
1983 *Beyond Method: Strategies for Social Research*, London, Sage.

Morris, M.B.
1977 *An Excursus into Creative Sociology*, Oxford, Blackwell.

Moser, H.
1977 *Methoden der Actionforschung*, München, Kösel Verlag.

Moscovici, Serge
1981 *L'âge des foules*, Paris, Fayard.

Muir, D.E.
1979 'SIMSIM: A Simple Simulation of Fundamental Social Processes', *Free Inquiry*, 7, no. 2.

Natoli, S.
1986 *L'esperienza del dolore*, Milano, Feltrinelli.

BIBLIOGRAPHY

Nedelmann, B.
   1984 'New Political Movements and Changes in Processes of Intermediation',
      Social Science Information, 23, no. 6.

Oberschall, Anthony
   1973 *Social Conflicts and Social Movements*, Englewood Cliffs (N.J.), Prentice
      Hall.
   1978 'Theories of Social Conflict', *Annual Review of Sociology*, no. 4.
   1980 'Loosely structured collective conflicts: a theory and application', in L.
      Kriesberg (ed). *Research in social movements, conflict and change*, vol. 3,
      Greenwich (Conn.), JAI Press.

Offe, C.
   1983 *New social movements as a meta-political challenge*. University of
      Bielefeld (Unpublished paper).

Offe, C., Keane, J. (Ed.)
   1984 *Contradictions of the Welfare State*, Boston, MIT Press.

Offe, C.
   1985 'New social movements: challenging the boundaries of institutional
      politics.' *Social Research*, 52 (4): 817–868.

O'Keefe, D.J.
   1979 'Ethnomethodology', *Journal for the Theory of Social Behavior*, 9, no. 2.

Oliver, Pamela
   1984 'If you don't do it, nobody will: active and token contributors to local
      collective action.' *American Sociological Review*, 49: 601–610.

Olson, M.
   1965 *The Logic of Collective Action*, Cambridge, (Mass.), Harvard University
      Press.

Oquist, P.
   1978 'The epistemology of action research', *Acta Sociologica*, 21, no. 2.

Parkes, D., Thrift, N.
   1976 *Making Sense of Time*, New York, J. Wiley.

Parsons, T.
   1975 'Some Theoretical Considerations on the Nature and Trends of
      Change of Ethnicity', in N. Glazer and P. Moynihan (eds.), *Ethnicity,
      Theory and Experience*, Cambridge (Mass.), Harvard University Press.

Perls, F.
   1976 *The Gestalt Approach and Eye Witness to Therapy*, New York, Bantam
      Books.

Pfohl, S.J.
1975 'Social Role Analysis: The Ethnomethodological Critique', *Sociology and Social Research*, 59, no. 3.

Pizzini, F.
1981 *Sulla scena del parto*, Milano, Angeli.

Pizzorno, A.
1978a 'Le due logiche dell'azione di classe', in A. Pizzorno, M. Regini, E. Reyneri, I. Regalia. *Lotte operaie e sindacato: il ciclo 1968–1972 in Italia*. Bologna, Il Mulino.

Pizzorno, Alessandro
1978b 'Political exchange and collective identity in industrial conflict,' in C. Crouch, A. Pizzorno (Eds.), *The Resurgence of Class Conflict in Western Europe since 1968*, vol. 2. London, MacMillan.
1983a 'Identita' e interesse', in L. Sciolla (Ed.). *Identita*, Torino, Rosemberg e Sellier.
1983b 'Sulla razionalita' della scelta democratica.' *Stato e Mercato*, no. 7.
1986a 'Sul confronto intemporale delle utilita', *Stato e Mercato*, no. 16.
1986b 'Some Other Kind of Otherness: A Critique of Rational Choice Theories', in A. Foxley, M. McPherson, G. O'Donnel, (Eds.), *Development, Democracy and the Art of Trespassing*, Notre Dame (Ind.), University of Notre Dame Press,

Pomian, K.
1977 'Ciclo' in *Enciclopedia Einaudi*, vol. 2, Torino, Einaudi.

Reali, P.
1982 *La psicologia del tempo*, Torino,Boringhieri.

Ricolfi, L., Sciolla, L.
1980 *Senza padri né maestri*, Bari, De Donato.
1981 'Fermare il tempo', *Inchiesta*, 11, no. 54.

Rochford, E.B.
1982 'Recruitment strategies, ideology and organization' in the Hare Krishna Movement', *Social Problems*, 29, no. 4.

Rositi, F.
1983 'Tipi di identità e tipi di mezzi', *Rassegna Italiana di Sociologia*, 24 no. 1.

Roth, R.
1985 'Fordism and new social movements'. Paper presented at the International Worskshop 'Analysis of Social Movements', Bonn, August.

Rucht, Dieter
1984 'Comparative new social movements.' Paper presented at the 'Egos Working Group on New Social Movements.' Aarhus, August 27–29.
1986 'Themes, logics and arenas of social movements.' Paper presented

at the International Workshop 'Transforming structure into action.' Amsterdam, June 12–15.

Sabbadini, A. (Ed.)
1979 *Il tempo in psicoanalisi*, Milano, Feltrinelli.

Saraceno, C.
1984 'Shifts in Public and Private Boundaries: Women as Mothers and Social Workers in Italian Daycare', *Feminist Studies*, Spring: 7–30.
1987 *Pluralità e mutamento. Riflessioni sull' identità al femminile*, Milano, Angeli.

Sbisa' M. (ed.)
1985 *I figli della scienza*, Milano, Emme Edizioni.

Schmitter, P.L., Lehmbruch, G. (eds.)
1980 *Trends Towards Corporatist Intermediation*, Sage, London and Beverly Hills.

Schott, S.
1979 'Emotions and Social Life', *American Journal of Sociology*, no. 6.

Schwartz, H., Jacobs, J.
1980 *Qualitative Sociology. A Method to Madness*, New York, Free Press.

Schutz,
1975

Sciolla, L.
1983a 'Differenziazione simbolica e identità', *Rassegna Italiana di Sociologia*, 24, no. 1.
1983b (ed.) *Identità. Percorsi di analisi in sociologia*, Torino, Rosemberg e Sellier.

Seguy, J.
1978 'Le phénomène sectaire comme revelateur social', *Autrement*, no. 12.

Sennet, R.
1976 *The Fall of Public Man*, New York, Cambridge, University Press.

Shorter, E.
1975 *The Making of the Modern Family*, New York, Basic Books.

Shorter, E., Tilly, C.
1974 *Strikes in France, 1830–1968*, Cambridge, Cambridge Univesity Press.

Simon, H.
1973 *The Art of the Artificial*, Cambridge (Mass.), M.I.T. Press.
1977 *The New Science of Management Decision*, Englewood Cliffs (N.J.), Prentice-Hall.

277

Smelser, N.J.
1963 *Theory of Collective Behavior*, New York, MacMillan.

Smith, J.L., Glass, G.V.
1977 'Meta-analysis of psychotherapy outcome studies', *American Psychologist*, 32.

Snow, D.A., Zurcher, L.A., Ekland-Olsen, S.
1980 'Social Networks and Social Movements: A Microstructural Approach to Differential Recruitment', *American Sociological Review*, 45, October 787–801.

Snow, D.A., Benford, D.
1986 'Ideology, frame alignment processes and cycles of protest.' Paper presented at the International Workshop, 'Transforming structure into action.' Amsterdam, June 12–15.

Snow, D.A., Rochford, E.B., Worden, S.K., Benford, R.D.
1986 'Frame Alignment Processes, Micromobilization and Movement Participation', *American Sociological Review*, 51, August: 464–481.

Snowden, R., Mitchell, G.D., Snowden, E.M.
1983 *Artificial Reproduction: A Social Investigation*, London, Allen & Unwin.

Stadsklev, R.
1975 *Handbook of Simulation Gaming in Social Education*, Institute of Higher Education Research, University of Alabama.

Stein, A.
1985 *Seeds of the Seventies*, Hanover, University Press of New England.

Stein-Greenblat, C.
1971 'Le developement de jeux. Simulations à l'usage du sociologue', *Revue Française de Sociologie*, 12, no. 2.

Stein Greenblat, C., Duke, R.D.
1982 *Principles and Practices of Gaming Simulation*, London, Sage & Jossey-Bass.

Stella, R.
1987 'Il contagio da AIDS come disastro culturale', *Inchiesta*, no. 4–5.

Tarrow, S.
1982 'Movimenti e organizzazioni sociali: Che cosa sono, quando hanno successo', *Laboratorio Politico* 2, no. 1.
1983 *Struggling to reform: social movements and policy change during cycles of protest*, Western Societies Occasional Papers no. 15, Ithaca, Cornell University.
1984 'I movimenti degli anni '60 in Italia e in Francia e la transizione al capitalismo maturo', *Stato e Mercato*, no. 12.

BIBLIOGRAPHY

1986a 'Comparing social movements participation in western Europe and the United States.' Introductory paper for the International Workshop 'Transforming structure into action,' Amsterdam, June 12–15.

1988b *Democracy and Disorder: Social Conflict, Political Protest and Democracy in Italy: 1966–1973*, Ithaca, Cornell University Press, forthcoming.

Thomas, L.V.
1978 *Mort et pouvoir*, Paris, Payot.

Tilly, C., Tilly, L., Tilly, R.
1975 *The Rebellious Century 1830–1930*, Cambridge, (Mass.), Harvard University Press.

Tilly, C.
1978 *From Mobilization to Revolution*, Reading, (Mass.), Addison-Wesley.
1986 *The Contentious French*, Cambridge, (Mass.), Harvard University Press.

Touraine, A.
1973 *Production de la société*, Paris, Seuil.
1978 *La voix et le regard*, Paris, Seuil.
1980 'Le methode de la sociologie de l'action', *Schweizerische Zeitschrift für Soziologie*, no. 6.
1982a *Introduction to Sociological Intervention*, Paper presented at the World Congress of Sociology, Mexico City.
1982b (ed.) *Mouvements sociaux d'aujourd'hui*, Paris, Editions ouvrières.
1984 *Le retour de l'acteur*, Paris, Fayard.
1985 'An introduction to the study of social movements,' *Social Research* 52, 4.

Touraine A. et al.
1978 *Lutte étudiante*, Paris, Seuil.
1980 *La prophétie anti-nucléaire*, Paris, Seuil.
1981 *Le pays contre l'Etat*, Paris, Seuil.
1982 *Solidarité*, Paris, Fayard.
1984 *Le mouvement ouvrier*, Paris, Fayard.

Useem, B.
1980 'Solidarity model, breakdown model, and the Boston anti-busing movement,' *American Sociological Review*, 45, no. 3.

Van Maanen, J.
1982 *Varieties of Qualitative Research*, London, Sage.

Vovelle, M.
1974 *Mourir autrefois*, Paris, Gallimard.

Wagner-Pacifici, R.E.
1986 *The More Morality Play, Terrorism as Social Drama*, Chicago, Chicago University Press.

Walsh E.J., Warland, R.H.
1983 'Social Movement Involvement in the Wake of a Nuclear Accident', *American Sociological Review*, 48, no. 6.

Watzlawick, P., Beavin, J.H., Jackson, D.
1967 *Pragmatic of Human Communication*, New York, Norton.

Watzlawick, P., Weakland, J., Fisch R.
1970 *Change: Principles of Problem Formation and Problem Resolution*, New York, Norton.

Webb, K. et al.
1983a 'Etiology and outcomes of protest: new European perspectives', *American Behavioral Scientist*, 26, no. 3.

Webb, K.
1983 *Social movements: Contingent or inherent phenomena*? Paper presented at Feltrinelli Foundation Conference, Milan, June.

Williams, R.
1978 'Le récit autobiographique. Analyse d'une "experience" de communication', *Recherches Sociologiques*, 9, no. 2.

Wilson, K. and A. M. Orum
1976 'Mobilizing people for collective political action,' *Journal of Political and Military Sociology*, 4: 187–202.

Wolpe, P.R.
1985a 'The maintenance of professional authority: acupuncture and the American physician', *Social Problems*, 32, 5.
1985b 'Medicine, Technology and Lived Relations', *Perspectives in Biology and Medicine*, 28, no. 2.

Wolton, D.
1974 *Le nouvel ordre sexuel*, Paris, Seuil.
1976 'La sexologie ou la guérison du désir' *Esprit*, no. 7–8.

Zald, M.N., McCarthy, J.D. (Eds.)
1979 *The Dynamics of Social Movements*. Cambridge, Mass., Winchrop.
1985 *Social Movements in Organizational Society: Resource Mobilization, Conflict and Institutionalization*, New Brunswick, Transaction Books.

Zeller, R., Carmines, E.
1980 *Measurement in the Social Sciences*, New York, Cambridge University Press.

Zerubavel, E.
1981 *Hyden Rhythms*, Chicago, Chicago University Press.

Zimmerman, D.H.
1979 'Ethnomethodology', *American Sociologist*, 13, no. 1.

Index